ALL IN A NIGHT'S WORK

The body of a red-haired woman was sprawled among a tangle of bloody sheets, pillows and covers. Her face and head had been smashed into a broken mass of bone, cartilage and tissue. The wall behind the bed was splattered with ugly, rust-colored stains.

Officers Kianka and Springer approached Spearman and asked him to tell them his story. Did he have any idea who might want to hurt his wife? Did either of them have enemies? When did he leave the house that morning, and what was he doing before he found her body?

Spearman invited the sheriff's officers to sit down. Then he himself slumped wearily into an armchair. "This has been a terrible shock," he said. Curiously, despite his remark, the detectives were aware that he appeared remarkably composed. . . .

GUN FOR HIRE

THE SOLDIER OF FORTUNE KILLINGS

Clifford L. Linedecker

AVON BOOKS ◆ NEW YORK

GUN FOR HIRE: THE SOLDIER OF FORTUNE KILLINGS is an original publication of Avon Books. This work has never before appeared in book form.

AVON BOOKS
A division of
The Hearst Corporation
1350 Avenue of the Americas
New York, New York 10019

First Avon Books Printing: October 1992

AVON TRADEMARK REG. U.S. PAT. OFF. AND IN OTHER COUNTRIES, MARCA REGISTRADA, HECHO EN U.S.A.

Printed in the U.S.A.

RA 10 9 8 7 6 5 4 3 2 1

Acknowledgments

Sometimes when acknowledging the help of others in preparing a book, it almost seems that the author could save time and space by pointing out those who didn't have a hand in it. Researching a book takes a lot of work.

But my friends and former colleagues Bob Abborino and Maureen Sikorski played an especially important role with their early efforts in helping me get the project off the ground.

Law enforcement agencies and individual officers, as well as members of the news media, were courteous and helpful in providing leads and information. They have my appreciation. And special thanks go to Sgt. John Kianka, Det. William Springer, and other members of the Palm Beach County Sheriff's industrious Rent-A-Wreck squad for their assistance and cooperation.

My thanks go as well to my agent, Adele Leone, for her loyal support and faith in me.

Violence is every bit a public health issue for me and my successors in this century as smallpox, tuberculosis and syphilis were for my predecessors in the last two centuries.

—U.S. Surgeon General C. Everett Koop

Contents

Introduction

When flamboyant Dr. C. Everett Koop was U.S. surgeon general a few years ago, he once remarked: "Violence in American public and private life has indeed assumed the proportions of an epidemic."

He knew what he was talking about!

Although it is one of the most technologically advanced nations in the world, with a sophisticated form of government, a literate, educated citizenship, and a living standard for most that few other countries can match, the United States is notorious for its violence and appallingly high murder rate. Statistics compiled by the United Nations show that four of every five countries that report their homicide totals to the international body have murder rates lower than ours.

Husbands and wives kill each other in fights over finances, children, or the family cat. A boyfriend beats his girlfriend to death because she's pregnant and he doesn't want to marry her. A girlfriend fatally stabs her boyfriend because he is seeing another woman. A teenager shoots her mother because she won't allow her to date until she's sixteen. A boy beats his father to death with a baseball bat because he has been denied use of the family car. A businessman runs his partner down with a pickup truck because he didn't want him to learn he has been embezzling their money.

An old man was recently beaten to death by his grown son in a fight over the last pork chop on the plate. A top college debater was stabbed to death by his coach during a quarrel because he hadn't prepared for an important match.

It doesn't require much of an excuse for some people to resort to murder as a temporary, or permanent, solution to their problems. And if they don't want to do the dirty work themselves, there's always a chance they can find someone else to do it for them.

For a time during the mid-1980s some Americans who were bent on homicide, but didn't want to fire the gun or wire the hand grenade to the car's undercarriage, did their shopping for a hit man in the classified pages of *Soldier of Fortune* magazine.

I consider *Soldier of Fortune* to be a fine magazine. I read it in the 1980s, and I still read it and enjoy it. I like the heady feeling of excitement when a writer recounts his stealthy trip through a Central American jungle with a band of dedicated and gritty companions who are armed to the teeth and ready for a fight. I admire the Contra freedom fighters who forced the Communist government of Nicaragua to permit free elections that ended that tortured nation's terrible civil war.

I like to read about the rugged courage of the underarmed and undermanned mujaheddin, who fought the Soviet-backed Red government of Afghanistan to a standstill, despite the staggering odds against them.

And I like the stories recounted by Vietnam veterans and others who put their lives on the line for their country and their country's interests, when that wasn't always the most popular thing to do.

But I especially like sharing in these adventures from the security and comfort of my favorite easy chair in my own front room with a copy of the magazine in one hand and a frosty can of brew in the other. At this point in my life, I'm satisfied with secondhand adventure. But not all of *Soldier of Fortune*'s readers feel the same way. Magazine executives have been quoted as saying a large number of their readers are law enforcement officers, or retired officers; and active-duty or retired military men.

But there are also gun enthusiasts—collectors and dealers—a dazzling smorgasbord of people who are fascinated with the raw power and lethal beauty of firearms and other deadly weapons. There are readers who are best described as survivalists. And there undoubtedly are some who have been, or are, mercenary soldiers.

True mercenaries generally don't get a very good press in America's conventional media today. But soldiering for pay has been a profession of both the high-minded and proud, and the low-down and scoundrelly, throughout history. Some students of history and warfare refer to mercenary soldiering as the world's second oldest profession.

Egypt's powerful Pharaoh Ramses II paid towering Nubian mercenaries to battle the Hittites thirteen hundred years before the birth of Christ. Caesar looked to the less-civilized areas of the world that are now Germany and France for fierce cavalry and foot soldiers to back his legions. Proud Hessian mercenaries fought for George III of England against the revolutionary American colonists. Even today fearsome Gurkha warriors from Nepal still serve Britain and India. And of course, the famous Foreign Legion still recruits soldiers from all over the world to fight in France's wars. Most recently, Legionnaires fought in the Persian Gulf War against the military forces of Iraq's power-mad dictator Saddam Hussein.

Some of the most famous mercenaries in the world hired themselves out to the belligerent lords of feudal Japan. They were samurai. The fearless swordsmen occupy much the same place in Japanese culture and entertainment today as the top shooters of the old wild West do in America. The samurai were Japan's steely-eyed top guns three hundred years ago and more, and they took special pride in selling their fighting services to the highest bidder.

Today most American mercenary soldiers fight not only for pay, but for a love of soldiering and adventure. And, until recently at least, because they believed in standing up to communism.

Soldier of Fortune doesn't claim to be the magazine of mercenaries. According to a cover blurb, it is the magazine of professional adventurers. But the fine line between mercenary soldier and daredevil adventurer can sometimes be difficult to draw. And the flavor of mercenary soldiering in *Soldier of Fortune*'s stories, and in the ads, can't be ignored. It's a man's magazine that appeals to men who like soldiering, guns, battle gear, and daring adventure.

Retired Col. Charles Beckwith, who led the tragic attempt to rescue American hostages from Iranian fanatics in 1980, has described the magazine in court as a military journal. I can live with that.

Soldier of Fortune is not a magazine for sissies. But it shouldn't be a magazine for hired killers, either. I'm convinced that was never the intent of either the publisher or the staff. But for a time a deadly fringe element of sociopathological losers and mental delinquents misused the publication in twisted schemes of murder and other criminal acts of violence.

Certain classified ads in the magazine's back pages were used by these grotesque misfits as contact points to link killers and clients. Those ads have now been discontinued. But they were pulled too late for some.

This story is about a few of the killers and their victims.

Clifford L. Linedecker
Lantana, Florida
June 1991

Chapter 1

An Intruder

Bay Circle was dark and quiet this early in the morning as the white Toyota Corolla turned off Prosperity Farms Road onto the one-way residential street.

Creeping along the road of compacted seashell and coral, the car slipped cautiously past the expensive homes before turning at the cul-de-sac and slowly retracing its route. As it approached 2367 Bay Circle on the right, it slowed, then stopped. The driver leaned across the empty passenger's seat to get a closer look, but the early morning darkness and protective trees and bushes shrouded the rambling three-bedroom cinder block structure like a cloak.

A glimmer of light appeared to flicker near the rear of the house, but a moment later it was gone, disappearing forever like a teasing chimera. The driver of the car couldn't be certain if he had really seen it or merely imagined it. Cursing to himself, he looked at his watch. It was nearly 4:00 A.M. Then he slowly eased

the car onto Prosperity Farms Road once again and
turned left.

The flicker of light hadn't been a chimera. Anita
Spearman was still awake in her bedroom at the rear of
the neatly landscaped ranch-style waterfront home at
2367 Bay Circle. It had been a long and exhausting,
although pleasant, evening. She and her husband, Bob,
had gone to dinner that night—their first dinner out together since her return from the hospital more than a
month earlier. And after returning home, they had made
love on the rumpled bed where she was now sitting
propped up against pillows stuffed against the headboard.

The lovemaking hadn't been entirely satisfactory.
Even after so long a time without making love to her,
Bob had seemed preoccupied, as if he couldn't wait to
get it over with. And that wasn't like him at all. Anita
slid out of the bed, smoothed the skirt of the new ruffled lacy red silk peignoir she was wearing, and walked
to her dressing table. There was a framed photo of her
husband, Robert R. Spearman, near the rear of the table next to the mirror. Several medication containers
were lined up in front of it, arranged in ragged for-
mation like a miniplatoon of cylindrical, brown toy soldiers. Quietly she studied the photograph, allowing her
mind to drift through both old and recent memories.

The twenty years that had elapsed since their marriage had taken a physical toll on her husband. He was
overweight, and his short, butch-cut hair was thinning.
The Florida sun had turned his face a dark, mottled
brown. She sighed. He looked every day of his fifty-
five years.

When she lifted her head to peer at her own reflection
in the mirror, it was obvious that the years had hardly

been any gentler to her. The once perky, pretty face had grown heavy, especially around the slumping jowls, and there were deep crease lines on either side of her mouth, giving her cheeks a paunchy appearance. She was forty-eight, but from her appearance, she might have been ten years older.

Anita and Bob had shared both good and difficult times since 1965, when they first met while both were working at the *Palm Beach Post—Evening Times* in West Palm Beach, Florida.

She was a bright, eager, and young cub reporter. She covered general assignments for a while, then moved to the city hall beat. He was older and more experienced. He had once been married to a woman named Beverly, but had been divorced for a long time. He was in charge of the *Post-Times* composing room.

She was twenty-eight and had never been married. He was thirty-five, and once divorced. She had earned her undergraduate degree from Winthrop College, a small but prestigious school in Rock Hill, South Carolina, and a master's degree in journalism from Northwestern University in Illinois. Northwestern is one of the most respected journalism schools in the United States. Bob had graduated from high school in Florida, and completed a year or two of college before dropping out. The remainder of his education was acquired the hard way, generated by the jobs he held and the work he did.

Born and raised in Gaffney, South Carolina, a stone's throw from the North Carolina border, she was a proper small-town southern girl, with a stable, economically comfortable, middle-class background.

He was from nowhere, and everywhere. Although he was born in the small south Georgia community of

Moultrie on New Year's Day 1930, he spent most of his childhood bouncing from one town to another in Florida, while his mother taught in the public schools. He rarely talked about his father, except to say that he left the family when Bob was still a boy.

Bob's background was so varied and full of adventure, he could have put a tramp dog to shame. Name the job, and there was a good chance that he had worked at it, especially if it called for muscle, unbounded energy, and a quick, facile mind. He was drawn to he-man, blue-collar work. He had been an oil field roughneck in Texas and dove off an oil rig in the Gulf of Mexico. In Florida he worked on construction and as an auto mechanic, and had tried his hand at a lot of other professions in between. As a young man he saw combat with the U.S. Marine Corps during the United Nations police action in Korea, the conflict we now call the Korean War. If the appellation "lady" applied to his wife, Bob might have best been described as a survivor. He was a rough-and-tumble man's man, who was a self-made success.

But Anita was no slouch as an achiever, either. She was also on her way up when she met her future husband. Newspaper management had already recognized her considerable executive and administrative abilities and begun grooming her for rapid promotion. She completed only a brief stint as a reporter before she was appointed city editor of the *Evening-Times*. Outgoing, friendly, and capable, she seemed to be destined for even more success than her rugged new sweetheart from the newspaper's composing room.

Much later a friend of the couple would recall to a news reporter that "Bob and Anita were like oil and water. He was a hardworking, tough-talking construction type, and she was a delicate, polite, well-educated business type.''

Although he was in charge of the composing room, by the time the couple met and developed a romantic relationship, Bob's success at the *Post-Times* had obviously peaked. He was at a dead end, professionally. Although he could be charming and personable in his own rough way when he wished, more often he was gruff in his dealings with other employees. And he lacked the polish, cheery sophistication, and friendly demeanor that helped Anita get along with colleagues from any of the newspaper's various departments.

Despite the litany of differences however, the unlikely couple had fallen in love, and on October 30, 1965, they were married at the Northwood Baptist Church in West Palm Beach. For the most part, the curious union had worked out—certainly as well as most marriages, and better than some. Bob's mother, Alberta, was delighted with her new daughter-in-law. And Anita's mother was impressed with Bob's seeming devotion to her daughter.

If the subsequent years hadn't been kind to the couple in the physical sense, they were generous to them in other ways.

Bob had proven to be an energetic and imaginative businessman. A short time after the marriage, he left the newspaper job, and with a financial assist from Anita's parents, he bought a parcel of land on Idlewild Road along the Intracoastal Waterway near the Jupiter Inlet and went into the diving salvage business. He was a tireless worker, and ten- or twelve-hour days were the norm to him, rather than the exception. He would accept just about any kind of job dealing with marine salvage or construction, and go anywhere he was asked to work. As the population burgeoned along South Florida's Gold Coast, he gradually converted his modest salvage operation into a profitable marine construction company.

The hard work paid off handsomely. After nearly twenty years of marriage, he and Anita were owners of a $3 million company that was one of the most successful businesses of its kind on Florida's sunlit Atlantic coast; they had a fine $240,000 home, a $270,000 yacht named the *Equalizer,* and their own airplane, a Beechcraft Bonanza worth $55,000.

Anita had kept pace with her industrious husband in the couple's race for success, however, and played a big hand in their good fortune. The skills, ready intelligence, and personality that had so impressed her superiors at the *Post* and *Evening Times* also caught the attention of Richard Simmons, West Palm Beach's city manager. A few years after her marriage, Simmons convinced her to quit the newspaper business and accept a job as city clerk. Despite her youth and inexperience, she excelled at the difficult and challenging job. It wasn't long before Simmons named her as his assistant city manager. It was the second most important and powerful administrative post in West Palm Beach. As coworkers and close friends, Simmons and his diligent protégée directed the city through the greatest growth period in its history.

When Simmons announced plans to retire, he recommended Anita for his job. Her closest competitor for the city's top administrative position conceded that she had earned first chance at the appointment, and West Palm Beach's political leaders agreed. But she turned the offer down. The job wouldn't be the same without her good friend Simmons. She submitted a formal notice that she planned to leave her job in city government and take early retirement. She also explained to a few close friends that her husband needed her help and expertise with the family business.

Bob was transforming their business from the small but profitable Spearman Marine Construction Company he had built up, into a full-fledged boatyard where boaters could tie up or dry-dock their prized watercraft for do-it-yourself maintenance and repairs. The new name was Bob's Boat Yard. But the boatyard business in Palm Beach County was highly competitive. Boatyards were sprinkled all along the Intracoastal, from Jacksonville south to Miami. It seemed that anywhere along the waterway where a condominium or a hotel hadn't already been constructed, someone was running a boatyard.

Converting the business to a boatyard nevertheless offered a potential for earning huge profits. But making the transition was an expensive process, that had faced the Spearmans with a serious cash flow problem. Consequently they'd had to refinance their boatyard on a second mortgage that raised the total indebtedness on the property from $450,000 to $500,000, and borrow another $50,000 on the *Equalizer*.

The idea of being so deeply in debt, even though they had the physical assets to cover the loan, with a million dollars or more left over, troubled Anita. She had learned from her father, who owned a furniture store in Gaffney, that indebtedness was something to be avoided. Furthermore, she suspected the money troubles involved more than a temporary cash flow problem, and that her husband was hiding something from her. During the past several months, he had appeared exceptionally tense and distracted. She telephoned his

bookkeeper at the business, Jean Tetta, and asked if
there was anything going on at the boatyard that was
bothering him. She said her husband was behaving like
a caged lion. He was pacing the floor, and having difficulty sleeping at night.

Ms. Tetta and other employes were already well
aware of their boss's perplexing change of tempera-
ment. He was getting on everyone's nerves. He was
unusually grumpy, finicky, and hypercritical. He complained of just about everything. It seemed there was
simply no pleasing him. But no one had a clue to what
was troubling him.

Concerned about his suspicious behavior, Anita had
driven to the office three months earlier and checked
the books. They revealed a discouraging picture. After
a three-year span of excellent earnings, income had
plummeted—more than a million dollars in the last year.
And the yard had less than a ten percent occupancy.
The alarming slump in earnings appeared to coincide
with the conversion of the business to a boatyard. But
there were also disturbing indications that some of the
qualities that had made her husband such a success in
the marine salvage and construction businesses were
now working against him.

He was a hands-on businessman who wanted to be
in the front lines where the action was. Yet he was a
jealous steward of the company's assets and kept a firm
hand on the expenditures, insisting that all bills be personally approved by him. He carefully monitored company supplies as well, keeping an eagle eye on
everything from pencils to acetylene tanks and diving
gear. He kept a rigorous watch on the company's nick-
els and dimes. If an employee made a personal telephone call outside the free call area that cost forty or

fifty cents, he made sure that the person paid back the long-distance fee. Jean Tetta, his secretary and book-keeper, would later publicly describe him as tight with his money, even cheap.

Somehow the business seemed to be veering danger-ously close to drowning in red ink. Anita resolved to use her background as a high-level administrator, as well as her personal contacts in the area business world, government, and the media to restore their company to the robust profitability it had enjoyed earlier.

But when she told her husband about her plans to assume an active role in the business, he objected. He didn't like the implication that he had somehow failed. Like many self-made men, he was sensitive to criti-cism, especially if it could be interpreted as implying that he was failing in his role as the family breadwin-ner.

Anita tried to explain that her decision to move into the administrative end of their business wasn't a reflec-tion on his own capabilities. Instead, it was a move that would free him from the day-to-day details, so that he could concentrate on what he knew and did best, su-pervising the boatyard workers and dealing directly with the customers—the lusty men who lived for boats and boating. It would be like the old days at the newspa-pers. They would be working toward the same end, but using different skills and holding down different jobs.

Bob still didn't like it. But Anita held the trump card. She was the majority stockholder in the company, and the preordained winner in any serious tug-of-war that might develop. There wasn't much that he could do about it if she continued to insist on the change. And it wouldn't be the first time that he had found himself forced to listen as she laid down the law.

There had been serious trouble in their relationship for the past year—ever since Anita discovered his long-term affair with another woman. She had become suspicious after realizing that he was spending an excessive amount of time away from home on business trips, or Caribbean cruises aboard the *Equalizer* with fishing or hunting pals and business associates. She was never asked to go along, even though she could have occasionally juggled her work schedule.

She confided to her boss that she suspected her husband of slipping off to the Caribbean islands with another woman, and was afraid that her concern over her personal problems would affect her work. She said she was thinking of hiring a private detective to do some snooping around for her. Then she followed through. Although she had half expected it, Anita was still shocked when she learned that he had been carrying on an affair since 1981 with Patricia Rozelle, an attractive, slender woman who was fifteen years younger than he was. The couple had met while he was constructing a seawall in North Palm Beach.

The private detective earned his fee. He produced evidence to show that Anita's husband had sailed to the Bahamas several times with the Rozelle woman aboard the *Equalizer*, spent weekends with her in New York and in California, and shared intimate dinners with her in restaurants along the southeast Atlantic coast from Jupiter to Miami.

Tipped off to one of the meetings, Anita confronted the couple while they were lunching together in a restaurant in the coastal town of Jupiter about twelve miles from the boatyard. She calmly said hello to her husband's companion, addressing her as "Pat." Then she told Bob she wanted to see him alone. He followed her outside the restaurant. It was the only time that Anita and her husband's mistress ever met.

Bob was profusely apologetic to his wife, and promised to end the love affair. When Anita later threatened to file for a divorce, and talked with an attorney, Bob assured her that the affair was over for good, and that there would be no more fooling around. He vowed that he was ready to become a good and faithful husband again.

But Anita was hurt. The husband she had been so loyal to had betrayed her trust, and she couldn't simply blink her eyes and pretend that nothing had happened. She told one of the office employees at the boatyard that she was thinking about getting a divorce. She vowed that if she went through with it, she would make sure she got her fifty percent of their assets. And, she bitterly added, she might even sell the business to one of her husband's competitors. "That would really get him," she said.

She wasn't sure she really wanted a divorce, however. So she went to her boss and trusted friend, Simmons, with her dilemma. Simmons suggested that she and her husband see his clergyman for marriage counseling.

Bob readily agreed to the suggestion, and seemed genuinely repentant during the counseling sessions. He insisted that he still loved his wife very deeply, and didn't want to lose her. Again he vowed that he had never loved Patricia Rozelle, and that the affair was finished for good. His sincerity and remorse seemed to be genuine. Although it was difficult to forget his betrayal, Anita resolved to forgive him. She was still in love with her husband.

The couple were still working out their new domestic

and business relationships when Anita discovered lumps in her breasts. It was breast cancer. She submitted to the trauma of a double mastectomy. But she was helped through the ordeal by her loyal family, which rallied to her side as soon as they learned of the diagnosis. One of the specialists who treated her was a favorite cousin who lived in a nearby community, Dr. Howard Parker.

Bob's loving support was especially comforting, although some aspects of his attitude were also undeniably troubling to Anita. Her husband had appeared as shocked and dismayed as she was when they first learned the results of the biopsy. In some ways, he had seemed to be even less willing than she to accept the ominous diagnosis. The news had numbed her at first, but then she accepted the verdict and grimly prepared for the operation. But her husband seemed to have simply refused to believe that the diagnosis was correct. He insisted on a second opinion, then a third. When the new tests also disclosed the cancer, he cried.

Despite his roving eye for beautiful women, Bob had always been an attentive husband. He brought Anita presents of fine jewelry on special occasions, and even when there was no special occasion. Only a few weeks before, he had surprised her with a shiny new Oldsmobile 98 that he said would be her own personal car after she was feeling well enough to drive again.

But now he was even more attentive. Suddenly he couldn't seem to do enough for her. He was so solicitous that it was sometimes annoying. He waited on her hand and foot. He protested whenever she exerted herself in any way. He didn't even want her to shop. He insisted on driving her to and from work. He held her and kissed her at every opportunity.

But there was a dark side to his attitude. At times he

appeared to be more concerned about Anita's appearance, and her breast reconstruction after the radical surgery, than whether or not deadly cancer cells might still be lurking in her body. When he talked with Dr. Parker, he didn't ask if the oncologists thought the cancer might have already spread to Anita's bones. He asked what she would look like after the operation. He wanted to know if she could wear a bathing suit, and if she would look as she had before the surgery. Dr. Parker would later be quoted as saying that Anita's husband seemed to feel that she would be "unalterably marred."

To neighbors and other friends and acquaintances, however, he presented an image of a picture-perfect husband, whose only concern was that his wife survive her dreadful illness. He not only fussed over her, but he also accepted her decision to become an active partner with him at the boatyard. And he began talking about a trip they would take to the Bahamas together on the *Equalizer* after she was well enough. When she shared the news with friends, she boasted that once her surgery was behind her, she would begin "to live again." She was looking forward to spending more time with her husband. And there would be more time, as well, to tend to her flowers. Anita loved flowers so much that she and her husband had built an addition onto the house where she could grow orchids and other exotic and beautiful plants. She had a green thumb, and could spend hours puttering around and fussing over her flowers.

When she returned home after her surgery at Good Samaritan Hospital in West Palm Beach, Bob asked Simmons, who was still her boss, not to telephone her or to allow anyone else to call. She was simply too weak to take calls, he explained. Bob especially didn't want his wife bothered by newspaper and television reporters, and he asked her boss to write a memo requesting that they leave her alone. He said she needed at least a week's rest. Simmons wrote the memo.

Bob also told Simmons that she was quitting her job immediately. It was time to find someone else to take her place as assistant city manager. Friends and colleagues at City Hall began to make plans for a retirement party in November after Anita was strong enough to attend.

When Anita returned from the hospital, and her mother, Louise Jones, moved in to help care for her for a few days, Bob was as pleasant as could be.

If he wasn't yet a perfect husband, the marriage nevertheless appeared to be back on track. With her operation behind her, her marriage apparently improving, and the prospects of working closely with Bob to rebuild their boatyard business, life appeared to be looking up for Anita Spearman.

Only two days earlier she had talked by telephone with a close friend, West Palm Beach City Commissioner Helen Wilkes, and chatted excitedly about the cruise to the Bahamas on the *Equalizer* that she and Bob were planning to take together. But terrible events had been set in motion that she knew nothing about, and could hardly have imagined.

If she had been awake at about 4:00 A.M., she might have heard a car slowly cruising along Bay Circle, then stopping momentarily before taking off again. A strange car moving through the neighborhood at that hour was something to be concerned about. Bay Circle was a sort of man-made peninsula that extended like a finger into a small bay connected to the Intracoastal Waterway, which, in some areas of northern Palm Beach County, was not much wider than a modest river. Bay Circle was the second of four such nearby land fingers that jutted into the waterway, with Azure Circle to the South, and Caribe Circle and Driftwood Circle to the north.

When the Spearmans first bought their house, the northern end of Palm Beach County wasn't yet heavily developed. The community that was later to be known as Palm Beach Gardens was then little more than a modest housing development between Military Trail and Old Dixie Highway. In twenty years, however, the community had grown considerably. Palm Beach Gardens, in fact, had already swallowed up Idlewild Road, a mile and a half away, where the boatyard was located. Shopping centers, restaurants, and a host of other businesses seemed to have popped up everywhere, until they almost outnumbered the houses constructed for families seeking to escape the bustle of West Palm Beach, Riviera Beach, Lake Worth, and other larger communities in the county.

Even with the advancing urban sprawl threatening to swallow them in the near future, Azure, Bay, Caribe, and Driftwood were still relatively secluded, private streets. With the exception of occasional guests and delivery people, about the only cars that entered Bay Circle were those of residents. And few of the Spearmans' neighbors were tooling around in their cars at four o'clock in the morning.

If Anita had been awake when the car stopped in front of her house, she might have telephoned the Palm Beach County Sheriff's Department. County Sheriff Richard Wille was a good friend, and many of his deputies knew her, as well. The sheriff's officers were well-trained members of a thoroughly professional law enforcement agency. And deputies could have sealed off Bay Circle within minutes. About the only way out for a burglar would be a wet and dangerous splash into one of the canals on either side of the street.

But there was no call to the Sheriff's Department. Anita was lying uncomfortably on her back, asleep. She had never been able to sleep well that way, but her recent surgery had made it necessary. And after twenty years of marriage, she wasn't used to sleeping alone. But her husband was a restless sleeper, and during her first week home from the hospital, he had accidentally struck her sensitive chest with a flailing arm as they lay side by side on the bed. Her doctor suggested separate beds until the healing process was completed. So she had moved into the guest bedroom at the rear of the house, while Bob continued to use the master bedroom.

The strange car had moved away from 2367 Bay Circle long before the comforting sounds of Bob making coffee in the kitchen began drifting through the darkened house. He was used to getting up early, and even before Anita's illness, he was usually awake and puttering around the kitchen long before she was ready to crawl out of bed.

She was curled up and sleeping soundly at about 6:00 A.M. when the bedroom door was cracked open and her husband peered through the predawn gloom of the shadowy room toward the bed. Anita was lying on her back, snuggled against the pillow, with the bed sheet pulled up across her chest. A clump of russet-colored hair stuck out above the sheet. She was still slumbering peacefully, and blissfully unaware, a few minutes later when the sounds of the garage door opening, followed by the engine of Bob's Chevy Blazer sputtering to life, drifted through the quiet house as he pulled the vehicle out of the drive and turned onto Bay Circle.

The crunch of the Blazer's tires against the compacted seashell and coral in front of the house had barely faded before Anita was jerked back to consciousness with a start. Someone else was in the bedroom. And it wasn't Bob. Her heart was pounding wildly as she opened her eyes in fright. Suddenly strong arms were pushing her deep down into the mattress. Then a hand was clamped over her mouth, and a pillow was being pressed down, hard against her face.

Panic-stricken, she struggled for breath and tried to push the pillow away. Kicking her legs and tearing with her fingers at the hairy arms above her, she fought desperately to escape the smothering embrace of the pillow. But the intruder was too strong, and a moment later a heavy, hard, blunt object crashed down onto the back of her head. She was struck a second, a third, and a fourth time with the bludgeon. Then she was being beaten with fists that crashed into her head through the thin pillow. The intruder slammed his hard knuckles into her face, and onto her chest, smashing and destroying the delicate tissue that was still healing after her surgery. He continued to beat her long after she lost consciousness and stopped breathing.

Chapter 2

The Rent-A-Wreck Squad

Robert Spearman rolled out of the huge bed in the master bedroom early on November 16, 1985. It would be an hour or two before the sun topped the horizon on the nearby Atlantic Ocean, but he had a full day ahead of him. Shuffling sleepily into the kitchen, he began to spoon coffee into the Mr. Coffee machine. But he clipped the edge of the basket with his spoon and spilled a streak of the dark brown grounds behind the filter.

For a moment he considered ignoring the spill, but knew from experience that if he did, the hole in the bottom of the basket would clog. Muttering under his breath, he pulled the filter and coffee from the basket, rinsed it out, and replaced the wet filter. Then, he slid the basket in place and turned the machine on.

It would take a few minutes. He padded to the refrigerator on bare feet and peered inside. There were some English muffins on the bottom shelf. He considered the time it would take to pop one into the toaster. As he reached for the package, he could hear the crunch of car tires moving slowly along the street in front of the house. Instead of grabbing the muffins, he withdrew his hand to look at his watch. It was barely past 4:30 A.M. The newspaper carrier?

He closed the fridge door, leaving the muffins where they were. Now he could smell the coffee as it dripped into the pot. There was no time to eat. He had to get out of the house. But he would have the coffee. He could eat later with the friend he planned to meet at Denny's restaurant. Still dressed in his pajamas, he filled his cup and returned to the master bedroom.

A shower and shave took less than fifteen minutes. By that time, the coffee was cool enough to drink. As he pulled on a pair of Jockey shorts, he glanced at himself in the mirror. He was just under five feet ten inches tall, and despite some thickening across his belly and a little sag to his chest muscles, he was in reasonably good shape for a man of fifty-five. He frowned at the expanding waistline and slumping pectorals. Cutting down on the beer and exercising more could help rectify that.

Nevertheless, he was proud of his body. It had taken him a long way, especially during the rough-and-tumble days of his youth. He shrugged his shoulders to loosen the tightness across his upper back, reveling in the flex and ripple of muscles across his shoulders and arms. He liked to think of himself as a man's man, capable of settling a disagreement with a menacing frown, or, when reason failed, with his fists. He knew some of Anita's friends considered him to be little more than a clever redneck. That bothered him sometimes, even though he didn't think much of many of them either.

It was Saturday morning, and there was no need for him to dress up. He was simply going in to catch up on some paperwork. He pulled the sweatshirt with the words "Bob's Boat Yard" printed across the front over his head. Then he slipped his bare feet into a pair of loafers. He looked at his watch. It was 5:30. Time to get moving.

It was still dark outside, but across the canal that separated Bay Circle from Caribe Circle, there was a light in one of the houses. Someone else was getting an early start. Closer to the house, at the dock some fifty feet away, Bob's prized yacht, the *Equalizer,* was bobbing ever so slightly on the morning breeze.

At the last moment before leaving the house, he cracked open the door to the guest bedroom and peered through the early morning gloom. Anita was snuggled up against her pillow, with the bed sheet pulled so far up over her chest and face that only a clump of her russet-colored hair showed. She was sleeping soundly. Quietly closing the door, he walked to the double garage, opened the overhead door, and moments later, he was guiding the Blazer away from the house.

At the far end of the street, turning onto Bay Circle from Prosperity Farms Road, the headlights of a car flashed in his face. Moments after they passed each other, Bob turned left on Prosperity Farms Road, took another left, and headed south toward PGA Boulevard. The Spearman home and business were only a few miles from the famous PGA National Resort and golf courses, which are the site of one of golfing's most prestigious tournaments. The PGA Seniors Championship there is known worldwide and has attracted such golfing luminaries as Jack Nicklaus, Arnold Palmer, Ben Crenshaw, and Gary Player. But Spearman wasn't a golfing fan. He preferred the more manly sports of shooting, boating, and fishing.

Whatever his thoughts may have been about at that moment, they weren't on golfing. Nor, apparently, were the thoughts of the person sitting quietly in the shadowy interior of a white Toyota he had just passed. The car had been pulled to the right side of Prosperity Farms Road, not more than ten yards from Bay Circle. It was easy walking distance to the Spearman home.

Ten minutes or so after Spearman's car drove off along Prosperity Farms Road, newspaper carrier Cherry James was startled by a strange man walking near 2367 Bay Circle. He was wearing some kind of uniform covered by a long coat, and had what appeared to be a duffel bag slung over his shoulder. There was nothing about the stranger's behavior that was especially alarming, but nevertheless, it was unusual to see an outsider hanging around that time of the morning. James made a mental note of the incident.

In the meantime, Spearman had pulled his Blazer into the parking lot at Denny's restaurant at the corner of Federal Highway and Northlake Boulevard in North Palm Beach and walked inside to have breakfast with a friend, Leon Hodge. He chatted for a few minutes with Hodge, who owned the E & H Boat Works next door to Bob's Boat Yard, and was a regular at Denny's. Spearman absently leafed through a copy of the *Palm Beach Post* as the men talked, before finally swallowing the last of his coffee and leaving.

Instead of heading straight for the boatyard, he pulled in at a nearby McDonald's, also along Federal Highway, and bought a sausage biscuit to go. Anita was still using a wheelchair around the house, and wasn't doing any more cooking than she had to. And she liked the fast-food breakfast snacks.

Finally he drove to the boatyard. It was Saturday

morning, and a few weekend boaters began showing up at the yard soon after he arrived. With a portable telephone hanging from his belt, Spearman poked around the yard for a few minutes, waved at a couple of his customers, then walked into the office.

Inside, he telephoned his girlfriend, Patricia Rozelle. She had just awakened a few minutes before, and they chatted for a while. He mentioned that he was at the office signing some checks, and talked about the problems he and his employees were having with the recent changeover of his company to a boatyard. Spearman would later recall that he also tried to telephone Anita. When she didn't answer the phone, he waited a few minutes, then tried again. Again there was no response, he would claim.

After the second unsuccessful attempt to contact his wife, he would add, he asked one of his employees to look after things at the boatyard, and drove the few blocks to his home to see if Anita was all right.

When he walked into the guest bedroom of his ranch-style home, he was confronted by a scene of horror. Anita was sprawled on her back. Her face was covered by a pillow, and her left leg was dangling limply over the edge of the bed. Her body was already taking on the ugly metallic tinge of death. Blankets and sheets were clumped and twisted in ugly snarls around her corpse.

Spearman retreated to the kitchen, where he picked up the telephone, which was already off the hook, and dialed 911. He blurted out that he needed an emergency rescue squad for his wife. "I can't wake her up," he told the operator. He said he thought she may have had a heart attack. Like all 911 calls, the conversation was automatically recorded. But Spearman talked only moments before ending the conversation and dropping the phone back onto its cradle. Then, without another look inside the bedroom, he dashed across the street to the house of neighbors, William and Pat Allen. He told the Allens that something was wrong with his wife, and that he had called for help.

Spearman was shaking, and at times seemed almost incoherent, as he babbled about Anita, his morning at the restaurant and the boatyard, and his terrible discovery. Mrs. Allen telephoned Bob's Boat Yard and blurted out to Robert Havlick, who was Spearman's general manager there, that Anita was dead. Havlick hurried to his pickup truck, slid into the driver's seat, and raced to the Spearman home.

In the meantime, Patricia Allen had hurried with her neighbor back across the road to his house. As Mrs. Allen followed Spearman into the bedroom, he began talking about a burglary. "I don't leave things like this," he apologized. "They took the gun." Then, pointing to jewelry boxes neatly stacked on top of the dresser, he added, "They took the good stuff."

Mrs. Allen was more concerned about the woman sprawled on the bed. It took only the briefest glance at the silent, still body, and she knew that Anita was dead.

A few minutes later when Havlick burst into the house, he found his boss slumped in a chair in the middle of the living room, rocking back and forth, with his head in his hands. Spearman was babbling: "Blood all over the walls. Blood all over everywhere." Spearman repeated the words over and over. Havlick never ventured into the bedroom. He stayed with his boss.

The Palm Beach County Fire Rescue Squad and Havlick arrived at the house in almost a dead heat. The paramedics were oblivious to the stacked jewelry boxes as they hurried into the bedroom. One look at the cold, blue-gray body in the frilly peignoir, and they knew it was already too late. There was nothing they could do for her. She was dead.

At first glance, it appeared that the woman might have suffered a fatal heart attack, as the caller had indicated when he telephoned for help. The paramedics were mulling that possibility over when one of them slipped on a sticky substance puddled on the floor and nearly fell. It was blood. Alarmed, one of the men leaned over the bed and gently lifted the pillow from the victim's face. It was a gory mess. The woman's face and head had been smashed into a broken mass of bone, cartilage, and tissue. Blood was smeared over her face and chest. When one of the paramedics glanced up behind the headboard of the bed, he saw more blood smeared and splattered on the wall. The dead woman was no heart attack victim.

As was his custom, Sgt. John Kianka of the Palm Beach County Sheriff's Department was at his desk early. Consequently, when the 7:30 A.M. call of a death at 2367 Bay Circle in Palm Beach Gardens came in, it was Kianka who answered the homicide division telephone. Kianka double-checked the address, then dropped the telephone back down onto the receiver, got to his feet, and called to Det. William Springer to join him. Fifteen minutes later the officers pulled up in a squad car in front of the Spearman house.

Uniformed deputies had already sealed off the house and yard. As soon as the homicide officers arrived and Havlick and the Allens identified themselves, the civilians were asked to leave. There would be plenty of time to interview them later.

As Kianka walked into Anita Spearman's bedroom,

Springer was only a step behind. Inside, a sheriff's deputy was talking with a barrel-chested, middle-aged man with a crew cut and graying hair. Another deputy greeted Kianka and Springer by name. He explained that he and his partner had arrived about twenty minutes earlier. Nodding toward the man talking with his partner, the deputy told the detectives that the middle-aged man was Robert Spearman. It was he who had made the telephone call for help.

"It's his wife," the deputy added, glancing toward the bed.

Kianka turned to the bed. The body of a red-haired woman was sprawled among a tangle of bloody sheets, pillows, and covers. The wall behind the bed was also splattered with ugly rust-colored stains.

Kianka and Springer approached Spearman and asked him to tell them his story. Did he have any idea who might want to hurt his wife? Did either of them have enemies? When did he leave the house that morning, and what was he doing before he found her body?

Spearman invited the sheriff's officers to sit down. Then he himself slumped wearily into an armchair. "This has been a terrible shock," he said. Curiously, despite his remark, the detectives were aware that he appeared to be remarkably composed.

As the officers listened, occasionally interrupting to ask a question, or to have something clarified, he filled them in on Anita's recent illness, and recounted his activities from the previous evening. It would be the first of at least four different accounts he would give in the next few days to law officers and friends. And each of the statements would have significant differences.

After awakening early, he said, he made coffee for himself, and took Anita a glass of apple juice before leaving the house. He said she had gotten up to use the bathroom when he gave her the drink, but planned to return to bed and sleep awhile longer. He promised her that he would bring her a sausage snack when he returned home in a few hours.

Spearman recounted chatting with Hodge over breakfast at Denny's, picking up the sausage snack for Anita, and driving to the boatyard to catch up on some paperwork left over from the previous night. He said that he became concerned after he was unable to rouse Anita by phone, and rushed to his home, which was only about a half mile from the business on Prosperity Farms Road. He called his wife's name several times as he entered the house, before hurrying into the bedroom and discovering her lifeless body on the bed. He said his wife, the bed, and the surroundings were splattered with blood.

While Springer continued talking with the husband, Kianka spoke with the deputy. The uniformed officer advised him that there were no pry marks on doors or windows, or other signs of forced entry into the home. When the deputies arrived, they had found three doors open: the front door, a back door to the garage, and an inner door connecting the house and the garage. The garage was at the front of the house.

Inspection of the garage door lock, based on the position of the bolt, indicated that it hadn't been forced. When the lock was opened, it was opened with a key. It wasn't inconceivable, of course, that Spearman might have left the doors unlocked or open when he left in the morning. Bay Circle was not in a high crime area, and although it may be unwise in these days, it's not uncommon for people who live in neighborhoods usually thought of as safe to leave the doors to their homes unlocked.

But a few feet away from Sergeant Kianka and the uniformed deputy, Spearman was telling Springer that he had locked the house up securely before he left home that morning.

Springer was having trouble with Spearman. Suddenly the victim's husband seemed to be having a serious problem controlling his emotions. He was remarkably composed only moments before. But now he was obviously having difficulty concentrating on what he was talking about. His emotions appeared to be flashing on and off as rapidly as the blinking of a neon sign. It was a curious reaction, but the experienced officers were aware that different people react to tragedy and deep shock in different ways.

Kianka asked the distraught husband to accompany him and Springer to the Palm Beach County Sheriff's Department headquarters for additional questioning. Spearman agreed. At the headquarters, Spearman and the detective team settled in for a long talk. The questioning continued for five hours.

Again the new widower went over the gloomy account of his wife's illness, and his activities late the previous evening and that morning. He said he left the house between 6:30 and 7:00 A.M., probably closer to 7:00, after looking in on Anita and assuring himself that she was sleeping soundly. Springer noticed that Spearman had left out the story of giving Anita a drink of apple juice. There were other glaring discrepancies, as well, but the detective merely made a mental note of the glitches in Spearman's stories. For the time being, he said nothing about it.

Spearman appeared to have again gained control of

his emotions, and replied to questions calmly and in detail. He said that his business was healthy. There were no financial problems. The business could hardly be better, he declared.

Springer asked Spearman how he and Anita had been getting along on a personal level. Did Anita have a boyfriend? Did he have a girlfriend? Spearman snapped, ''No,'' to both questions. He said he and his wife had been very much in love. Except for concern over Anita's recent illness, their marriage was untroubled. He insisted that their union was never stronger than in the months immediately preceding her operation, and just after the surgery. He pointed out that they had made love late the previous night, in fact, for the first time in several months. He didn't mention Patricia Rozelle, nor did he say anything about telephoning her from his office that morning.

Continuing to respond to questioning, Spearman said that although he hadn't had an opportunity to make an efficient inventory, only a few things appeared to be missing from the house. Apparently the most valuable items that he could immediately identify as missing were his wife's five-thousand-dollar keepsake diamond ring, and her gold wedding band. The band was inscribed with the words ''I love you forever.''

Spearman said that an Ithaca twelve-gauge Model 37 pump-action shotgun he owned was also gone. He explained that he sometimes used the scattergun to hunt birds in North Florida with his pals, and kept it in a gun stand outside his wife's bedroom. Spearman said he last noticed the gun on Saturday, the day before Anita's slaying. He had purchased it at Tuppen's, a West Palm Beach sporting goods store, a year earlier, but unfortunately hadn't recorded the serial number.

The missing shotgun set off an alarm bell in Springer's mind. Based on his cursory examination of the dead woman, it seemed that the butt of a shotgun or rifle may have been the weapon used to bludgeon her to death.

But that brought up another troubling point. If the killer had taken the shotgun from the stand before entering her bedroom, did he already know that she was there? And if he knew she was there, did he intend to kill her regardless of whether she was asleep or awake? If the killer was a burglar who merely wanted to steal the shotgun instead of using it as a murder weapon, it would seem more logical for him to leave it where it was until he finished searching the bedroom for valuables, then pick it up on the way out.

At first glance, Anita Spearman's death might have appeared to be a tragic, although routine murder that occurred during a burglary. Almost an accidental homicide. A burglar could have broken into the house, perhaps after lying in wait outside and watching Robert Spearman leave, then slipping inside, only to be surprised by Anita Spearman. It wouldn't be the first time that a frightened thief had committed murder after breaking into a house he thought was empty, only to be surprised by one of the residents.

Curiously, however, except for Anita's rings, the shotgun, and possibly a few other articles of jewelry, nothing else appeared to be missing from the house. A hurried burglar, who killed in a moment of alarm, might well have not stuck around to rummage through drawers looking for valuables. But it was difficult for the investigators to understand how he could have missed scooping up a .357 Magnum that was lying on the top of a nightstand next to Anita's bed, especially when he had taken the shotgun.

And there were other easily transportable valuables in plain sight. Jewelry and cash were still lying on top of dressers when police arrived. The victim's gold and silver Rolex watch, worth at least two thousand dollars, was still on her wrist, although the killer had taken the time to strip the valuable ring and the wedding band from her fingers. And there was a television set and a VCR, both appliances that were unlikely to be overlooked by burglars. Her purse, with credit cards and cash inside, was still lying on a coffee table. The detectives were bothered by the perplexing departure from a pattern burglary at the crime scene, as well as by Spearman's sudden mood shifts.

Kianka and Springer didn't learn until much later in the day that Anita was an important official in West Palm Beach city government, and that she had friends in high places—including their boss, Sheriff Richard Wille. They learned as well about her local newspaper background.

When the municipal offices in West Palm Beach opened to resume regular business on the Monday morning after the slaying, the flag at city hall was flown at half-mast. Black ribbons were attached to the doors of county offices. Former colleagues, who only a few hours before were happily planning her retirement party, were now in deep mourning. Anita Spearman had been a women with numerous friends. But somewhere, she also had at least one remorseless and deadly enemy.

The shocking news of Anita's murder was splashed on the front page of the *Sunday Palm Beach Post* in screaming headlines. Hundreds of murders in Palm

Beach county are recorded in the newspaper every year, but most are part of the mindless violence of the slums, fallouts among junkies and narcotics traffickers, or domestic spats that turn deadly. As tragic as they are, there is little that is unusual—or especially newsworthy—about them. Even though most editors would be unlikely to admit it to outsiders, they are treated by the media as nickel-and-dime homicides, worth only the bare minimum of space in newspapers, and probably no air time at all on the television news. But this slaying was not one that would be kissed off in a four-inch story in either the *Post-Times* or the competing *Miami Herald* and *News and Sun-Sentinel* from nearby Fort Lauderdale. And the story was featured prominently on the newscasts of every commercial television station in the viewing area.

Anita was not only a law-abiding and prominent citizen who was brutally murdered in her own home, she had also at one time been a respected member of the local news-gathering community. Even though she had left her career in journalism years ago, she was still considered to be one of their own. And now her grisly murder had turned her into a reluctant and helpless subject of big news.

In one of the first stories carried in the *Post,* the newspaper reported that there were no suspects. It was a straight, factual statement, yet one that might also have been interpreted as an accusation or implication that the Sheriff's Department was, in some undefined way, not doing its job.

The investigation was only a few hours old before Sheriff Wille was on the telephone to Sergeant Kianka. He wanted to know if, indeed, there were no suspects, and who was assigned as lead investigator.

Kianka told him the only suspect at the moment was Robert Spearman; not so much because they had any evidence implicating him, but because he was the last person known to have seen his wife alive. And although it went unsaid, every experienced homicide investigator knows that many, possibly most, homicides involve people who are emotionally close to each other—most often as family members or lovers. When a married or recently divorced man or woman is murdered, in many cases the spouse almost automatically becomes a suspect.

Kianka advised his boss that Springer was the lead investigator in the case. He also pointed out that Springer had been a detective with the department for two years, and was an experienced and able lawman. Wille was satisfied, and hung up the telephone after asking Kianka to keep him informed about the progress of the investigation.

Kianka wasn't bothered by the fact that his boss had expressed an active interest in the case. The Palm Beach County sheriff's job is an elected office, and Wille was a politician as well as Palm Beach County's chief law enforcement officer. But the men in his department respected him—many even admired him. He was supportive of his officers and rarely interfered with an investigation.

Wille had held his job for twelve years, not simply because he was a good politician, but also because he was a good administrator. And he knew the business of law enforcement. During the dozen years he had been in office, he transformed the Palm Beach County Sheriff's Department from a modestly small, local law enforcement agency into one of the best in the state. He hired the best men and women available, and provided them with up-to-date equipment and training. By 1985 the sheriff's department had nearly fifteen hundred employes, and the annual budget was close to $100 million. Sheriff Wille wasn't presiding over a nickel-and-dime operation.

Palm Beach County had nearly tripled its population and economic base during Wille's tenure as sheriff. The county had come a long way from the mosquito-and-alligator infested swamp it was in 1890, when the multimillionaire railroad builder and cofounder of Standard Oil, Henry Flagler, built a railroad station on the mainland so that the rich would have a convenient way to reach the plush resort town he had built up on Palm Beach. Today the barrier island separated from the mainland by the Intracoastal Waterway is world-famous as a home and playground for the genteel—and sometimes not so genteel—rich.

The city of West Palm Beach was originally established in the late 1890s to house servants who worked for the wealthy northerners wintering in Palm Beach. Except for the railroad station in West Palm Beach, the country was undeveloped, mostly swamps, grubby farms, and sprawling ranches with scraggly herds of skinny cattle.

In the 1920s things began to change in Palm Beach County and other coastal areas of South Florida. The county experienced an economic boom as real estate hucksters sold affluent Yankees on the notion that South Florida was a tropical paradise, an Elysian fairyland that would soon be teeming with people who were desperate to escape the harsh northern winters.

The Roaring Twenties was a period of optimism and flamboyant affluence throughout the nation, in fact. Confidence men and silver-tongued hucksters touted re-

tirement communities, fanciful cities not yet on drawing boards, and incredibly enticing opportunities for
earning big money and finding a better, more comfortable life in Florida. There was barely time, they
warned, to get in on the ground floor of a surefire real
estate boom that would make current land prices in the
North seem like candy-store bargains. Millions of dollars rolled into the accounts of the land promoters.
Some of the big talkers even actually bought land,
cleared it, and marked off streets. A few went so far as
to build homes.

But even the honest developers went belly-up when
the Great Stock Market Crash of 1929 occurred and the
nation slumped into a devastating economic depression. Cinderella dreams turned to bitter ashes overnight. The Great Florida Land Boom was one of the
first casualties of the stock market crash. Swampland
that had sold just a few months earlier for five thousand
dollars was suddenly being offered for a few dollars.
Usually there were no buyers, even at those prices.

The extravagantly promoted population and economic boom had been doomed from the beginning,
however. Older Americans looking for a warm climate
in which to retire found more warmth than they had
counted on, or could tolerate, especially during the
sticky, humid summer months. Younger men and
women fared little better. Not only was the summer
heat oppressive, the promised jobs simply weren't there.
With the exception of Miami at the far tip of the peninsula, South Florida slipped back into tropical lethargy
for another thirty years. It was the 1950s before the
arrival of the air conditioner began changing all that
forever.

Once more, most of the new citizens were northerners. Again, many of them were senior citizens, retirees fleeing the frigid winters of Indiana, Michigan, Pennsylvania, New Jersey, and New York. But there were also doctors, lawyers, accountants, shopkeepers, tradesmen, and legitimate developers, solid, middle-class citizens who were still active members of the work force but were seeking new opportunities and escape from the oppressive taxes and local laws that were beginning to strangle small and moderate-sized businesses in the North.

Some were also running from the burgeoning crime of the northern cities. But the criminals came right along with the Yankee refugees, or followed close on their heels. Fast-growing Palm Beach County must have seemed to be an ideal haven for the scalawage.

The county offered special opportunity for burglars. Skilled professionals could prey on the palatial homes of the very rich in luxurious Palm Beach, and in other nearby exclusive communities such as South Palm Beach and Manalapan. For those with less ambition, skill, or nerve, there were the homes of the middle- and upper-echelon executives, lawyers, doctors, and bankers in communities such as Boca Raton, and later Atlantis, Wellington, and a host of other plush developments.

Winter homes of wealthy northern executives, businessmen, and professionals are scattered throughout Palm Beach County and the entire Gold Coast area of South Florida. Many are left unattended and generally lightly guarded, if protected at all, but fully furnished, throughout much of the year. Without an efficient, alert, and vigorous police force to stop them, Palm Beach County and the neighboring area would be a burglars' paradise.

Armed robbers, purse snatchers, muggers, sneak thieves, and rapists also help keep police busy and on their toes in Palm Beach County, as they do in any community. But in the past decade narcotics traffickers, street-corner dealers, and drug abusers have become responsible for an alarming share of the crime. Despite the backbreaking influx of small-time criminals and big-money drug smugglers and dealers, however, by the 1980s the Palm Beach County Sheriff's Department was holding its own.

Wille had confidence in his officers to keep one leg up on the criminals. And forty-eight-year-old Sergeant Kianka had confidence in the men assigned to his squad, as well. He was an experienced lawman who had little patience with maverick or flashy cowboy types. He believed in teamwork, in each member of the squad working together. And he was a stickler for details, who knew the importance of legwork and checking out every lead.

Colleagues on other squads liked to pass the word around when they did a good job and solved a good case. Police are human, and everyone likes recognition and a compliment when it is deserved. But Sergeant Kianka enjoyed reminding his men of the cases that they hadn't yet solved, or might never solve. Let them take the bows, Kianka told his men, when discussing the others. "Let them think they're the Hertzes and Avises around here. We're the Rent-A-Wrecks. We may not be as flashy, but we're going to get the job done without worrying about how we look."

His men liked that catchy name tag. And thereafter they were proud to refer to themselves as members of the Rent-A-Wreck squad.

The men of Kianka's squad were treated equally.

When a big case, such as the Spearman murder, came up, he didn't assign it to the most experienced investigator or to his closest friend on the squad. Assignments were doled out on a rotation basis, and when Anita Spearman was bludgeoned to death, it just happened to be thirty-nine-year-old Springer's turn to head the next murder investigation. Kianka assigned the case to him without hesitation.

Both Kianka and Springer were themselves reflections of what was taking place in Palm Beach County's once predominantly Florida-born population. Both had come to the county from northern police departments. In fact, they had cut their law enforcement teeth working with police agencies in adjoining states.

At the time of the Spearman murder, Kianka was in his fourteenth year as a Palm Beach County sheriff's deputy. Previously, the veteran officer had worked with police departments in Ocean City, Atlantic City, and Pleasantville, all in New Jersey.

Springer put in ten years with the Pennsylvania State Police before taking an early retirement in 1981 and heading south. After a short stint in Florida as a probation officer, he joined Wille's growing department. When he took over as lead investigator in the Spearman murder, he had been a member of the Rent-A-Wrecks for two years. He was a cautious, methodical investigator.

Springer knew there was a host of possible motives that could be explored in the killing. Burglary, of course, was the most obvious. But violence in Florida is often tied to the flourishing drug-smuggling trade, and there was a disturbing possibility that one or both of the Spearmans could have been somehow tied in to the ruthless narcotics business—either as willing or unwilling participants. The boatyard, the *Equalizer,* even the couple's Beechcraft Bonanza airplane, could have attracted the attention of dope smugglers anxious to use the facility or equipment in their blood trade. Murdering Anita could have been a warning to Bob to cooperate in a smuggling scheme, if he didn't want to be the next to die. Bob, Anita, or both of them may have had a personal or business enemy. All those possibilities would have to be checked out.

But Springer needed to eliminate Spearman himself as a suspect before he could begin focusing on other possible killers and motives. And when Spearman at last walked out of the homicide division headquarters after the marathon interrogation, on his way home to drown his troubles in an uncharacteristic whiskey drunk, he had left some perplexing and unanswered questions behind. Springer was troubled by the inconsistencies in the two statements.

There were other things that disturbed the seasoned homicide investigator, as well. Why, for instance, had the killer taken only Anita's rings and the shotgun, and overlooked other valuables that could have been so easily added to the loot? And he puzzled over the widower's sudden mood shifts. Springer had by no means settled on Spearman as the prime suspect in Anita's slaying. But there was no question that the boatyard owner's statements would have to be carefully checked out. There were too many inconsistencies and puzzles to be cleared up.

While Spearman was being questioned in the Sheriff's Department homicide division offices, evidence technicians were busy at his house. Photographers snapped pictures of the crime scene. They took pictures of Anita's body from various angles, made close-up shots of the dreadful damage to her head, and photographed the bloody bedclothes, the wall, the night-stand, and the dresser.

Other trained evidence technicians dusted furnish-ings and doorknobs for fingerprints, and took carefully detailed measurements and locations of blood splatter patterns. Sgt. Gregory Richter, a crime scene special-ist, and another detective even dropped to the floor and went over the carpet on their hands and knees with magnifying glasses in their careful search for evidence. They were looking for anything from telltale threads and buttons, to ripped-off fingernails and foreign strands of hair, whatever might be helpful in solving the murder or later useful as evidence in a criminal trial.

At last Anita's body was lifted onto a gurney, cov-ered with a sheet, wheeled out of the house, and trans-ported to the Palm Beach County Medical Examiner's Office for an autopsy. The autopsy confirmed the ob-vious. Anita's death was the result of massive brain damage caused by four smashing blows to her skull with a blunt instrument. The beating had left triangular and moon-shaped wounds—like injuries that might be left after bludgeoning with the butt of a shotgun, rifle, or handgun. The medical examiner estimated the time of death as between 3:00 A.M. and 6:00 A.M.

Ironically, the examination confirmed that Anita was completely free of the cancer that had led to her double mastectomy. And the scars from her breast implants were healing properly. She had been well on her way to resuming a healthy life when she was brutally beaten to death.

Spearman's statement that he and Anita had made love the night of the murder was also confirmed by the report. A gynecological examination revealed the pres-ence of semen, but no sperm. Bob Spearman mentioned during the interview that he had undergone a vasectomy.

Springer frowned as he continued to study the report. The autopsy showed that Anita Spearman had not eaten for at least eight hours prior to her death. But Spearman had said in his initial statement that he had brought his wife a glass of apple juice before leaving the house. If she had drunk the juice, Springer wondered, why was there no trace of it in her stomach?

Springer and his colleagues had been busy. Detectives had begun looking through their records for cat burglars who might have previously worked the quiet residential area. They checked for other reports of crimes in the neighborhood. They knocked on doors and talked to neighbors, questioning them about any strangers recently seen in the quiet suburban residential area, and seeking any other information that might provide leads in the mysterious slaying.

Neighbors talked with police, but they were cautious about opening their doors to other strangers. The people on Bay Circle and nearby streets were scared. And most of those who did talk to inquiring journalists and other strangers who approached them about the murder wouldn't reveal their names. No one knew who had killed Anita Spearman, or why, and there was no reason to think that whoever was responsible might not return to the neighborhood to seek out new victims. It wasn't the time to be passing your name and address around to anyone who asked.

Some residents changed locks on their homes, or consulted crime prevention specialists about how they could improve their personal security. Then they followed up on the recommendations. A few who didn't already have personal handguns in their homes bought weapons. In Florida there was no waiting period for handgun sales. Florida's gun laws were among the most lenient and relaxed in the nation. The state wouldn't even initiate a program to check for criminal records of would-be gun purchasers for five years, until early 1991. At the time of Anita Spearman's murder, a citizen in Florida could go into a gun store and walk out with a new .357 Magnum or 9-mm Smith & Wesson in thirty minutes or less.

Springer and his colleagues had been busy trying to run down the missing shotgun. He checked with Tuppen's sporting goods store in West Palm Beach, where Spearman bought the gun. Since there was no weapons registration law in Florida, the dealer would be the only source for the shotgun's serial number. The dealer easily located the sales slip, but he didn't have an organized filing system. If Springer wanted the number, he would have to dig it out the hard way, by sifting through boxes of records. Stoically a Rent-A-Wreck squad detective launched into the backbreaking task.

The homicide investigators were also busy talking with colleagues, employes, friends, and acquaintances of the Spearmans from outside the neighborhood, about the couple and the tragedy that had so abruptly ended the near twenty-year marriage. Most of the people the detectives talked with had only good things to say about the Spearmans and their marriage. They drew glowing word pictures of a couple who were deeply in love. The childless couple worked well together, friends agreed. And Anita had proven to be just what Bob needed to curb his former roughneck ways, and smooth his rough edges. They were successful teammates and best friends.

One woman who was a leading Palm Beach county

politician said she was especially impressed by the concern Bob had shown about his wife after it was learned that she had cancer. A neighbor and longtime friend said he had never seen anything other than love and devotion from Spearman toward his wife. He never observed the husky boatyard owner speak harshly to her or mistreat her in any way. The woman who helped Anita out with household chores as a once-a-week cleaning lady for the Spearmans said she worked for them for years, and they always impressed her as a loving couple. The glowing testimonials were convincing. Robert Spearman, it seemed, was an especially loving and devoted husband.

At first glance it seemed that Spearman loved his wife far too much to have murdered her. He just wasn't the type to kill anyone, most of the couple's friends and acquaintances agreed. Furthermore, they couldn't conceive of a motive. He had no obvious reason they knew of to kill her. He had nothing to gain and everything to lose.

As much as most of the people who knew the couple liked and respected Spearman, no one tried to describe him as another Phil Donahue. He was a man who expected and demanded the dominant role in the marriage. And he was not only a careful monitor of expenditures at the boatyard, but he also extended his tightfisted control to the home front. Although Anita and her family had contributed a lion's share of the money to establish the salvage company, he had always insisted on making the business decisions.

Just as his employees had to run every bill past him at the marine construction company, and later the boatyard, Anita had to get his personal okay before making any major expenditure for the household. One time when the garbage disposal broke down, she had to put up with the crippled device for almost six months before her husband permitted her to have it repaired. This was the same spontaneous gift giver who at other times surprised his wife with expensive presents. Bob, it seemed, was a man of curious contrasts.

Spearman regularly left Anita at home alone while he went away with his cronies to fish, or to hunt birds. She also stayed behind in the house on Bay Circle while he sailed off on week-long trips to the Bahamas. He took other frequent overnight or weekend jaunts to Miami, Fort Lauderdale, the Florida Keys, and out of state, almost always without inviting her to come along. And he disliked many of her friends, dismissing them as intellectual or social snobs, without backbones or common sense.

Most of Anita's friends and relatives nevertheless believed him to be a good and loyal husband. Only a few of the couple's close friends knew that he treated her as though she were little more than a bright child. Some complained that he treated her more like a daughter than his wife. He ridiculed her decisions, both personal and in her job, and was convinced that she didn't have any real business sense. It was true that she had difficulty understanding the complexities of the marine salvage business, or how to handle a boat. But he would never admit that she was knowledgeable in areas that he knew nothing about, and would be unlikely ever to master. "He was always chewing her out for one thing or another," one of his close friends would eventually recall.

As the detectives continued to dig into the couple's background and domestic relationship, they began to turn up an even more ominous side to the macho boatyard owner that most of the Spearmans' friends knew nothing about, or so much as suspected. For one thing, they learned that his business wasn't as healthy and shipshape as he had presented it to be. Shortly before Anita's death, the couple had been faced with some serious financial problems to work out.

For another thing, they learned that Spearman was an outrageous philanderer. He loved illicit sex, and was known at various times to have taken off on secret sexual flings with prostitutes. And he had carried on a back-alley romance with another woman for years. They first heard of the affair when a West Palm Beach private detective telephoned Springer after reading newspaper stories about the murder, and revealed that Anita had hired him a few years earlier to find out if her husband had a girlfriend. He did, and her name was Patricia Rozelle.

And although Spearman had vowed to his wife after the confrontation at the restaurant that the romance was over, inspection of his telephone bills indicated that he had continued to stay in close touch with the woman. He had made numerous calls to her home over the past year. And, in fact, he telephoned her apartment early on the morning of the murder.

When homicide investigators went to her apartment and asked to talk to her, she slammed her door in their faces. The next day, however, she voluntarily showed up at the Sheriff's Department with an attorney and said she was ready to answer questions. It would be the first of two statements she would give, first to police, then to police and a deputy state's attorney, approximately two months apart. Both times she would be accompanied by her own lawyer.

As the lawyer sat nearby, monitoring the conversation, she admitted to the long-term relationship with Spearman that began in 1980. She insisted, however, that the affair had ended several months earlier. After that, the relationship had evolved into one of nothing more than good friends, she said.

Later in her statements to investigators, however, she said that several times during their relationship, Spearman mentioned divorcing his wife. Ms. Rozelle stated that her former lover had said during those conversations that he wanted to be fair to Anita. Then, she added, after Anita's breast cancer was diagnosed, he said he could never leave his wife while she was ill.

Ms. Rozelle said that she and her longtime lover had never discussed marriage to each other. "If he ever got free, I suppose we would," she observed. "We haven't talked about that. No, we've made no plans."

She also disclosed that Spearman contacted her after Anita's murder and told her he wanted to explain to her face-to-face what had happened. At the subsequent meeting, he told her of getting up early and going to Denny's, then on to the boatyard to catch up on business, the woman stated. She quoted him as saying that he stopped at McDonald's on the way home from the boatyard to pick up the sausage snack. He had told investigators that he picked up the snack after leaving Denny's and going to the boatyard. It appeared to be a minor detail, but the inconsistency was curious, nevertheless. Police cases are sometimes solved by paying attention to minor details.

According to Ms. Rozelle's statements, Spearman told her that when he walked into his wife's bedroom, "there was blood all over. Anita wasn't covered right, he couldn't arouse her." After he went to the neighbor's house and they returned with him, she said, he told her that they walked in the bedroom and wouldn't let him come in. She quoted him as saying they warned him, "Bob, don't come in here."

"He said he didn't do it. He wanted me to know that, which I never doubted," she told the detectives.

The woman said Spearman apologized to her. "He said he was awfully sorry that he had involved me in this and he didn't want to do that, and he said he felt real bad about it."

It appeared to Springer that another talk with the perplexing widower was in order. On Tuesday, November 18, two days after the murder, Spearman was asked to come in to the homicide division headquarters for another round of questioning. He reluctantly agreed, but he was plainly annoyed. He complained that he was busy preparing to accompany his wife's body back to Gaffney, South Carolina, for her funeral. She was to be buried in the family cemetery in her hometown.

The Miranda warning was read to him before questioning began. He was formally advised that he had a right to remain silent if he wished, that anything he said could later be used in court, and he had a right to have an attorney present, even to have a lawyer appointed for him if he couldn't afford his own. Based on a 1966 decision of the U.S. Supreme Court, headed by liberal Chief Justice Earl Warren, that reversed the conviction of a confessed kidnap-rapist, the warning had become a requirement before police could question suspects. Although Spearman showed some signs of anxiety and impatience, he agreed to talk. And he waived his right to have an attorney present. Like his earlier statement at the Sheriff's Department, the new interview with Spearman was also tape-recorded.

Reading of the warning was ominously significant.

The Miranda warning is read to people suspected of criminal offenses, or who might later be charged with crimes. Since the warning hadn't been read to Spearman before the earlier questioning, he apparently hadn't been considered to be a solid suspect at that time. The attitude of investigators toward him had obviously changed. This time two of Springer's colleagues conducted the interrogation.

Spearman seemed surprised when he was asked about his romance with Patricia Rozelle, and he was indignant. At first he angrily denied the affair. But when he was confronted with telephone company records of calls from his offices to her apartment, and with statements from the private detective and from Mrs. Rozelle herself, he grudgingly admitted that it was true. However, he insisted, as she had when she was questioned earlier, that the affair had ended long ago.

He explained away his business difficulties as nothing more than a temporary cash-flow problem tied to the changeover from a marine salvage and construction operation to a do-it-yourself boatyard. Although he conceded that the change of direction had led to a decrease in business, he said he expected the economic difficulties at Bob's Boat Yard to be resolved as he built up a new clientele. He told the detectives that he decided on the business change so that he could gradually withdraw from the daily operation and have more time to spend with his wife.

He said that Anita's will provided for half of her share of the business to go to her mother and sister if she died before they did.

Spearman seemed to be nervous as he told his story once again. But that was understandable. People are usually uncomfortable when they are being questioned by police. As he talked, however, troubling discrepancies again began to emerge between his newest account and statements in the earlier interviews.

For example, in his earlier account at the Sheriff's Department, he had told Springer that he had breakfasted with a friend and read a newspaper at Denny's on the morning of the murder. In his latest statement, however, he said he ate breakfast and read the newspaper at McDonald's. He also eliminated his account of giving Anita a drink of apple juice altogether. In the newer statement, he said he had merely looked into her room, and seen that she was still asleep.

The detectives pointed out the inconsistencies between the statements to the widower and asked if he would consent to take a lie detector test. Spearman agreed, but said he was too upset at that time. He told the investigators that he would submit to questioning with a polygraph after returning to Palm Beach County from his wife's funeral. The homicide officers had no choice but to settle for the promise, and Spearman left to accompany his wife's body back to South Carolina.

As Spearman and Anita's family were preparing the next day for her funeral, the persistence of the Rent-A-Wreck squad paid off. After sifting through hundreds of receipts from the sporting goods shop, Det. Van Garner found the sales slip for the shotgun. At last investigators had the serial number. Four days after Anita Spearman's murder, the shotgun, properly identified with serial number, was entered into the National Crime Information Center (NCIC) computer base as a stolen weapon.

A few hours later, Anita Spearman's family and friends bid their last good-bye to the woman who had left her South Carolina home for a new life in Florida

more than twenty years earlier with her head and heart
full of dreams. The widower didn't attend the visita-
tion, but slipped into the packed church through a side
door for the services. His eyes were misted over with
tears as he looked at the flower-covered casket. He
didn't chat with any of Anita's friends, and quietly left
with members of her family after the services were concluded. It was raining when Anita's casket was lowered
into the soggy grave.

When Robert Spearman returned to Palm Beach
County, he welched on his promise to take the lie detector test. Instead, he hired a leading criminal defense
attorney from West Palm Beach, David Roth, to represent him. One of the experienced attorney's first bits
of advice to his client was not to take the polygraph
test. A short time later, Roth formally notified the Palm
Beach County State Attorney's Office of his client's refusal to submit to the examination.

On December 2 a reporter with the Palm Beach
Evening Times telephoned Spearman and asked for an
interview. At first Spearman refused, but about ten
minutes later he called back and said he had changed
his mind. Even though his attorney wouldn't like it, he
said, he would talk to a reporter. Spearman told the
reporter that the sheriff's investigators considered him
a prime suspect in his wife's murder. And he claimed
the Sheriff's Department homicide detectives were
bumblers who were picking on him as a scapegoat because they couldn't find the real killer. Then he added,
in a voice that was shaky with emotion, "I didn't do
it. Anita and I were very devoted to each other. I feel
like my whole life has ended."

When Spearman was approached by another reporter
two days later, he did an about-face, refusing to answer

any questions. "I opened my big mouth once," he said, "and I'm not going to do it anymore."

On December 5 Roth formally requested that sheriff's officers provide him with written transcripts of the statements his client had made to investigators. And Roth wrote a letter to Assistant State Attorney Paul Moyle, the chief homicide prosecutor, that basically resulted in a near news blackout on the case. Referring to an earlier conference with the authorities, he said he was writing to confirm that neither he, state attorney's officers, nor Spearman would talk further with the media about the case.

"In light of Mr. Spearman's emotional condition and the nature of this investigation, we both have agreed that this would be the best course of action," he wrote.

Moyle agreed, and issued a statement to the press pointing out that no one from the State Attorney's Office or the Sheriff's Department would discuss the case with reporters.

But the lawyers couldn't keep other people from talking about the mysterious case. At the Denny's, McDonald's, and other restaurants frequented by Bob, customers discussed the Spearmans, and some speculated about his possible involvement in his wife's murder.

Customers at Bob's Boat Yard and nearby marinas gossiped about the case as they worked on their boats or gassed them up before leaving to spend a day on the ocean.

The three-block-long street that was Bay Circle had never seen so much traffic. Strange cars turned down the little street almost daily, cruising slowly by the quiet house at 2367, then continuing on and around the circular turnaround to pass by the structure once more on the way back to Prosperity Road. Occupants of the cars craned their neck and pressed their faces to the windows of the vehicles, staring at the house as if they half expected to see Anita's shrouded body wheeled out the front door on a gurney.

By this time Springer was firmly convinced that Spearman had somehow played a hand in his wife's murder. He suspected that even if Spearman wasn't the killer himself, he knew who the killer was.

Springer's industrious homicide team had been checking Spearman's bank statements, and learned that he had withdrawn large sums of money from his account shortly before the murder of his wife. But there was no indication of what he had done with the money. The lawman also learned that Spearman had telephoned his old flame, Patricia Rozelle, on the morning of the murder. And he had continued to telephone her almost every day after that. The detective's suspicions were also piqued, however, by the large number of long-distance telephone calls Spearman had made in the six or eight weeks immediately preceding the murder. Investigators had tracked calls to New Jersey, Indiana, Arizona, Georgia, and Tennessee. Seventeen of the calls were to the same two numbers near Knoxville, Tennessee.

The boatyard owner's continuing relationship with Ms. Rozelle, and the puzzling long-distance telephone calls, were intriguing information. But it was by no means the kind of hard evidence that investigators needed to break the case or make an arrest. And with Spearman now shielded by his attorney from further questioning, the investigation inevitably slowed.

Gradually Spearman appeared to be regaining his confidence. On New Year's Day 1986 he celebrated his fifty-sixth birthday. He was continuing to bunk on the

Equalizer, and he put the house on Bay Circle up for sale. He told friends he was thinking of buying a condominium.

On January 23 Roth mailed a letter to Moyle, advising that he had arranged for a lie detector test to be privately administered to Spearman by Roy Strohacker, a former police officer from the Palm Beach County town of Lake Worth. His client, Roth said, had passed. "I trust that this information will assist the Sheriff's Office in pursuing the person or persons responsible for Anita Spearman's murder," the lawyer wrote.

Roth also wrote that Lt. Pat McCutcheon, a Sheriff's Department detective, had consented to permitting an independent polygraph operator to administer the test. McCutcheon responded to the letter by confirming that it was true the lawmen had consented to a test by an independent operator. But the investigators were supposed to be in on selection of the operator. Roth, however, had left them out of the decision making, picked the operator himself, and gone ahead with the test without further consulting them, he said.

The Sheriff's Department officer stressed that he wasn't questioning Strohecker's qualifications. But because of the events leading up to the test, the polygraph results wouldn't be considered in the investigation.

The men of the Rent-A-Wreck squad agreed. They weren't impressed by the defense lawyer's disclosure that Spearman had passed a private lie detector test. They pointed out that not only were they shut out of the testing procedure, but they had no way even of knowing what questions were asked by the operator. As far as they were concerned, the test wasn't worth the graph it was printed on. Spearman was still a rock-solid suspect in his wife's murder.

Chapter 3

Sean

It was a slow Sunday morning on November 17, 1985, in Maryville, Tennessee, when the late-model black Chevrolet Camaro stopped at a red light next to Police Sgt. Michael D. Johnston's patrol car as he was preparing to stop at a fast-food restaurant for breakfast.

Maryville is a quiet little southern college town of about twenty thousand in the foothills of the Chilhowee Mountains, and the bespectacled, soft-spoken traffic patrol officer had heard his share of Andy Griffith and Mayberry jokes.

But he was an experienced lawman, and he immediately recognized the vehicle as closely resembling a car that local police had been on the lookout for since receiving a tip a few weeks earlier from a tow truck driver.

The tipster telephoned police on October 27 and reported that he had just hauled a white Toyota rental car into a Maryville shop after a minor traffic accident. The Toyota driver explained that the insurance company would be in touch, and prepared to leave. But as he was unloading his personal property and transferring it to a late-model black Camaro, he removed what appeared to be a MAC-10, the tow truck operator said. MAC-10 machine pistols are compact and are the most rapid-firing weapons manufactured. They can be fired with one hand. And they are favored by narcotics traffickers and other violent criminals who use them in bloody shootouts with competitors—and sometimes with police. The deadly weapons aren't used for hunting birds or deer.

The tow truck operator said he asked the stranger if he had a license for the weapon, and the man replied that he did. But the tow truck driver wasn't convinced he was telling the truth, and telephoned police with the tipoff about the gun. He also provided license numbers and descriptions of the damaged Toyota and the Camaro.

When Maryville police ran a computer check on the Toyota, they learned that it was listed as stolen. It had been driven from a Hertz Rent A Car agency in Houston, and never returned.

Now, by an incredible stroke of luck, it appeared that the Camaro was stopped in the next lane, close enough for Johnston to reach out and touch if he had been in the passenger seat instead of behind the wheel. As the light changed and the car pulled ahead of him, Johnston peered at the license plate to see if the tag number matched the one they were looking for. But the plate was bent over, obscuring the number. Failure to properly display the tag provided sufficient excuse to stop the car, even if it hadn't resembled the Camaro Maryville police were on the lookout for.

Johnston reached for his car mike, and ordered the

motorist to pull the Camaro to the side of the street. Then, as the Camaro veered to the side of the street, slowed, and stopped, the police sergeant guided his own vehicle to a stop a few feet behind it.

Maryville is small-town-friendly, but it has its share of crime. And, although the thirty-four-year-old officer may have shared an Andy Griffith southern drawl, he was well aware that he wasn't working in Mayberry. Maryville was a bare fifteen-minute drive north along U.S. Highway 129 to Knoxville, and had its share of criminals and crime. And Johnston was well aware that anytime someone who might be carrying MAC-10s was stopped, the situation called for extreme caution. He had already been in one roadside shootout, and that was more than enough to last him for a while.

Barely two years earlier, in 1983, he made a pullover that had looked like nothing more than a routine traffic stop, and it ended up in a shootout. The driver had been teasing police all night, challenging them to car chases, before Johnston finally pulled him over. Years later, Johnston would remember that when he began walking toward the stopped car, he was thinking how emotionally pleasing it would be to grab the troublemaker by the hair and tell him, "Boy, you don't do that in my town."

But he never had the chance. The driver came piling out of the door with a scattergun. Johnston proved then how good he was at quick draw. He pulled his service pistol and put three shots into the motorist. The man with the shotgun never had time to pull the trigger. Even with the pressure on, however, Johnston was careful where he laced his shots. He put the troublemaker temporarily out of action, but he didn't kill him.

So when Johnston approached the black Camaro, he

already knew from experience how quickly even the most innocent-appearing traffic stops can quickly turn violent and deadly. Consequently, he approached the car cautiously. The flap on his holster was unbuttoned, and his right hand was poised close to the butt of his gun, as a handsome, curly-haired young white male opened the door of the vehicle and slid from the driver's seat. A petite and pretty young black woman and two children remained quietly seated inside.

After Johnston asked the young man to walk over to the patrol car with him and produce his driver's license, the motorist apologized and said he didn't have the permit or any other identification with him. He said his name was Sean Trevor Doutre, but explained that he was on his way to church with his wife, Linda, and her two children, and he had forgotten to bring his billfold. "Well, that's better than nothing," Johnston observed, and began following the motorist back to the car for a look at the young woman's identification.

Johnston stayed right on the motorist's heels, and kept his hand poised near his holster as they approached the vehicle. If the curly-haired driver was indeed the man seen at the body shop with the machine pistol, there was a good chance that he could be carrying a weapon.

There was, indeed, a weapon. But the motorist wasn't carrying it on him. It was in the car. As Johnston peered through the front window, he spotted a sleek pump-action twelve-gauge Model 37 Ithaca shotgun propped, barrel up, between the front seat and the driver's door.

Johnston wasn't about to take any unnecessary chances. "I pulled my weapon, and got his attention," he would later matter-of-factly explain. Keeping his eye on the driver, the police sergeant ordered him to slowly back away from the car, and told the people inside to press their hands on the ceiling over their heads, and to sit still. Continuing to keep a watchful eye on the man and his passengers, Sergeant Johnston returned to his car and radioed for backup officers.

While Doutre and his passengers were transported to the Maryville Police Department headquarters for further questioning, quick computer checks confirmed that not only was the Camaro the car they had been looking for, but the driver had a criminal record and was an ex-convict.

Doutre had a 1982 conviction on his record for petty larceny and burglary. He served a short term behind bars after a 1983 conviction in Panama City, Florida, for car theft. And the previous July he was nabbed in Gainesville, Florida, on charges of larceny to a motor vehicle, and driving without a valid license.

A search of the Camaro, meanwhile, had turned up two more weapons. A 9-mm Uzi with fifty-two rounds of ammunition, and a .45-caliber pistol with a silencer, were found stashed in the glove compartment. Not only were silencers illegal in every state, but as a convicted felon, Doutre was legally barred from the possession of any guns at all.

Johnston and his fellow officers were also curious about $6,080 in cash, and several pieces of expensive jewelry, including a pearl necklace and a pricey bracelet, that were found on Doutre and in his car. That seemed to be a suspiciously large amount of riches for a twenty-year-old knockabout and ex-convict to be carrying around.

Doutre simply didn't have the type of background that would likely account for his acquiring so many riches by legal means. He had told Johnson that he grew up in Colorado, moved around the country for a

while, and came to Florida when he was a teenager.
He said he worked on fishing boats before leaving the
Sunshine State for Tennessee.

Maryville police permitted the woman and children
to leave, while they continued to check out Doutre.

One of their first moves was entering the serial numbers and descriptions of the guns in the National Crime
Information Center (NCIC) computer. The NCIC computer carries a national listing of stolen property, as
well as descriptions of fugitives, missing persons, un-
identified persons, and an exhaustive index of federal
and state criminal history records. It even includes a
listing of fugitives wanted on warrants from Canada.
But the computer check was disappointing. None of the
weapons had been reported stolen. Consequently, the
shotgun and the two smaller guns were tagged and
stored in the police property room.

The Maryville law officers, however, notified the
U.S. Bureau of Alcohol, Tax, and Firearms (BATF) in
Knoxville that they were holding a young man the federal agents might like to talk to. Notification of the
BATF is standard procedure when police agencies are
confronted with silencers, or semiautomatic weapons
such as the Uzi.

Doutre had an outlandishly shocking story to tell
when the BATF men dropped in on him at the lockup
in Maryville. But they had to work for it. At first he
couldn't even settle on his address. And at various times
over two different sessions with the agents, he alternately listed addresses in Florida, Knoxville, and elsewhere in Tennessee and in Louisville, Kentucky. It
seemed that he was a drifter.

Initially he claimed that the shotgun and the 9-mm
Uzi machine pistol were his. The pistol with the si-

lencer had been left behind in his car by a hitchhiker, he said. It wasn't a very believable story, and the BATF agents told him so.

Doutre responded to their disbelief by breaking into tears. He blubbered to Agent H. Russell Alford that he had more to say, but wanted to talk with a lawyer first. Doutre didn't telephone a lawyer, however, and the interrogation was temporarily stopped.

When the talks resumed, Doutre had a completely different story to tell. He said that he worked for a man named Richard Savage, who ran a tough girlie bar named the Continental Club, near the edge of Knoxville. The weapons, Doutre said, belonged to his boss. And he explained that Savage owned the weapons because he was the head of an interstate murder-for-hire gang. It was a startling and shocking admission.

If there really was such a thing as a code of honor or silence among thieves and other criminals, apparently no one had told Doutre about it. Once he began talking, it was as if a floodgate had been opened. He told the federal agents things they hadn't even dreamed of asking about.

The agents were very much interested in what the young man had to say. They had heard about Savage, and were already quietly checking out reports that guns were being illegally mailed to and from the stripper bar.

Doutre said that he met Savage through an ad he answered in a magazine for professional adventurers called *Soldier of Fortune*. Savage used the same magazine to advertise the services of his gang for contract killings, the former car thief declared.

He told the agents that he had been looking for excitement and adventure when he answered the maga-

zine ad, and thought it would be fun to live the life of
a mercenary. He said he worked for Savage for about
three months, first as a bouncer at the club, then as a
hit man. He said that Savage had dispatched him to
Georgia, Texas, and Kentucky on murder contracts.
Doutre claimed, however, that he didn't follow through
on any of the killings. He explained that he had traveled
with some other gang members who were planning to
kill a man. And he said that he lied to his boss another
time, telling him that he couldn't find the targeted victim of a hit, because he didn't have the heart to go
through with the contract murder.

The self-described sensitive young man claimed his
boss had even ordered him to murder his wife, Linda.
He explained that Savage was worried that she knew
too much about the murder-for-hire operation and
couldn't be trusted to keep her mouth shut. Consequently, Doutre claimed, he and his wife were on the
run from Savage. He said he was sure that the murder-
for-hire gang leader was looking for them both. Doutre
sniveled that he was afraid of what Savage would do to
the two of them if he learned about the talks with the
BATF.

He talked of other criminal activities as well. Curiously, however, all were either in the planning stage or
were contracts that were never carried out. He said that
Savage had once sent him to Florida to pick up drugs,
but he returned empty-handed. Now, he said, his boss
was putting together a plan to hijack a gold shipment
in Alaska that would take at least a dozen men to carry
off.

The information was intriguing, but in no way provided the kind of solid evidence that either the BATF
or local police agencies could use to file criminal

charges against the mysterious club owner. Agent Grant McGarrity asked Doutre if he could help catch Savage with automatic weapons, or weapons with silencers.

Doutre suggested that they might be able to get the goods on his boss by placing an undercover agent inside the gang. All the spy would have to do was telephone the number listed in the magazine ad, and pose as a would-be hit man, he explained. The agents would think about it, but there were no immediate steps to act on the young car thief's scheme.

Doutre had provided a lot of freewheeling talk about shadowy murder plots, multimillion-dollar gold heists, and other sinister schemes, but the hard facts were missing. And he had been especially careful not to incriminate himself. Two days after he was pulled to the side of a Maryville street by Sergeant Johnston and taken into custody, he was released on ten thousand dollars bail. He was scheduled to appear in court later on charges of illegal possession of weapons, and possession of a silencer.

When Doutre walked out of the Maryville police station, he took the jewelry, including the bracelet and an expensive pearl necklace, with him to give to his wife.

Information that would eventually be put together by the BATF, Maryville Police Department, and other law enforcement agencies would reveal a picture of a tragic youth whose childhood was a horror. The young man's mother would eventually be described by Sean's father and stepfather, and by social workers and others, as a former doper, boozer, and kleptomaniac who twice rejected her son when he was still an infant. According to his father, Lee Perry, Sean's mother often left home for days at a time. Finally, when the child was about nine months old, she walked out for good.

Perry said that when he returned to his home in Salt Lake City after work that day and discovered that his wife was gone, he walked into their bedroom and found his infant son lying on the floor behind the door. The baby was quietly tearing wallpaper from the wall and eating it.

According to Perry, he moved to Los Angeles with his son after his wife left, and got a job there. But one day while he was at work, Sean's mother showed up at the baby-sitter's and took the child away. But Perry recalled that he tracked the mother and son to her parents' home in Arizona. He said he picked the boy up once more, and returned with him to Salt Lake City. He took care of him for two years, until Perry was arrested and sent to prison for two years on bad check charges. The three-year-old boy was returned to his grandparents in Arizona, and Perry didn't see his son again for nineteen years.

The grandparents reportedly didn't want the boy, and he was returned to his mother. She had married Robert Swetich, and the couple was living in Nevada when the boy moved in with them. Sean's stepfather would later recall a troubled two-year marriage during which his wife drank heavily, and once overdosed on drugs. During that time, she gave birth to a girl. Swetich was at work one day when the brother and sister wandered into a local tavern. Their mother was gone again.

Once more Sean went to live with his grandparents, this time accompanied by his little sister. But it was only a short time before the grandparents returned the children to Swetich. They wanted nothing to do either with their daughter or with her children, he would later declare. But taking care of two small children was too big a job for the abandoned husband. He couldn't work and care for both of them. Reluctantly he sat down for a talk with his six-year-old stepson and explained that he couldn't take care of him anymore. Sean was turned over to the Nevada State Welfare Department. The child accepted the decision stoically. It wasn't the first time that there hadn't been room in the homes or lives of people he loved.

Sean was placed with foster parents, who were so taken with the dark-eyed, curly-haired boy that they asked for permission to adopt him. But Nevada state law did not permit couples in the foster parent program to adopt their charges. The child was returned to custody of the state.

He was seven years old when a couple named Doutre decided that they wanted the winsome waif for their own. Child welfare workers warned the couple that there was a good chance of serious troubles developing for families adopting a youngster as old as Sean. But the Doutres had made up their minds, and they were permitted to adopt him. At last, it seemed, the little boy who had been bouncing around from home to home with all the permanency of a tumbleweed had a real family that would care for him. But two years after they had adopted him, the Doutres returned him to the custody of welfare authorities. It seemed they had belatedly decided that the warnings of the social workers were on target.

Sean Doutre was back on the public treadmill. He was shuttled from one orphanage, foster family, boys' school, and home for emotionally disturbed children to another in Nevada, Arizona, Utah, California, and Washington State.

The youngster desperately wanted a man he could look up to as a role model. He was fourteen and living at a center for emotionally disturbed teenage boys in Cypress Island, Washington, when he met Donald Burrell. For a short time it appeared that Sean had found just the right adult to help provide the caring guidance that he so desperately needed. The young teacher-counselor was kind, concerned, and was impressed with young Sean, as well. Sean was different from the other boys. The others had family and friends in the area, someone on the outside with an interest in them, whom they could visit or receive visits from. Sean had no one, so it wasn't surprising when he latched on to Burrell.

Despite all his shuffling around, Sean was a quiet and well-behaved youngster, who was bright and talented, as well. He was athletic, had a flair for art, and was an excellent student. Burrell was especially impressed at how well the youngster had mastered the intricacies of chess. He had a quick, inquisitive mind. But however devoted to his young charges Burrell may have been, he had his own life to live. He resigned from the program and left Washington State to travel in Africa.

The time would come when psychiatrists and psychologists would talk about the devastating effect of what must have seemed to the boy as one more act of rejection. Sean's lack of roots and repeated rejection took an emotional toll. He didn't trust other people, and he seemed to be afraid to love.

A few years later when Sean tried to enlist in the army, he was rejected once more. Even the military didn't want him.

Life in the Southwest and Northwest hadn't been especially good to the young man, so he drifted around for a while, and eventually found his way to Florida. He found occasional jobs there on fishing boats, but it was hard, hot, dirty work with low pay. He tried construction for a while, but again the pay was low. The good money in construction went to skilled professionals who were carpenters, plumbers, electricians, or heavy equipment operators. Unskilled laborers barely earned enough to live day to day. And bosses didn't worry when they quit. There was always someone else who was desperate to take their place.

While he was living in institutions, Sean had become fascinated by some of the music that black youngsters listened to. He was crazy about reggae, the lilting Caribbean tunes developed and popularized by the Rastafarians, who consider the late emperor of Ethiopia, Haile Selassie, to have been a living god. Jamaica is the stronghold of Rastafarians, who call themselves Rastas, smoke huge amounts of the powerful locally grown marijuana called ganja as part of their religious rites, wear dreadlocks, and play and listen to the storytelling reggae music.

Two brilliant island musicians, Bob Marley and Peter Tosh, exported the music and the Rasta message throughout the Caribbean, North America, and Europe. Suddenly Rasta and reggae were no longer mostly confined to Jamaica and Jamaicans. The music, along with the religion and the dreadlocks, had become popular throughout much of the world. There was no need to spread the message of ganja.

Sean loved reggae and the two musicians so much that he adopted the alias of "Peter Tosh Marley." Friends who knew him by that name called him "Pete." It was one of various aliases that he would use, but it was his favorite.

Regardless of whichever name he was using, Sean didn't have much money. Like most young men his age, however, he had an eye for shiny new cars. And he didn't care if they belonged to him or to someone else. It wasn't long before he found himself in a Panama City courtroom, listening sullenly as a judge sentenced him to prison for car theft. He was sentenced under the name Peter Tosh Marley.

When he was released, he went back to the fishing boats. Then he answered an advertisement in the classified section of *Soldier of Fortune* magazine. The ad was placed by Richard Savage and carried the telephone number of the Continental Club. A few days later, Doutre was hired to work as a bouncer at the club—and to take care of other assignments.

Chapter 4

Doc Savage

Richard Michael Savage never had much luck settling into a job that he could make a success of. That was surprising, because he tried hard. And failure wasn't a habit in his family.

He spent his earliest years in Kentucky and Tennessee. He was born in Knoxville, but was adopted when he was six months old.

Raised in a loving family that also included a sister and a brother, he attended elementary school in Paducah, Kentucky, before the Savages moved to nearby Oak Ridge. Oak Ridge is a picturesque east Tennessee mountain city that became famous after World War II for the work done there, first in developing the atomic bomb, then the hydrogen bomb. Today it is the site of the Atomic Energy Museum.

But as a boy in Oak Ridge, young Richard was more interested in sports than in such esoteric subjects as atomic energy research. And he was good enough at sports—starring in football, basketball, and track in junior high school—that he could realistically set his sights on an athletic scholarship to the University of Tennessee. A knee injury, however, shattered that dream before he finished high school.

Consequently, instead of continuing his education at the university, after graduating from high school, Savage enlisted in the army. He joined just in time to be sent to Vietnam.

By the time he was in Oak Ridge Junior High, he had already acquired the nickname "Doc," and the tag followed him through high school and into the army. It would, in fact, stick to him for the rest of his life. The nickname was neither uniquely imaginative, nor surprising. Young males whose family name happened to be Savage have been acquiring the same nickname since the mid-1930s when a rugged fictional adventurer named "Doc Savage" was created by writer Kenneth Robeson, and became a popular hero of pulp magazines, books, and movies.

Richard "Doc" Savage would have a hard time living up to the reputation of his barrel-chested fictional namesake. But he would try.

He was a good soldier. During the six years he remained in the army, he served two one-year tours of duty in Vietnam as a courier with the Signal Corps. He was there during the bloody Tet Offensive of 1968, and would later talk with pride of working as a courier for the U.S. commanding general, William Westmoreland. He would also mention that he once shot to death a Vietcong guerrilla, and insist that the enemy soldier was the only man he ever killed.

When Savage left the army with an honorable discharge, he returned to the United States obsessed with a fantasy world of guns and glory. He enjoyed the company of other virile, adventurous men, the kind of companions who appreciated the eloquent simplicity of the finely polished blue steel of a handgun or rifle. A good precision weapon could be as smooth, lovely, and aromatic as the skin and body of a beautiful woman to people who appreciated such things. But he had had his fill of the army. His eyes were set on a career in law enforcement, and he took advantage of the GI Bill to enroll at the University of Eastern Kentucky in Richmond. He liked the independence that police work seemed to offer, and didn't want a job that would stick him in an office or on a factory production line.

A city of some twenty thousand people about a half hour's drive south of Lexington in the heart of Kentucky's bluegrass country, Richmond would play a prominent, sometimes sinister, role in Savage's life for the next fifteen years.

He married while he was in school, and became the father of a son. And despite the help of the GI Bill, he quickly found himself mired in financial troubles. He got himself a part-time job with the school's Department of Safety and Security as a guard. Even that wasn't enough, however, and there were times when he had to pawn or sell some of his modest trove of personal possessions. One time he sold a chain saw he owned to his boss at EKU.

By 1975, when he graduated with a bachelor's degree in law enforcement after four years at the school, he was already in debt. Financial troubles would continue to dog him for the next decade.

After graduation, Savage moved his family to the little red-clay town of Lindsay, Oklahoma, where he had found a job on the police department. Lindsay is about thirty miles due south of Oklahoma City, and the eager young apprentice lawman hadn't exactly moved into big-time police work. Lindsay was a small town of about four thousand people, and Savage found himself tied to a low-paying job that offered little excitement and even less of a future. He wrote a few traffic tickets, drove a few drunks home, played peacemaker in a few family fights, and rounded up a couple of stray dogs and wandering cows before he decided it was time to move up to a job as a state trooper. When he failed the entrance examination by a hair, he concluded he had had enough of the Sooner State and quit his job in Lindsay. He had been a police officer for six weeks.

It was time to move east, away from the red clay, the dust, and the boring flatland of the Southwest, back to the rugged but beautiful hill and mountain country where he had grown up. But there simply weren't any jobs available in law enforcement, so he drove a truck for a while. And he tried his hand as an insurance adjuster. Then the young husband and father moved into corrections, taking a job as a guard in the Kentucky State Prison system. It must have seemed at the time that if a position in law enforcement wasn't available, corrections was the next best choice. But the pay of state prison guards is notoriously low, and when it appeared that after two years, his career wasn't going anywhere, Savage shifted to a job at the Federal Correctional Institution in Lexington. A minimum-security prison, it was once a lockup and treatment center for drug addicts. The grim prison is smack in the middle of Kentucky's horse country, where sleek thoroughbreds can be seen at almost any time, grazing contentedly in the lush pastures and fields, or working out on tracks at private farms.

But all the beauty of the Kentucky bluegrass country

was outside the walls of the FCI. Inside, it was cold, grim, and depressing. And sometimes it must have seemed to the guards and other employes that they were almost as hopelessly trapped as the convicts. The pay and working conditions at the FCI weren't much better than Savage had experienced in the state prison system. He stayed there a year.

After leaving prison work, Savage was employed for a while with a loan company in Lexington. Then he got a job as an insurance adjuster in Knoxville. But less than a year after he gave up his aborted career as a prison guard, he returned to EKU and earned himself another degree, this time in criminal justice. He had acquired excellent educational credits in his chosen field, he had no criminal background, he worked hard, and he was a family man. Even with two degrees, however, he still couldn't find himself a good job in law enforcement. It was frustrating.

Savage's domestic life wasn't progressing any better than his professional life. In 1980 he and his wife were divorced. She kept their son.

It appeared that it was time for a change of direction and a new start. So he moved to Gatlinburg, Tennessee, at the edge of the Great Smoky Mountains, and went into the motel business with his mother, Muriel Savage. The mother and son were hoping to take advantage of the highly touted World's Fair in nearby Knoxville to get them off to a good start in their new business. But the fair was a flop. So was the motel. Mrs. Savage had been widowed for about five years, one year longer than the ill-fated business partnership lasted with her son. After he gave up on the motel, he tried to convert the property into a rest home. That effort also failed. So did a restaurant he opened in the nearby town of Kingston. Savage blamed the restaurant swoon on ex-convicts he hired as kitchen help.

One business reverse after another had left Savage mired deep in debt and on the edge of bankruptcy. He lived with his mother in Gatlinburg for a few months, then rented an apartment in Knoxville and moved in with his thirteen-year-old son. Muriel Savage followed suit, and rented an apartment in the same complex.

Savage was getting sick of his rolling-stone search for a profession. He had been a good soldier, but he didn't want an army career any more than he wanted to spend the rest of his working life as a truck driver or insurance adjuster. Law enforcement, his first career choice, however, hadn't worked out well for him. Nor had corrections, his second choice. And the economic depression of the early 1980s that threw the tourism business into a temporary swoon had helped put him and his mother out of the motel business.

A dark cloud seemed to dump black rain on every job or business venture he tried. Yet his brother was a successful attorney in Lexington, Kentucky. And his sister was the happy wife of an Episcopalian priest she had married in Georgia. His siblings were leading stable, satisfying lives. But here he was, thirty-five years old, and it seemed that he couldn't be successful at anything.

At last he heard about the Continental Club. Not everyone would have seen the club as an opportunity to better themselves. It had a reputation as a sleazy strip joint that attracted a rough crowd of bikers and mountain-country hooligans who came to the club to guzzle booze, fight, and ogle the naked dancers. It was the kind of river-town hangout that the late hero Sheriff Buford Pusser of *Walking Tall* movie fame used to storm into and bust up with his baseball bat. And it was just what Savage was looking for.

Alongside a country highway, the club was surrounded by hills that bloomed with flowers and flowering trees throughout the spring, summer, and early fall. There were the bursting white and pink blossoms of dogwoods, and vivid color splashes of redbuds, daisies, and violets. And right in the middle of all that natural beauty was the nudie bar. It was run down and squat ugly.

The physical ugliness didn't bother Savage a bit. He realized he had at last found a business he could succeed in. There was money to be made in naked women.

So he took out a lease on the club at the south edge of Knoxville, and began sprucing it up. He had a new stage constructed for the girls, and installed improved lighting. But the spruce-up was confined to the physical surroundings, the property itself. The girls still danced naked, and patrons still occasionally fought with their fists and boots. But Savage had been adding some new titillating twists to the entertainment menu at the Continental Club. He encouraged the girls to do more than merely prance around naked onstage. The acts of many of them moved closer to—many observers would likely say clearly beyond—out-and-out obscenity. Good customers or high tippers were permitted to touch, as well as look. Savage wasn't in charge of the Continental long before local police agencies began taking an even greater interest in the club than before and investigating complaints about widespread prostitution and dope dealing on the premises.

Nevertheless, the Continental Club prospered and earned a good profit under Savage's stewardship. The first month he was in charge, he grossed twelve thousand dollars. But he also hardened the tawdry water hole's already seedy reputation among the Knoxville area's vice squad police—and local good ol' boys and yahoos. It became known as an oasis where just about anything from booze and dope to sex-for-pay was reputedly available for a price. All this, as well as the titillation of bleach-blond and tattooed sirens with bruises on their thighs who proved during several performances nightly that they could do au naturel bump-and-grinds and chew gum at the same time.

Although Savage was tall, with a lanky masculinity about him, it seemed that he was an unlikely person to be the operator of such a rough and disreputable place. He was soft-spoken, outwardly unaggressive, and had a long-standing relationship with Debra Mattingly, a plump young woman he had begun living with after his divorce. Debra knew her way around, and when he took over the club, he put her to work as his assistant manager. He even loved little animals, and had a carefully groomed and affectionately pampered toy poodle he named "Duke." Duke was hardly the breed of dog that a he-man would select as his personal pet.

Savage was an enigma. At times he talked tough, but more often, it seemed there was almost nothing anyone could do that would provoke him. He liked to stand around at the bar and visit with his customers, casually exchanging gossip and observations in his soft Tennessee twang about the club, the customers, and the girls. Sometimes he would buy drinks for the regulars. When they bought drinks for him, it was poured from a personal bottle of Maker's Mark that he kept behind the bar for himself. He had never had trouble with alcohol, but he drank more at the Continental Club than he had ever drunk before.

David MacMahon knew Savage then and would later recall that the club operator was easygoing and went out of his way to sidestep trouble. He would rather joke around with people than quarrel with them. MacMahon described Savage as meek, a man who did everything he could to avoid confrontations. He preferred to let his bouncers handle any quarrels or fistfights that developed. Or he telephoned local police for help. Law enforcement officers made frequent visits to the club. If they weren't already dropping in to check out reports of drug sales, prostitution, other obscene acts, or liquor violations, it wouldn't be too many days before Savage would call them to settle a dispute, or to break up a fight.

Despite his background in the military, law enforcement, and corrections, the rangy club owner wasn't much of a fighter. One time when the jealous boyfriend of one of his nude dancers decided that her boss had been paying her too much personal attention, Savage was given a terrible beating in his own club. It was a humiliating experience.

Even though he may have had trouble keeping his eyes and hands off some of the girls, Savage also kept a close watch on the cash register. He had already failed at too many businesses not to pay attention to his ledgers. But much of the appeal to him of running the club seemed to be the rough-and-tumble clientele.

As soon as he took over the club, he began surrounding himself with hooligans and whores. Outlaw bikers, ex-convicts, petty thieves, penniless drifters, strippers, and prostitutes; all became part of the new in crowd at the Continental Club. It seemed that as far as the new owner was concerned, the more seedy and sinister someone was, the better. Some of his friends, employees, and clientele could have made a fit of the dry heaves look good by comparison.

That bothered MacMahon. His brother-in-law owned the club property. And MacMahon worried about the bouncers and some of the other street people and drifters whom the new owner of the club hired. About all anyone had to do was to show up and ask for a job, and Savage would hire them. It didn't matter if they had just gotten out of prison, or looked as if they had lost a fifteen-round fight to ''Smokin' Joe'' Frazier or ''Sugar Ray'' Leonard. Some of the dancers joked that their new boss would hire Jack the Ripper or Charlie Manson if they showed up at the club and said they were looking for work.

The bar owner lived in a fantasy world. He told outrageous lies about himself, and of the wildly adventurous life he claimed to have led. It was often difficult for even those closest to him, who were familiar with his fanciful stories, to separate truth from fiction. Wib Ogle, owner of Ogle's Floor Coverings, which was next door to the ill-fated motel, was impressed with Savage's intelligence and apparent business acumen. Ogle had served as police chief of Gatlinburg for more than sixteen years. Savage told him that he was a police lieutenant in another Tennessee city.

Savage was also a dreamer, and he loved being surrounded by virile, gutsy men and easy, sexy women. He wanted adventure and action—and if he could make some money while satisfying those desires, it was even better.

As 150,000 to 200,000 or more other American men, including a large number of Vietnam War veterans and law enforcement officers, were doing every month, Savage liked to thumb through and read *Soldier of For-*

tune magazine. *SOF*, which is subtitled *The Journal of Professional Adventurers*, had been published in Boulder, Colorado, since 1975 by retired Army Reserve Col. Robert K. Brown. And it was designed for the kind of men who are interested in such things as the brushfire wars raging around the world, unconventional warfare, clandestine operations, weapons, and exotic fighting gadgetry that can cripple or kill.

Colonel Brown has a master's degree in U.S. history, and is foursquare American, patriotic, and anxious to stand up and say so. In the pages of past issues of *SOF* he had offered ten thousand dollars in gold for the capture of Idi Amin, the bloodthirsty former dictator of Uganda. And he once offered $1 million to anyone who could capture a Soviet M-24 helicopter gunship and deliver it from Nicaragua. His magazine reflects his attitude. It attracts men who like rugged adventure, guns, throwing knives, other paramilitary paraphernalia, unarmed martial arts, and challenge.

Many of the readers are undoubtedly Walter Mittys, who prefer their adventure from the safety of their armchair, with a glass of Jack Daniel's straight up, or a frosty can of Bud in their hand. But others are doers—men of daredevil courage, or reckless foolishness—who sign up to fight as mercenary soldiers in the brushfire wars of foreign lands, work as bodyguards to unpopular businessmen and political leaders, or get themselves tangled up in harebrained schemes to invade other countries and to topple foreign governments.

In 1976 four Western mercenaries were executed by the winners of the civil war in the southwest African nation of Angola. One of the unlucky soldiers of fortune was Daniel Gearhart, an American veteran of the war in Vietnam. He had signed up to fight for what turned out to be the losers, after responding to an advertisement in *SOF*.

The executions, which sparked worldwide publicity and widespread condemnation of the new Soviet- and Cuba-supported Marxist government, led to an FBI investigation of Brown and his magazine to determine if they might be involved in violations of the Neutrality Act. Brown insisted that *SOF* was in the information business, not the business of recruiting mercenary soldiers. The message was obvious; *SOF* had no more control over what people did with the information they read in the magazine that the *New York Times* or *Time* and *Newsweek* had over the actions of people who read their publications. The probe died.

The magazine's macho, unapologetically pro-American, and fiercely anti-Communist stance, has put it at odds with much of the liberal-leaning conventional American press. The open enmity of *SOF*'s colleagues in the media, however, seems to have much to do with its popularity among its readers. While the conventional press was painting ugly word pictures of the anti-Communist Contras in Nicaragua as CIA-sponsored thugs, *SOF* identified them as dedicated freedom fighters and raised money for their support. At the same time that columnists in other magazines and in newspapers were fretting about human rights abuses by government forces in El Salvador, *SOF* was concerning itself with the mass killings and other atrocities committed by Red guerrillas operating in the civil-war-torn Central American nation.

One of Colonel Brown's pet concerns was American prisoners of war (POWs) believed by many to have been left behind when the United States was forced out of Vietnam in 1975. And when *SOF* set a sales record with the June 1985 issue, a bare-chested machine-gun-firing Sylvester Stallone was featured on the cover as the fearless ex–Green Beret who returned to Communist Vietnam after the war to rescue American POWs.

The cover story featured an interview with Stallone by *SOF* Executive Editor Dale A. Dye that was timed with the actor's movie *Rambo: First Blood, Part II.* In the interview, Stallone confirmed that he, too, believed that Americans were left behind as POWs in Southeast Asia. Other stories dealt with members of an *SOF* training team, including Dye, who slipped into Nicaragua to get together with the anti-Sandinista Contras; the civil war in Afghanistan; Col. Otto Skorzeny, the German commando who led the dramatic glider rescue of Italy's deposed dictator, Benito Mussolini, during World War II; and knowledgeable pieces about combat weapons.

That blockbuster tenth-anniversary issue was also the first to carry an ad placed on the last page of a six-page classified section by "Doc" Savage. Wedged between offers for a nonlethal chemical weapon to repel rapists or other attackers, and plans and materials for converting an automatic Ruger 10-22, the anonymous ad read:

GUN FOR HIRE: 37 year old professional mercenary desires jobs. Vietnam Veteran. Discrete and very private. Body guard, courier, and other special skills. All jobs considered.

The classified also gave telephone numbers for business and home, and an address in Gatlinburg, Tenn.

The night number belonged to the Continental Club. Savage either didn't know that the word *discreet* had been misspelled in the ad, or it didn't bother him. Serious shoppers would understand the message.

Five other ads, some even more cryptic than the Gatlinburg entry, appeared on the same page of the anniversary issue offering what appeared to be somewhat similar services. But many of the key words and phrases were the same as those used by Savage. He had looked over other ads before composing his own, and copied from those he liked. The sinister personal services notices were spotted throughout the classified section, as well as ads offering everything from brass knuckle "paperweights" and spiked dog collars, to bumper stickers calling on Hollywood actress-activist Jane Fonda to go back to Hanoi and stay there.

Display and classified ads in the magazine have offered crossbows, exploding arrows, deadly Ninja throwing stars, pineapple grenades, blowguns, instructions for making your own napalm, and confidential mail drops. *SOF* isn't a magazine for sissies or typical Sunday afternoon golfers.

The same words cropped up repeatedly in the personal services classifieds. *Mercenary, high-risk, weapons expert, explosives expert*, and *discreet* or *private* were words used in one ad after another.

One of the ads offered the intelligence services of a "female" who claimed to have trained under a Green Beret and was looking for an assignment in Europe. Obviously the magazine's appeal isn't exclusively male.

Advertising rates were printed on the first page of the classified section: fifty cents a word for personal classifieds, and a dollar per word for other ads. There was also a disclaimer notifying readers that *SOF* did not have the resources to verify the validity of each ad. Readers dissatisfied with products or services contracted through the ads were advised to notify U.S. postal inspectors. It was noted as well that the magazine was distributed nationally and internationally, and some products offered there might be prohibited or require special licenses in certain areas. The magazine recommended purchasers consult local law enforcement authorities about any items they were in doubt of.

Savage left his advertisement in the monthly magazine for six issues. It cost him a total of eighty-seven dollars. At fifty cents a word, or approximately fifteen dollars each time the ad ran, he got his money's worth. Within a few days after the *Rambo* issue hit the newsstands, there were almost more calls and letters streaming into the Gatlinburg address and telephone numbers he had listed than he could handle.

Not all the calls were from prospective clients with jobs to carry out. Many were from men looking for work. Most of them had more bluster than brains, and they paraded into the club like a shell-shocked troop of ragged zombies. They were schemers, conspirators, drifters, and law enforcement rejects.

It wasn't long before Michael Wayne Jackson, a forty-two-year-old former police chief from little Tatum, Texas, showed up at the bar. William Clayton Buckley, a former security guard and Vietnam veteran, also found his way to the seedy nightclub on the outskirts of Knoxville. Eighteen-year-old Dean DeLuca from Toronto, Canada, was the youngest member. And of course, there was Sean Trevor Doutre, as well as a handful of others. Doutre was still playing with his Peter Tosh Marley persona, and insisted that people who worked or hung around the club call him ''Pete.''

Jackson had run his own classified in *SOF*, looking for the same kind of work his new pal was advertising for. It was Jackson's ad that brought the two men together. Savage called him at his home in Linden, Texas, and asked if the ad had brought him any business. When Jackson replied that it hadn't generated a very encouraging response, Savage made a couple of suggestions. He recommended dropping in subsequent ads any mention of Jackson's former job as a chief of police, and instead emphasizing his experience in Vietnam as a sniper.

Jackson took the advice, and his telephone began ringing with offers of work by people who wanted someone killed. The ex-lawman would later claim that he turned down all the contract murder offers because he really wanted security jobs. Nevertheless, he agreed to work some assignments he got from Savage.

The ex–police chief did indeed describe himself in his ads as a "Nam sniper." But if that was true, he must have been incredibly good on long-distance targets, because when he was in the military service he didn't get any closer to Vietnam than Guam, the largest of the western Pacific Ocean's Mariana Islands. And he wasn't even in the army. He was a navy fire fighter. Both Savage and Jackson, it turned out, liked to spin tall tales.

Jackson and Savage had much in common, in fact. Like Savage, Jackson had earned a bachelor's degree in criminal justice. He was a graduate of the State University of California at Hayward. Of course, he had also been in law enforcement for a while, but not for as long as Savage. Jackson wasn't very popular with his employers during his abbreviated career as police chief of the rural east Texas town. He had an embarrassing habit of handcuffing prisoners and marching them through the city council chambers, while the council was in session. The performances weren't appreciated by his bosses.

The eccentric lawman found others means of grandstanding that were equally frowned on. He liked to sling his handgun low on his hip, and practice quick draws. Harrison County Sheriff Bill Oldham would later describe the former Tatum police chief to a newspaper reporter as a "gun nut" who would "see how fast he could draw and then shoot his barn door."

The Tatum city councilmen got their fill of Chief Jackson in a hurry. And they proved they could also be quick on the draw when the situation called for fast action. They fired him. His tenure as a Texas lawman lasted only three weeks, half the time Savage put in on police work in the neighboring state of Oklahoma. Texans love cowboys, but not on twentieth-century police departments.

Before he left town, Jackson was arrested for one of the nastiest acts committed during his short stay in Tatum. He was standing in his own front yard when he sadistically shot a dog to death, as the two young brothers who owned the pet watched helplessly and screamed in horror. Jackson later tried his hand at several jobs, none in law enforcement, and eventually settled in Linden, another little windblown town in northeast Texas. He was handy with tools, and when he hooked up with the new boss of the Continental Club, he had been working as a maintenance man.

Buckley was also handy with tools. He was a quiet man, who liked to tinker with mechanical things—like guns, bombs, and hand grenades. He was from Nicholasville, Kentucky. Nicholasville was a town of six thousand to seven thousand people located between Richmond, where Savage had gone to college, and Lexington, where he had worked as a prison guard. Buckley may have become a security guard because he couldn't get into police work. When he was fifteen he spent six weeks in an area mental hospital, after school officials accused him of plotting to murder a classmate.

He had managed to stay out of trouble since then, however. And only a couple of years earlier he was issued a card identifying him as a Knox County Sheriff's Department special deputy. He had requested the card from the office of Sheriff Joe Fowler in Knoxville, because he said he was a private investigator and needed the identification for professional reasons. Curiously, a few months after the card was issued, Buckley asked that it be canceled because he no longer needed it.

Ostensibly most of the coarse and hungry newcomers to the Continental Club worked at the bar as bouncers along with other shady characters who had found their way there earlier, people like Ronald L. Emert. Emert was a big-bellied, full-bearded small-time criminal who had been in and out of jail most of his life before wandering into the club. Emert had sold some stolen property, and bought some stolen property. And he occasionally dealt in a bit of dope. Savage gave him a job as a part-time bouncer and gofer. MacMahon would later tell a newspaper reporter that Savage hired about fifteen bouncers. Then he added: "He could have hired fifteen more to watch them, they were so stupid."

Doutre appeared to get along especially well with Savage, at least in the beginning. Some of the men, as well as the girls, made fun of the relationship. They joked that the husky club owner had become a father figure to the young onetime fisherman from Florida.

But if Doutre looked up to Savage, he was even more taken by one of the dancers. It made no difference to him that Linda Smith was black and he was white.

Doutre thought Linda was just about the cutest thing he had ever seen.

Linda had been adopted by loving parents in Knoxville, but had been living pretty much on her own since dropping out of high school when she was eighteen. She was working part-time at the club when Doutre breezed into town and into her life. She was as love-smitten with the handsome, dark-haired bouncer as he was with her. He was a classic hunk: tall, dark, and handsome, with long eyelashes that, instead of detracting from his heady masculinity, simply added to his appeal. He was a snappy dresser, and looked especially dashing when he wore his favorite Indiana Jones–style hat. It was white, like the good guys in the movies wear. Pete was the kind of take-charge, masculine sweetheart that girls who work in walk-in, drag-out bars like the Continental Club dream about.

A few days after his arrival in town, Linda took him home to meet her family. He introduced himself as Peter Tosh Marley. He added that he was born in Jamaica, and he was adopted after his mother died giving birth. By heartwarming coincidence, it seemed, he and Linda—two adopted children—had met and fallen in love.

But Doutre seemed almost too good to be true, so good that the Smiths couldn't help but be suspicious. They were protective of their daughter, and worried about the young man's puzzling wealth. He drove a shiny new black Toyota Celica, and sported a gold necklace that had to be worth thousands of dollars. And he was very generous to Linda. He seemed to be awfully young to have already achieved the kind of success that would have enabled him to accumulate such expensive toys legitimately.

When Linda's mother, Annie Ruth Smith, asked him what kind of work he did, he replied that he was in the security business in Florida. He wouldn't be any more specific than that, and said nothing about just where in Florida he worked, or who he worked with in the Sunshine State.

Whether or not the Smiths believed him, there wasn't much that they could do about it. Linda was infatuated with her new boyfriend. And there was no question that he was well mannered and polite. He was courteous to his elders, attentive to Linda, and respectful of the Smiths and their home. When the young couple stayed overnight, Linda always slept in her own room, and he bunked on the living room sofa.

He didn't bunk on a sofa at the 330-square-foot efficiency apartment in Knoxville that he and Linda moved into, however. The young couple and some male friends rented the three $150 downstairs studio apartments in a sixteen-unit complex. They all made themselves noticed as soon as they moved in. And they left mixed impressions on their neighbors.

Doutre earned the gratitude of just about everyone when he rushed into a burning apartment and helped a neighbor's children escape. But he didn't make many friends with some of his other activities. There was no indication that it bothered Doutre in the least when Linda would stumble next door and, between sobs, complain to a friendly neighbor that Sean was trying to force her to turn tricks so they could pay their bills. Eventually the sympathetic woman helped both the young people obtain jobs at a local motel: Linda as a maid, and Sean doing maintenance work. They kept the jobs two weeks.

Neighbors worried that Doutre was selling drugs

while the couple and their mysterious pals lived in the apartment complex. The couple had barely moved in before strangers in cars began showing up either late at night or in the early hours of the morning, stopping in the parking area in front of the apartments and honking their horns. In a minute or two, Doutre or someone else would come outside, walk to the car, hesitate a few moments, then return to the apartment.

There was no evidence that Linda was involved in either prostitution or drug dealing. And she was never accused or charged by police with committing criminal offenses while she and Doutre lived in the apartment.

Even if Doutre and his cronies weren't big-time drug dealers, however, they were up to something that was downright curious. Men went in and out of the apartments at all hours of the night and day, and there was some speculation that a prostitution ring was being operated there right under the noses of the neighbors. But if prostitutes were working out of the apartments, they had some strange clients.

A few times the strangers unloaded large plastic containers, the kind bleach is bottled in, and lugged them from their cars or vans into the apartments.

One time several men gathered in the parking lot, then climbed into a black car and drove away. When they returned later and left the car, the man who led them through the lot was wearing radio earphones. A couple of others were outfitted with heavy belts with loops in them, the kind that telephone linemen use for climbing poles.

The men returned a few days later on a Sunday morning togged out in military camouflage outfits. One of the strangers, who behaved as if he were the leader, had a large patch on the shoulder of his shirt that looked like an Army First Cavalry Division insignia. A man was also frequently seen lurking around the apartments in a blue uniform like those commonly worn by police officers. He told a woman who lived in the complex that he was in the security business. People hired him to protect them, he explained.

The woman later identified the "security man" as Savage, after looking at a photograph. Other neighbors said the camouflage-garbed man with the insignia also looked like Savage, but they couldn't be sure. Savage, as it turned out, was paying the rent on the apartments.

There were simply too many suspicious characters hanging around the apartments. Neighbors were convinced that the newcomers in the complex had to be up to something no good.

A few times a neighbor surreptitiously jotted down the license plate numbers of the cars parked in the lot by groups of strangers. He scribbled a few notes. And he pulled the venetian blinds back from his front window and snapped some photographs of the men wandering around in the linemen's gear and the military camouflage outfits. Then he telephoned the Knoxville Police Department and talked to an officer with the Organized Crime Bureau (OCB) about the strange goings-on. He gave them the license numbers, and offered to turn over the photographs.

The OCB responded by assigning a couple of men to keep the apartments and surrounding area under periodic surveillance. And when the OCB ran a check on the license numbers, they learned that one of the cars was registered to Muriel Savage. They tracked another license plate number to William C. Buckley, the one-time security guard.

But the OCB never turned up any proof of illegal

activity at the apartments. The BATF hadn't been any more successful checking out reports that Savage was illegally moving firearms in and out of the Continental Club through the mails.

Doutre's neighbors nevertheless had taken all they were going to take of the sinister goings-on. Sean was accused of being tied to a prostitution operation, and he and Linda were kicked out of the efficiency.

Despite Linda's complaints to her neighbor about Sean's efforts to pay their bills by making her work as a prostitute, and the troubles with their living arrangements, the couple were just as emotionally attached as they had been from the beginning of their relationship. And a few months after they first met, they were married in the living room of her parents' modest home in Louisville, Tennessee, by the minister of their church, the Reverend Stone Carr.

It wasn't until the couple began preparing for the wedding, in fact, that Linda's parents learned that they hadn't even known the real name of their prospective son-in-law. Sean had to have a copy of his birth certificate in order to obtain the marriage license, and when he sent away for it, he used the address of his future in-laws. When a birth certificate in the name of Sean Trevor Doutre arrived in the mail, Mrs. Smith almost sent it back because she had never heard of the young man before. Even the place of birth seemed to be wrong. Instead of Jamaica, the man named on the birth certificate had been born in the United States. Linda's mysterious fiancé stopped her mother just in time, and admitted that his legal name was, indeed, Sean Trevor Doutre.

The clergyman also had some early reservations about marrying the couple because Sean wasn't consid-

ered to be a Christian. But Linda's father was a deacon
in the Rest Haven Baptist Church, served by the minister in the nearby Chilhowee Mountain foothill town
of Alcoa, and it was difficult to refuse to perform the
ceremony. The Reverend Carr relented and agreed to
preside at the rites. Sean helped sway the minister when
he announced that he wanted to be saved, promised to
join the church the day after the wedding, and allowed
himself to be baptized. After his baptism, Doutre told
friends that he planned to reform his new bride.

As it turned out, the bridegroom and his unscrupu-
lous friends had many secrets, although they didn't always guard them very well. But they kept some better
than others. At that time the Knoxville Police Department's OCB didn't yet know that Doc Savage was one
of the furtive strangers whom the neighbors at the apartment complex had been so worried about—although they
were already quietly checking into his activities at the
Continental Club.

Doc Savage, of course, was busy fielding telephone
calls generated by his gun-for-hire ad in *SOF*. The
variety of dangerous, clandestine, or purely unconventional jobs offered to the strip club owner and would-
be adventurer were mind-boggling. There was the call
from the man who wanted a *Dirty Dozen*-like team of
gunslingers to hijack the gold in Alaska. Another caller
wanted a few good men to pull off a surprise assault
against the Sandinistas in Nicaragua. He said he would
supply the transportation, guns and ammunition, camouflage clothing, and jungle equipment, as well as
rubber dinghies for landing, and pay fifty thousand dollars to each man—or to their survivors—at the conclusion of the dangerous operation.

A couple of callers wanted Savage to arrange for

Rambo raids on Vietnam to look for American soldiers missing in action there. Another caller wanted him to pull together a few good men to help hijack an army payroll in South America. There was a scheme for a helicopter-led prison breakout. Others wanted him to help smuggle and transport marijuana, cocaine, and other illegal drugs. A woman wanted her husband murdered because she had found out he was a homosexual. And a husband in the Midwest offered Savage $150 to beat up on the man's wife. But they could only deal, the caller explained, if Savage would agree to arrange the time and place so the husband would be present and could watch the beating.

Savage was embarrassed after a brief talk with one caller who left him feeling like less than a professional. The prospective client asked the club owner if he did wet work. When Savage responded that he didn't know anything about scuba diving, the caller angrily barked into the telephone: ''You stupid son of a bitch. I want you to kill somebody.''

Wet work was a pet phrase used by certain elements in the espionage business when they were discussing assassination or clandestine acts of murder. Almost every profession has its own unique lingo, pet words and phrases that are especially useful or favored by those in the business. Savage hadn't mastered all of them yet. But he was learning fast.

The calls and the schemes were exciting. Some offered the kind of real-life adventure that is the stuff of Hollywood blockbusters, and little boys' dreams. A majority of the calls, however, were more sinister. The prospective clients were looking for a murder broker. And most of the calls were from people like the hot-tempered man who inquired about wet work. They wanted someone killed: a business associate, a mother, father, girlfriend, or boyfriend. Most often, however, they were husbands looking for someone to murder their wives.

Savage was amazed, but intrigued. Much later when talking to a newspaper reporter, he would marvel: "I didn't know there were that many nuts in the country."

Chapter 5

Bombs and Bungles

It didn't take many telephone calls before Savage had digested the message. Homicide was where the opportunity was. Calls were coming into the club at the rate of about one every other day, and a majority of the prospective clients were looking for hired killers. Most of those who didn't want to hire killers contacted him because they wanted to become hit men.

He was fortunate that there was so much available labor, because there was too much work for him to handle alone. Savage decided to become a murder broker. He would scout a few jobs himself, but more often he would coordinate the negotiating and planning, while sending out teams of hired guns to do the actual wet work. Now that he knew that wet work had nothing to do with scuba diving, he liked the word. It had a sinister, occult ring to it that made him feel and sound like an insider when he used it.

He used it when he was talking with employes or friends at the club. He dropped the phrase into the conversation casually as if he expected his listeners to be already familiar with its ominous connotation among men who moved in the furtive and murky world of clandestine contracts, covert actions, and professional assassins.

Savage treated the Continental Club almost as if it were a special sanctuary, where he could say or do anything he wanted, and his secrets would never pass beyond the walls. He was neither discreet nor private when he was talking with employes or patrons at the bar. It wasn't long after his first classifieds were published in *SOF* before he was openly bragging about being in the contract murder business and recruiting killers.

Seventeen-year-old Bradley Tipton was a high school dropout who had worked at the club only three nights as a disc jockey, for twenty dollars a night, when his boss asked him how he would like to make a quick two thousand dollars. All he had to do for it was to go on a contract hit Savage had lined up and kill someone. The shaken teenager turned him down, even though it was a top-dollar offer. Savage usually quoted a price of twenty thousand dollars to customers for each contract, and passed on a flat one thousand dollars each, plus expenses, to members of his murder squads. It left him a tidy profit margin.

One night Savage may even have been checking out MacMahon as a potential recruit. MacMahon recalled later that they were drinking a couple of beers when Savage casually asked him how ruthless he was. It was a curious question, which MacMahon replied to with a simple "I get by." Savage smiled, and dropped the subject.

When the new boss at the Continental Club was talking with prospective clients on the telephone, however, he was more cagey. The men and women who responded to his classified were not yet part of his world. If Savage talked to a caller who stated flat out, without beating around the bush, that he or she wanted someone murdered, he would act shocked. He would say that wasn't the kind of work he was looking for. He wasn't in the killing business.

If the caller sounded sufficiently cautious, but sincere, Savage would usually ask for a thousand-dollar good-faith downpayment, and a round-trip airline ticket. Then he would book a flight for a personal meeting with the prospective client. The meeting would give each a chance to look the other over, before making a solid and dangerous commitment to a killing.

Savage soberly confided to his cronies that you had to be careful when you were dealing with murder for pay. You never knew when the law might be on the other end of the telephone, trying to set you up. He explained that he had been in the law enforcement business himself, and was too cunning to fall into a police trap. Besides that, the classifieds were generating more than enough response. There were plenty of jobs available, so that he didn't have to take unnecessary chances.

Of course, he didn't tell his mother what he was up to. She knew about the *SOF* classifieds, but he assured her that the ads had nothing to do with anything illegal. He explained that he was looking for courier jobs, or work as a bodyguard. He had never been in any kind of trouble with the law before, and Muriel Savage accepted his explanation.

He would later insist that he did, in fact, do some interstate traveling on legitimate courier work. But he didn't provide details about the reputed assignments, and no one made any serious efforts to check out his claims. Other activities he became involved with after placing the ads were of more immediate interest to law enforcement authorities.

Savage had tried his hand at enough businesses to seek out expert advice from someone who had more experience in the world of big-time criminal enterprises than he did. A seventy-five-year-old career criminal and ex-convict who hung around the club became his adviser on the gun-for-hire venture. The people around the bar generally addressed the grizzled old-timer by his nickname: "Hit-Man."

Savage reportedly drew on the Hit-Man's knowledge and advice at critique sessions that were held after each outing by the murder squads. There was plenty to criticize, especially after the first few clumsy assassination attempts by his outrageous amateurs.

Forty-three-year-old Richard F. Braun, who was president of an oil and gas investment firm in suburban Atlanta's Cobb County, was marked for death in the first contract accepted by the leader of the ragtag band of ne'er-do-well killers and creepy crawlies in training. Bruce M. Gastwirth, an associate and former owner of the company, had seen Savage's ad in the June issue of *SOF* and telephoned to ask if he could handle a murder for hire. Savage agreed to accept the assignment for ten thousand dollars, only half of what would quickly become his standard fee. It would be a learning experience for everyone, a ludicrous and clumsy attempt at contract murder that was unbelievably inept.

The Reliance Capital Services Corp., in the suburban north Atlanta town of Smyrna, was undergoing troubling times, and was under investigation by the FBI for possible fraud. Braun ran afoul of his sinister associate after testifying before the Securities and Exchange Commission. He was preparing to break his ties with Reliance Capital Services and pull his money out of the company.

On June 9 Buckley slid beneath Braun's van as it was parked outside the businessman's home in the exclusive suburb of Sandy Springs, and wired a hand grenade to the undercarriage. But it exploded before Braun climbed inside the vehicle the next morning.

The Braun hit was a disappointment for the fledgling murder gang, but Savage had other jobs lined up. A bar owner in Rochester, Minnesota, had seen the gun-for-hire ad in the June issue of *SOF*. And he wanted him to burn down a barn owned by an Iowa chicken farmer whom he blamed for short-changing him in a six-thousand-dollar business deal. The job sounded as if it was tailor-made for the gang's line of work, and he had just the man for the assignment: Buckley, his explosives expert. But first he wanted to look things over for himself. Besides, he and his girlfriend, Debra, had never been to Minnesota. He told her to pack suitcases. They were heading west, where he had a job to talk over.

Debra didn't want to be the only woman on the trip, so her friend, Linda Smith, was invited to go along. Linda wasn't told what the trip was all about. Early in June the adventurers set out on the long drive west in a shiny Lincoln Continental. The incongruous chums from the Continental Club were as happy and excited about the adventure as if they were setting out on a trip to the Emerald City in the mystical land of Oz.

Many, perhaps most, visitors to Rochester are drawn to the southeast Minnesota city because of the famous Mayo Clinic, which is known for the healing work done there on ailing and broken bodies. Savage was heading to Rochester to discuss the gang's first venture into big-time arson. They were going to burn down a chicken house.

Richard Foster worked on road construction until 1982, when injuries suffered in a traffic accident forced him to look for another line of work that was less physically demanding. He had a longtime fascination with guns and other weaponry, so he opened F&J Arms, a survival camp supply business. Along with the survival gear he supplied to clients in Iowa, Michigan, and Minnesota, he also sold rifles, handguns, and a variety of other weapons. And he worked at building up his collections of antique slot machines and exotic weapons. An Uzi submachine gun would eventually become one of his prized possessions.

In 1984 he bought The Pub, a bar in downtown Rochester. From most appearances, he was a classic hardworking small businessman, determined to make a success of himself. Most of the people who knew the thirty-one-year-old bar owner liked him. He was easygoing, took good care of the pets he kept at his apartment, occasionally traveled to places like Las Vegas, where he once participated in a big-time pool tournament, and treated his girlfriends well. To the women who cared for him and knew him as ''Rick,'' he was a loving son, a devoted big brother, and an attentive boyfriend who was leading the life of a happy bachelor.

But law enforcement authorities had begun to become aware of a more ominous, shadowy side to his character and activities. Law officers would later learn he could be a nasty person to cross in a business deal.

Debra Mattingly and her friend Linda Smith spent most of their nights in Rochester in their motel rooms, while the men were away talking business. One time

Ms. Mattingly's boyfriend asked her to leave the room for a while so that he could talk privately with a man who had just knocked on the door. The stranger was Foster. Savage accepted the job, and assigned Jackson to go along with Buckley to burn the poultry barn.

On the night of June 22, one of the huge barns at a poultry farm in rural Fertile, Minnesota, about a half-hour drive from the North Dakota state line, exploded in flames. No one was hurt in the explosion or fire, but thousands of capons, castrated roosters raised for their sweet, succulent flesh, were incinerated. Local fire investigators quickly determined that the blaze was deliberately set. And the owner of the chicken barn suspected that he knew who was responsible: Richard Lee Foster. But there was no way to prove it.

The poultry prince had run into financial troubles in 1981, and accepted a loan from another area farmer who knew Foster. The chicken farmer would later testify in court that he subsequently became involved in a business deal with Foster that went bad. He said Foster was outraged, and demanded he make up a $3,000 loss out of his own pocket.

A few days later, two strangers jumped the distressed farmer and beat him up. Then a smoke bomb was set off near one of his farm buildings. Finally his poultry barn was burned.

Foster was elated with the success of the arson caper. So were Savage and his two-man arson team. The two bar owners were so pleased, in fact, that they continued to talk off and on over the next few weeks by telephone and exchange confidences. Savage even traveled to Minnesota a couple of more times to chat with his new chum about such things as guns, arson, and other areas of common interest.

But Savage couldn't waste all his time gloating over the gang's first big success. He contracted for another hit.

Alice V. Brado, a forty-eight-year-old terminally ill widow in Aurora, Colorado, wanted the would-be gang of want-ad killers to carry out a hit on a man she blamed for a business deal that had cost her life savings. She identified the target as Dana Free, a young building contractor with offices in Marietta, Georgia. Mrs. Brado said Free was her boyfriend in 1984 when she gave him the money to invest, and he took out a half-million-dollar life insurance policy on himself as a guarantee. He named her on the document as his fiancé and beneficiary.

But they fell out over the ill-fated business deal. And shortly after Free arrived in Georgia, he began receiving telephone messages from anonymous callers advising him that he was "a dead man." Free was never accused of or charged by authorities with committing a criminal offense.

Savage agreed to take the murder contract on Free's life for twenty thousand dollars, and selected Buckley, the same explosives expert who had been so successful in Fertile, to handle the hit. On July 13 Mrs. Brado gave Savage a five-thousand-dollar down payment for the killing. Eleven days later a truck driver friend of hers from Colorado, Ward C. Lambeth, passed another fifteen thousand dollars on to the leader of the want-ad killer gang. Lambeth not only lent her the blood money, but acted as her unpaid courier and delivered it.

Although Savage enlisted Buckley for the job, he decided to scout out the area himself. Accompanied by his girlfriend, he drove to the Atlanta area to check out Free's movements and to find his car. When he was satisfied that he had collected all the information he needed, he passed it on to his explosives expert. Early on the evening of August 1, Buckley waited in the darkness outside Free's apartment building in the far north Atlanta suburb of Smyrna, until he was certain he would not be seen. Then he slid under the contractor's car and attached two hand grenades to the underpinnings. The next morning Free climbed in his car and drove away. There was no explosion. Unaware that he was only inches from death, the Georgia businessman drove around all day with the deadly grenades hanging underneath his car. But they never exploded, because the pins were still attached.

Savage was furious, and he gave Buckley a ferocious chewing out. "Idiot" was among the least insulting names the gang leader called his bumbling underling. It was a humiliating experience for Savage to explain to his client that one of the hired guns he had personally selected had bungled such a simple job. Buckley had no defense. He had fouled up, and when his boss told him to return and do the job right, he agreed to try again.

But Savage had temporarily lost faith in Buckley, and asked Jackson to go along and take care of wiring the grenades. He wanted them rigged so that they would explode as soon as the car's ignition was turned on. Jackson didn't want to do the wiring, but he agreed to stand guard while Buckley rigged the grenades. That night after Free parked his car and retired inside his home, the chastened bomber slipped under the vehicle to rewire the grenades. Once more he secured them to the underside of the car, and this time attached the pins to the drive shaft. When Free climbed inside the next morning, turned on the ignition, and began to move the car out of the parking lot, the pins would be yanked out and the grenades would explode. It was a foolproof plan. Or so it seemed.

Buckley and Jackson were hiding in bushes nearby the next morning when Free walked out of his house, climbed into his car, and turned on the ignition. The engine started, then died. Free turned the ignition key again, and the vehicle lurched into motion and moved about fifteen feet. There was a plopping sound, and he peered out the driver window. A hand grenade had just bounced off the concrete surface of the lot and was rolling toward a row of bushes. As the second grenade exploded, Free scrambled clear of the car. He watched in shock and horror as the vehicle burned. He had just survived an assassination attempt for the second time in little more than twenty-four hours.

Unseen by their intended target, Buckley and Jackson had also made a successful scramble for their lives, as the live hand grenade unerringly bounced toward their hiding place in the bushes.

Unlike the first attempt on the Georgia businessman's life, the second bungled effort hadn't gone unnoticed. Free went into hiding. The ex–police chief and the explosives expert hadn't racked up a very impressive performance as hired killers. Not only had they bungled the second attempt to murder Free, but they had tipped their hand and sent him underground.

There was little that Buckley and Jackson could say in their own defense when they got together with Savage and others for the critique of their miserable showing in Georgia. But it was Savage who had to telephone Mrs. Brado and tell her that his contract killers had messed up the hit a second time. He promised to eventually carry through on his murder commitment. But the vengeful widow would have to wait awhile until they could track the frightened man to his hiding place, and he let his guard down, before they could try again.

In the meantime, Foster had come up with another job for them. He was so impressed by the team's performance in Fertile that he decided to even the score with a competitor in the bar business. His target, in fact, was Harold H. Hayes, the same man he had purchased The Pub from. After selling out to Foster, Hayes had opened another bar named Harry's 63 Club. And Foster was convinced that the 63 Club was taking business away from him. That was especially grating to Foster because he had been friends with Hayes for years and assumed that his chum wouldn't open a competing business nearby.

Foster wanted revenge, and was anxious to see that his competitor's business was crippled or destroyed. At first there was some talk about breaking Hayes's kneecaps. But the unsuspecting bar owner could never be tracked down when he was alone.

The conspirators quickly settled on another bombing and arson job. It would be just like the poultry barn in Fertile. Savage tapped Buckley, his explosives expert, for the job, and the two men drove once more to Rochester to meet with Foster. The Rochester bar owner handed over a thousand-dollar payment to Savage. Foster also pointed out some bushes near Harry's 63 Club where the bombers could hide while they were preparing to make their move on the competing bar.

But Savage and Buckley didn't like the plan. It was too dangerous. They returned to Knoxville. A few days later, however, Foster talked them into returning to Rochester to carry out the contract. This time Savage telephoned Jackson at his home in Linten and instructed the former police chief to meet him and Buckley in Rochester, where he had a job waiting. Jackson had some expertise of his own in the bomb-making business. And the arson contractors had also provided themselves with a handy booklet of printed instructions explaining how to set off an explosion.

Under Jackson's expert direction, the conspirators collected a volatile devil's brew of fertilizer, ammonia, and a rolling pin. Then they placed their unconventional bomb inside a garbage can, and set it outside the tavern. Savage and Buckley said their good-byes and began the drive back to Knoxville, while Jackson and Foster waited for the explosion. Nothing happened! Several hours later when the coast was clear, Jackson sneaked back to the garbage can and gingerly carried it away.

Foster was furious, and he insisted that Jackson try again. The bar owner enlisted a local man into the scheme. Then he drove Jackson on a shopping trip to buy some model rocket engines and an igniter from a local hobby shop. And he observed closely as Jackson assembled the new, improved bomb, for a second try at wiping out the competing bar.

When the bomb was assembled, Jackson and his local companion drove back to Harry's 63 Club, and left it just outside the building. This time the makeshift bomb fizzled, spit, and popped—but there was no explosion, and no destructive fire. Foster was enraged. He couldn't believe that Savage's hand-picked bomb expert had failed again. Swearing and fuming, he insisted that Jackson do the job right. Once more Jackson sneaked back to the trash can and carried it away for another try the next day.

This time Jackson picked up two one-gallon cans of

Coleman fuel, and assembled a new bomb containing explosive black powder. After the new, improved bomb was assembled, the conspirators waited for darkness before Foster drove Jackson to the bar. There, the former police chief attached the new bomb to the inside of a door to an auto repair shop located under the tavern. Incredibly, the caper went awry once more when the bomb fizzled and sparked, sending a thin stream of black smoke into the air. The smoke set off the fire alarms.

Rochester firemen, rapidly followed by members of the police department's bomb squad, speeded to the auto repair shop and bar. Officer Val Stevens saw the bomb as soon as he peered through a broken window pane in the garage door. He let himself inside and defused it.

Now that police had been alerted that someone was trying to set off a bomb in the building, Savage's bumbling hireling was forced to call off the efforts to eliminate Harry's 63 Club. No matter how much Foster might rant and rave over the foul-up, there was no way that even Jackson could be bullied or shamed into again trying to blow up the bar. Savage and his cronies were left with another embarrassing failure to critique.

But Savage was persistent. And he was determined to shape his gang members into true professionals capable of carrying out the contracts assigned to them. Contracts like the hit on Victoria Morgan Brashear.

Mrs. Brashear was a special education teacher in Lexington, Kentucky, married to a man whom another woman wanted for herself. So the other woman, Mary Alice Wolf, paid Savage five thousand dollars to have her killed. Ms. Wolf was twenty-four-year-old former Louisville waitress who had just begun working across the Ohio River in Jeffersonville, Indiana, as a home nurse helping care for a man who was a quadriplegic.

Ms. Wolf was bitter, and consumed with desire, envy, and hate. She was obsessed with Alan Brashear. She had dated him off and on since 1979, when they met while they were working at Kamp Kysock, a summer camp for handicapped children sponsored by the Kentucky Easter Seal Society. She was a nursing student then. They were still going together when he met Victoria Morgan at the same summer camp the following year. Victoria Morgan was a beauty, much prettier than Mary Alice, who was a plump, moon-faced, dishwater blonde. But Alan Brashear and Victoria Morgan didn't begin dating until the Fall of 1981, after they had met again that summer.

Alan had been having trouble breaking up with Mary Alice. He told her that he didn't want to go with her anymore, but she continued to telephone him, pleading to resume the romance. Sometimes she threatened. One time she even told him that if he died, she would dig him up after he was buried, to make sure that he was really dead.

He was afraid of her. He was not only worried about his own safety, but about the safety of the people he loved. He would later say that she made it clear that if he stopped speaking to her, people he cared for would be hurt. Consequently, there were times when she showed up at his apartment that he gave in and talked with her. A few other times, however, he would insist that she leave. He claimed that he even sent her money to leave him alone.

The onetime nursing student was heartbroken and furious when she learned that her former boyfriend was dating the pretty girl he had met at the camp. And she was bitterly determined to find a way to somehow break them up, or to lure Brashear away from his new sweetheart. Early in 1982 Victoria Morgan received a letter from Mary Alice claiming that she was pregnant, and Alan Brashear was the father. She said she thought that Victoria would want to know just what kind of a man she had been dating. The outrageous letter was upsetting, but unconvincing. It didn't work.

Just because the pregnancy sham had failed to break up the young lovers, however, didn't mean that Mary Alice was ready to give up. Instead, she launched a telephone campaign, repeatedly calling Victoria at her home and at her office. She said that Victoria was stupid to become involved with someone like Alan Brashear. Sometimes she would telephone five times a day. At other times a week might pass without a single call. Then the harassment would begin all over again. Victoria Morgan was upset and frightened.

Mary Alice telephoned and wrote letters to her rival's clergyman, to Victoria, and to members of her family, including an eighty-one-year-old aunt. She pestered Alan's family with letters, cards, and calls, as well. And she told other people that Brashear had gotten her pregnant, and she had given birth to his child.

At last the desperate couple passed word to the driven young woman that they had broken up; they weren't dating anymore. The harassment stopped. But it started again when she learned that she had been hoodwinked. The couple had not only continued to date, but they had gotten engaged and were planning a June wedding. The young lovers were merely learning to live defensively. When the bride-to-be announced the engagement in the Edmonton *Herald News,* her hometown newspaper in Metcalfe County, Kentucky, she left out the date and time of the wedding, even the church where the ceremonies would be performed. The caution was justified.

Mary Alice's frenzied emotional assault on her former sweetheart and his fiancé was exhausting, and unending. There seemed to be no end to it. So Victoria Morgan finally appealed to the local courts for help. Mary Alice reluctantly agreed to a court-mediated understanding prohibiting her from telephoning or writing to the couple or to their relatives.

A few days before Christmas, Victoria drove to Richmond, about twenty miles south of Lexington, to visit her boyfriend at his apartment. She had barely arrived before her plump nemesis showed up across the street. The young schoolteacher was looking out the window of her boyfriend's home when Mary Alice backed her car into Victoria's vehicle. The jilted woman had resumed her obscene pursuit.

There was simply no way that the couple could plan their wedding without making provisions to deal with the distraught woman who had been constantly harassing them for almost two years. And despite the court-mediated agreement, there seemed to be good reason to fear she was planning an ugly incident to ruin their wedding day.

Two weeks before the wedding, on June 9, 1984, a birth announcement appeared in the *Herald-News* claiming that Alan Brashear and Mary Alice Wolf were the parents of a son. Mary Alice mailed a photograph of a little boy who appeared to be about a year old to Victoria's mother. Victoria went back to court and obtained a restraining order to keep Mary Alice away from the wedding and reception. And an off-duty policeman was hired as a guard, to provide additional protection.

The new Mrs. Brashear had been hopeful that once she and her husband were married, his spurned former lover would give up. They were false hopes. The couple returned from their honeymoon to learn that Mary Alice had filed a paternity suit against her onetime boyfriend. And in December she telephoned from California and told Alan that she had given birth to his son, but the boy was ill and in the hospital. Later, she said the little boy had died.

The near nonstop harassment was nerve-racking enough. But the young couple had no way of knowing that their tormentor was about to become more lethal. Mary Alice had read Savage's "gun for hire" ad in *SOF*, and realized that she had found the solution to her problem. Or so it seemed to her at the time.

The Brashears were preparing to move from their home in Richmond to Lexington by the time Mary Alice began putting her sordid scheme in motion to have her rival murdered. She telephoned Savage, and he said he would take the assignment. But although she now had a team of contract killers lined up, she didn't have the money to pay for the job. The young woman and Savage began driving back and forth across the Ohio River between Louisville and Jeffersonville, working out the details. Soon a romance developed between them, and they found themselves mixing business with pleasure.

Mary Alice had been working for Paul Hickerson for about three months when she borrowed six thousand dollars from the forty-seven-year-old quadriplegic, and handed over five thousand dollars to Savage as his retainer. There would be another ten-thousand-dollar payment after Victoria Brashear was dead, she promised. Mary Alice had told Hickerson she needed the money to pay bills, and promised to work off the debt by continuing her home nurse duties. She considered it an advance payment on her work, more than a loan.

It was the first time that the murder-for-hire gang leader had taken a contract on a female. But Savage wasn't touchy about having a woman killed, and he didn't anticipate any serious problems with the contract. The woman who was fingered for death had no idea she was targeted for murder. And Savage knew the Lexington-Richmond area as well as he knew Knoxville. He had worked in one of the central Kentucky cities as a prison guard, and attended college in the other. He was convinced that the Brashear contract should be an easy hit. Instead, it was the beginning of a ludicrous comedy of errors that might even be funny if his objective hadn't been so deadly.

Savage drove to the Lexington-Richmond area, and followed his quarry around for a couple of days to learn her habits and scout out the hit. It was easy to find her, and she was easy to tail. He followed her to church on Sunday, and to church again Wednesday night for choir practice. And he followed her when she shopped, and visited with friends. One time when their cars stopped side by side at a traffic light, the young woman turned her head toward him and flashed him a sunny smile.

But the gang leader had a job to do. Returning to Knoxville, he talked to Jackson about taking the assignment. He said he thought the best plan would be to shoot the unsuspecting young woman on a Sunday, when she could be counted on to go to church. If Jackson couldn't shoot her then, Savage suggested, he would have a second chance on a Wednesday night when she sang with the choir. He said she was most vulnerable on church days. But Jackson didn't want the job. He refused to have anything to do with killing a woman.

So Savage turned to Buckley and Doutre, and sent them to Richmond to murder the friendly special education teacher. Before they left, he gave them the guns they were expected to use in the execution. One of the handguns was outfitted with a silencer. Savage always provided the weapons.

But the hired killers returned to Knoxville a couple of days later and reported they hadn't been able to carry out the hit. They claimed they had scoured the city of approximately twenty thousand people, but couldn't find the teacher's apartment. They were lying.

They had found the apartment without any trouble at all. And they had already settled on their plan when they pulled their car into a visitor's space in the complex's parking lot. The plan called for Doutre to immobilize the victim with a stun gun, then press a pillow over her face, and shoot her to death at close range. The sound of the gunshot would be muffled when he pressed the muzzle into the pillow.

Buckley waited in the car, parked outside the apartment building, while Doutre left to make the hit. A few moments later Doutre rang the couple's doorbell, and the woman he had been sent to kill responded by asking what he wanted. The hunter and his quarry were separated only by a locked sliding glass door. Doutre said he was there to see her husband, but he was vague about the purpose of the talk. Alan Brashear wasn't at home anyway, and his wife didn't like the appearance of the rough-looking stranger, or the sound of his awkwardly stammered story. She refused to open the door. Her suspicions probably saved her life. She had stared into the black eyes of death, and survived.

Doutre gave up and returned to the parking lot where Buckley was waiting for him inside the getaway car. He told his cohort that he couldn't go ahead with the hit because he was interrupted. He claimed he had successfully talked his way into the apartment, and was just ready to shoot the twenty-four-year-old woman when a neighbor walked out of another room. No one had offered to pay him for two killings.

Savage was disappointed by the failure, but he was determined to get the job done. He made a couple of telephone calls, and sent his triggermen back with orders not to return until they had completed their job. This time he sent Dean DeLuca, the Toronto teenager who had drifted into the bar looking for work as a hired gun, along with them as insurance.

By that time the couple, still unaware that a contract had been taken out on Mrs. Brashear's life, had moved to Lexington, a bustling city of nearly two hundred thousand people that is home to the University of Kentucky, and is about ten times as large as Richmond. Nevertheless, the hit team had no trouble finding the Brashear apartment.

But once more, they decided that conditions weren't right for murder. The three would-be hit men returned to Knoxville a few days later, and reported that they still hadn't been able to carry out the contract.

Mary Alice Wolf was getting impatient. She complained that her love rival was still alive long past the time she was supposed to have been murdered. She reminded Savage that they had made a deal, and she expected satisfaction. Savage agreed. But by that time he had given up on Buckley and Doutre. Even sending DeLuca along with them hadn't helped. So he tapped a couple of men who worked for him at the club to make the hit. He had never called on them to carry out a kill-for-pay contract before.

The neophyte hit men drove around Lexington, checking out the apartment and nearby streets that would provide a getaway route. They even swung by the elementary school where their quarry worked. One of the designated triggermen moved close enough to touch her, but he didn't. And he didn't use the gun that Savage had provided him with to shoot her. Later he would say that the woman was just too pretty to kill.

But the men weren't prepared to admit that to their boss. When they returned to Knoxville, they claimed they had good news. They told their boss that the woman had been shot to death as planned. At last Savage was able to telephone his client and tell her that the contract had been carried out.

A few days later, however, Mary Alice telephoned Savage at the club. She had learned that Victoria Brashear was still very much alive. There was no indication that any attempt had ever been made to kill her. The plump home care nurse was furious.

It was one more embarrassment for Savage in what was becoming a string of embarrassments. He had sent three teams of hired killers across the state to murder an unsuspecting woman. And no one had so much as fired a shot at her. Savage's normally mellow personality began to change. His temper became as prickly as summer cactus, and he snapped at his employees at the club, grouching that he couldn't trust anyone to do their job without hanging over them to make sure that they followed his orders. He even grumped about his dancers and the bartenders. But he saved most of his pique for the crackpot cadre of rowdies, hooligans, and police groupies that he called his murder-for-hire gang.

Finally he and Buckley drove to the Hickerson home in Jeffersonville to talk things over with Mary Alice. Savage had hatched an alternate scheme that could pay big money for himself and his client.

He recommended that instead of having the pretty schoolteacher murdered, Ms. Wolf should marry her employer. Then Savage's dial-a-killer crew could stage a break-in at the Hickerson house, murder her new husband, and they could all profit from the property and insurance left to the widow. She thought it was a rotten idea.

Mary Alice didn't want to hear about the outrageous murder-for-profit scheme. Even the silver-tongued Savage couldn't talk her out of her deadly obsession that easily. She was determined to have her former boyfriend's wife killed. She told the men that she was convinced that once her love rival was permanently removed from the scene, the heartbroken widower would turn to her for consolation, and she could rekindle their old romance. She was stubbornly determined, and wouldn't be talked out of the killing. But Savage was already a three-time loser. He tried to reason with Mary Alice. He argued that if Brashear loved her, he would simply walk away from his wife. The woman didn't have to be killed.

And although he didn't mention it to Mary Alice, he thought it would be a shame to murder someone as nice as Mrs. Brashear. He hadn't forgotten the time he was personally scouting out the hit, and she had smiled at him. Savage called off the murder plot against the unsuspecting teacher—at least temporarily.

He had other unfinished business to attend to. Bruce Gastwirth still wanted Richard Braun killed. And the troubled Georgia businessman was still ready to pay top dollar for the job.

Chapter 6

The Comedy Ends

Late in August, Savage returned with Debra Mattingly and Doutre to the Atlanta suburbs to murder Richard Braun. The gang leader had selected a 9-mm MAC-11 semiautomatic machine pistol, outfitted with a silencer and plenty of ammunition.

MAC-11s are devastatingly lethal weapons. They are such favorites of big-time narcotics traffickers that they are sometimes referred to on the street as "Miami choppers." Police are generally not allowed to use them. That kind of hellish firepower is usually reserved for the people in the black hats.

Savage's plan called for him and his girlfriend to park in the getaway car a short distance from the Braun home, and serve as lookouts. Doutre was designated as the triggerman. The onetime fisherman turned hit man dressed professionally for his latest assignment. He togged himself out in a dark ski mask and a new set of camouflage clothing, and hid behind a tree a few feet from the driveway at Braun's house in Sandy Springs.

The Braun home was in a neat and tidy upscale neighborhood, a pleasant and presumably safe place to live. Sandy Springs was far away from the mean streets of Atlanta with its rampant crime and violence. Yet the community was close enough to the lure of Atlanta's cultural and economic attractions to entice professionals, the doctors, lawyers, accountants, and successful businessmen who settled their families there. The quietly comfortable suburb offered good neighbors, good schools, and good living. It was a place where horror and violent death seldom intruded.

Savage's scheme called for Doutre to wait until Braun started his car and drove past the tree. Then Doutre was to leap from his hiding place, and spray his target with the high-velocity 9-mm shells. The ambush had been carefully calculated and organized, so that this time there would be no room for mistakes. The gang's ringleader was even on the scene to supervise personally.

Savage and Debra waited in the getaway car a few yards from the house as Doutre took his place behind the tree. It was early morning and a faint mist of silvery dew still glistened on the short grass of the neatly manicured lawn when Braun stepped out of his front door at about 9:00 A.M. He appeared with his sixteen-year-old son, Michael, and they planned to go shopping. The teenager had not been targeted as part of the murder plot. It was simply a stroke of bad luck. But it didn't affect Doutre's determination to carry out the contract.

He stood in a half crouch behind the tree, with his right hand tightly gripping the MAC-11, as the father and son walked to the late-model Mercedes and eased themselves into the front seat. The forty-three-year-old Smyrna businessman turned the key in the ignition, and a moment later the vehicle was backing slowly down the driveway toward the street. The car and its occupants never made it.

Braun probably wasn't even aware of the camouflaged and masked figure who stepped from behind the tree until the first bullets slammed through the glass and metal of the luxury car and smashed into his body. Perhaps not even then. Doutre already had the gun leveled at the windshield when he cleared the tree. Shell casings flew in every direction, bouncing and rolling willy-nilly on the lawn and driveway, as Doutre squeezed off a hail of metal at the man in the car.

The silencer muffled the normal sounds of the shells exploding from the weapon. The only noise was the rip of the shells as they tore into metal and flesh—and the abbreviated scream of the victim. The real horror was visual.

After the first mad flurry of shots, Braun tumbled from his car and staggered toward the house, holding his side. Then he fell facedown, sprawling helplessly on a small embankment. The shattered Mercedes continued to roll slowly down the driveway as the gunman stalked over to the injured man on the ground and trained the muzzle of his MAC-11 at him. Then he squeezed off two more shots into the back of his head, execution style.

A few feet away, the Mercedes had stopped, and Michael was wrestling the door open and lurching outside. He had been shot in the leg. As the ski-masked killer turned in his direction and pointed the MAC-11 at him, the teenager desperately pleaded for his life.

Surprisingly, the gunman hesitated. Then he dropped his gun hand, and pressed a finger to his lips. The sound of the soft "Shhhh! Shhh! Quiet! You didn't see nothing!" could barely be heard, before the long-legged killer turned and loped away, disappearing in the tree-lined and bushy area where he had been hiding moments before. By some miraculous twist of fate, the killer had spared the boy's life.

Michael Braun was hurt, but he was alive and conscious. And there was nothing he could do to help his father as he helplessly watched him die. The elder Braun was struck four times; twice in the side, and twice in the head.

Savage and his girlfriend picked the gunman up a short distance from the house, and the team made their getaway. They were still within sight of their victim's house when they slowed the car and Doutre tossed the MAC-11, and the silencer that was still attached, under a bridge. The next day Gastwirth turned over ten thousand dollars in hundred-dollar bills to John H. Moore, his helpful friend and go-between from the Kentucky drilling company. Moore kept three thousand dollars for himself, and delivered the other seven thousand dollars to Savage.

Savage's gang had at last spilled human blood. Even then, however, the hit hadn't been carried off without a serious glitch. Doutre's inexplicable act of mercy had left a witness alive. It was one more of the confoundingly unprofessional acts that the gang had been making a habit of. Instead of basking under the congratulations of Savage and other gang members when they gathered at the Continental Club for the debriefing and postcontract hit critique, the first-time killer was called on the carpet. His colleagues were disappointed in him, and they made sure that he knew he had let them down.

Although the shooting itself was carried out with

ruthless precision, Savage and his blood-crazed disciples had made other mistakes from the very beginning that enabled experienced law enforcement officers to recognize the hit as the work of amateurs. When Fulton County Sheriff's Department homicide investigators arrived at the shooting scene, they found the shell casings scattered all over the lawn and driveway.

Det. R. C. Wiley would later point out to reporters that an experienced and better-trained professional hit man would not have used a MAC-11 machine pistol for that very reason. The rapid-fire weapons eject the casings and toss the shells all over. And shell casings can provide important leads to investigators, and devastating physical evidence in criminal trials.

A more professional hit man would probably have used a .22-caliber revolver or similar weapon, Wiley pointed out. The small-caliber handguns do not eject the shell casings as the weapon is fired. And more skilled professionals would not have disposed of the murder weapon so close to the crime scene. A short time after the killer team's getaway, Ms. Mattingly went back to the bridge to retrieve the handgun, and found it exactly where it had been tossed. It was returned to Savage's personal murder arsenal. Keeping a gun that had already been used in a killing was yet another mistake.

Buoyed by the success of the Braun slaying, Savage sent a male-female murder team to carry out the aborted contract on Dana Free. Mrs. Brado still wanted him killed, and Savage had tracked the frightened businessman to Pasadena, Texas, where he was thought to be hiding out in the home of his fourteen-year-old son and former wife.

Pasadena is a suburban southeast Houston city of more than one hundred thousand people, mostly blue-collar families, that for nearly fifteen years had been trying to live down unwanted notoriety as the former home of one of America's most ruthless serial killers. Dean Arnold Corll, a sadistic homosexual who preyed on adolescent boys, was the ringleader of a cruel kidnap-and-murder gang responsible for the torture-sex slayings of at least twenty-seven youngsters during a spree thought to have begun in 1970 or 1971. The killing didn't end until late summer 1973, when one of Corll's young cohorts shot him to death during a paint-sniffing and sex orgy.

Police came under heavy criticism at the time for not paying more attention to worried parents who reported their sons missing, and insisted that they must have come to some harm. Police claimed just as insistently that the boys were most likely runaways—until they began digging up the bodies. So by early fall of 1985, no one in Pasadena was looking forward to making national news with another high-profile crime. But it wasn't their choice to make.

Buckley had been given another chance to kill. His teammate on the hit was Sherry Lynn Breeden. The rugged young woman worked at a Kentucky coal mine before finding her way to the Continental Club, where Savage gave her a job as a bartender and bouncer. The hard work in the coal-mining business had helped make her tough and sinewy, and she could hold her own in physical face-offs with any of the women at the club, and with most of the men.

Savage provided the hit team with an Uzi semiauto-matic, a .45-caliber automatic pistol with a silencer, one hundred rounds of ammunition—and as deadly backup, two fragmentation grenades. He told them to shoot the elusive businessman, and to make sure that he was dead. He wanted a hit that was clean and final. But Buckley had his own ideas. He thought things over while he and his companion were traveling to Houston, and decided against using the guns on the job. There was something about the noise and destructive force of hand grenades that he liked.

The hit team spent a couple of days staking out the house in Pasadena, waiting for just the right time to strike. Three times while waiting for the hit, Savage wired fifty dollars to them through Western Union as expense money.

The assassination team waited outside the house for the early morning darkness of October 12. Then at about 3:00 A.M., when the street was deserted and everything was quiet, Buckley pitched a hand grenade through the living room window. A couple of seconds later, his companion lobbed another grenade through a kitchen window. Their getaway car jerked forward and they headed off down the street at full speed as twin explosions blew the front off the darkened house.

Damage to the house was severe, but it could have been even more devastating. BATF explosives experts determined that the blasts were caused either by inert or practice grenades that had been reloaded by hand. Regular military fragmention grenades would have been many times more destructive.

Savage wasn't aware of that problem, but he was upset anyway when they returned to Knoxville and reported they had taken care of their assignment with a couple of grenades. He was even more disturbed when they were forced to admit that they hadn't waited around in Houston to learn the results of their handiwork. But they were pretty sure that Free was dead, they said. Buckley pointed out that they had used two grenades—doubling their chances of success.

The post-hit critique of the Pasadena caper was brutal. Savage wanted his hit squads to follow his instructions to the letter, and he had told them to use guns. He wasn't satisfied with being pretty sure that Free had been killed. He couldn't close out his contract with Mrs. Brado until he could prove for certain that her former sweetheart was dead. And no one had seen a body. His hit squad hadn't even seen Free inside the house before they tossed in the grenades. It was sloppy, unprofessional work. Savage groused that one of the advantages of using a gun was that you saw the victim before and after the shooting. With a grenade, you couldn't be sure. He pointed out that the gang should have already learned that lesson with the earlier unsuccessful attempts to kill Free and Braun by wiring grenades beneath their cars.

It was about two weeks after the grenades were tossed into the Pasadena house before Savage learned that his worst fears had been justified. Free had escaped again. He hadn't even been in the house when the oddball hit team tossed the grenades inside. The nervous businessman had cleared out of town before Buckley and his partner even arrived in Houston. Although both Free's son and the boy's stepfather were in the house that night, they were asleep in their bedrooms and were uninjured. Three times Savage had sent hit squads out to murder Dana Free, and each time the elusive businessman had escaped without a scratch.

Savage realized that if Free had been frightened into hiding out after the earlier attempts on his life, he would have burrowed even deeper underground after the latest effort. There was no telling where he was now. Reluctantly the Free contract was once more put on hold. Savage also put the payment to his erstwhile hit team on hold. Sherry Breeden would later tell law enforcement authorities that she didn't receive a dime for her part in the sorry debacle.

Savage was becoming frustrated. None of his hired guns appeared to be able to carry out a murder on the first try, and he was falling behind on his contracts. He had already been negotiating with a businessman from Palm Beach County, Florida, who had read his "gun for hire" ad in *SOF* and had telephoned, saying he wanted his wife killed.

The two men talked by telephone several times before Savage caught a flight for Florida to meet with the prospective new client. Robert Spearman readily agreed to Savage's twenty-thousand-dollar fee for the hit, and handed him a two-thousand-dollar down payment in crisp new hundred-dollar bills. A few days later, Savage sent Doutre and Emert to West Palm Beach to collect the rest of the fee. Spearman explained that his wife's body was riddled with cancer, and she was in agonizing pain. Murdering her would, in effect, be an act of mercy. Spearman made it clear that he was anxious to get on with the slaying. But the hired hit men would take their time.

Savage had another contract in Arkansas that his hit teams had been having trouble with. The man who had been targeted for death there was every bit as elusive and difficult to kill as Free, although he was easier to find.

Norman Douglas Norwood was a thirty-one-year-old law student at the University of Arkansas in Fayetteville. Like Savage, he had tried his hand at law enforcement and corrections. He had been a policeman in the asterisk-sized Florida panhandle town of Alford, held a job as a security guard, and worked for a while as a prison guard. He had even earned a degree in criminology and law enforcement from Florida State University before beginning law school to train for a courtroom role in the criminal justice system.

He was easygoing but anxious to move back into the working world as soon as possible. As a law student, he was kept busy hitting the books and didn't have a lot of spare time. He had a rifle in his apartment for hunting or target shooting, but few leisure hours to use it in. When he wasn't attending classes, or studying, he was often talking by telephone with his pretty friend and eventual fiancée, Kathy Smith Gray.

Norwood and the Tulsa woman met through her sister, Holly Smith, who was a fellow law student at the university. The relationship got off to a rocky, violent start in July when the sisters, their mother, and three other passengers tumbled off the edge of a cliff in a pickup truck. Norwood and two other men riding in the back of the truck were thrown out, and he landed on a boulder, temporarily paralyzing himself.

Kathy and her mother became two of the injured student's most faithful visitors at the hospital in Fayetteville. After his recovery and release from the hospital, he and Kathy continued to stay in touch by telephone. Often the conversation centered on Norwood's health or his progress at school. At other times it veered into the deteriorating state of Kathy's eight-year marriage to Tulsa businessman Larry Gray.

Eventually Kathy told her husband that she wanted a divorce. He was upset, but it wasn't the first time that he had experienced a failed marriage. Although he had a son by a previous wife, there were no other children, and he told her that he wouldn't contest the divorce so long as she didn't already have a boyfriend. Kathy replied that she didn't, and it was true. At that time her relationship with Norwood consisted of nothing more than the fateful outing in the pickup truck, the hospital visits, and frequent telephone calls.

There seemed to be no reason to suspect that the divorce troubles of the couple in Tulsa would lead to a murder contract on the mild-mannered law student in Fayetteville. Norwood seemed to be about as unlikely a candidate for targeting by a hit man as there could be. He was older than most of his fellow students, and he had his feet planted firmly on the ground. He hadn't returned to college to play. He was studious and serious about his career and future, and he looked the part. He wore glasses, dressed neatly, though inexpensively, sported a neatly trimmed red beard and mustache, and drove a three-year-old car. There wasn't much to differentiate him in appearance from many of the other male students or instructors on the campus. But that had already begun to change. Presumably no one else on campus was about to be targeted for murder.

But Larry Gray had bugged the family telephone, and he learned that his wife was in frequent touch with Norwood. When Gray learned that the law student planned to visit his parents in North Florida during the semester break, he put out a murder contract on him. And he notified Savage of Norwood's travel plans.

Norwood's first close brush with death at the hands of Savage's deadly gang occurred in a motel in the outskirts of Memphis, Tennessee, in late August—only two days after Braun was gunned down in his driveway.

Norwood received a telephone call while visiting his family from a woman who told him that she was calling from the dean's office at the law school. She asked if he could pick up a fellow student on his way back to Fayetteville and give her a ride. Norwood consented to the request, and it was agreed that he would pick his passenger up at a motel in Memphis, which was convenient to both of them.

When he was a few miles from Memphis on his return trip to the campus, Norwood telephoned the motel to let his passenger know that he would be arriving in a few minutes. But a man answered, explained that he was the brother of the student, and said she was taking a shower and couldn't talk with him at that time.

But Norwood's mysterious passenger wasn't at the motel when he arrived. Instead he was met by the man he had talked to on the telephone. The tall, handsome young man explained that his wife and sister had left a few minutes earlier to get something to eat, and he suggested that they wait in the room for the two women to return. The women never showed up.

It was a perplexing development. Norwood still had an approximately six-hour drive, and although he had plenty of time, he was anxious to get back to the campus. He couldn't understand why his passenger would simply leave the motel and stay away so long when she was depending on him for transportation back to school. And curiously, although she had supposedly taken a shower only a short time before, he noticed when he walked into the bathroom that nothing was disturbed. There was no sign that either the shower or the sink had been used. And all the towels were clean and hung neatly in place.

It was an awkward situation for both men to be in,

and after chatting uncomfortably for two or three hours, the brother suggested that they drive around and look for the missing women. When that failed to turn up any trace of them, he suggested that Norwood stay overnight. It was already late and Norwood reluctantly agreed. He stayed in the motel room that had already been signed for, and his new acquaintance took another room.

The women still hadn't shown up the next morning, and the brother of Norwood's missing passenger made a belated confession. He explained that his sister hadn't been at the motel at all the previous day. He admitted that she was simply late, and he had merely been trying to delay Norwood until she showed up.

But Norwood had run out of time and patience, and he left Memphis without his passenger. He was unaware, as he made the long drive back to Fayetteville by himself, that, in fact, there had never been a passenger. It was only due to some strange quirk on the part of the young man he had spent so many uncomfortable hours with at the motel that he hadn't been murdered. The young man was Sean Doutre, and he had been sent to kill Norwood.

The telephone call from the law school dean's office was bogus, a ruse engineered by Savage. The strip club operator's girlfriend, Debra Mattingly, had made the call, posing as the secretary for the dean.

Although Norwood had walked into the trap set for him, for some reason never explained, Doutre simply decided not to go ahead with the contract killing. He returned to Knoxville and told Savage that he had left the motel for a few minutes to drink a beer, and missed meeting with Norwood. It was all a matter of bad timing, he lied.

Even though luck was on the unsuspecting law student's side in Memphis, the murder-for-hire gang wasn't yet through with him. Doutre's perplexing reluctance to kill again so soon after the Georgia slaying had provided only a temporary reprieve. Savage was still determined to carry out the murder contract. The day after Norwood returned to the campus, the gang leader dispatched a two-member hit-man team to make another try.

It was a hot and typically humid late summer morning in Fayetteville when someone knocked on the door of Norwood's off-campus apartment while he was talking on the telephone. He continued his telephone conversation as he opened the door, and motioned two men standing at the entrance to follow him inside. One of the men was middle-aged, with a belly just beginning to peep in a gentle sag over his belt. He wore cowboy boots. The other was much younger, and looked as if he might still be in his teens. He was slender, well muscled, and was wearing blue jeans. Norwood had no way of knowing, but his guests were William Buckley and Dean DeLuca. Buckley and DeLuca waited patiently in the living room a few feet away until he concluded his conversation and hung the telephone back on the receiver. Then they finished explaining that they were private detectives from Knoxville gathering information for a law firm about another student who had applied for a job. They weren't especially imaginative, and claimed the law student they were checking out was named ''Bob Jones.'' They added that they would appreciate it if Norwood would talk with them for a few minutes and answer some questions about the young man.

Norwood had never heard of Bob Jones. But he offered to give them the names of law school officials who were more likely to know the student. He was just easing himself into a chair when Buckley suddenly lunged at him. Without a word, the man tried to press a hand-sized electronic device that looked something like a doctor's beeper to his neck and chest. Norwood was taken by surprise. He wasn't a physically imposing man, and Buckley towered over him. Norwood's attacker probably outweighed him by at least forty pounds. But the startled law student was scared and feisty, and he had every reason to believe he was fighting for his life.

He had recognized the hand-held device as an electric stun gun. There are several varieties of stun guns, but all are designed to temporarily disable and were initially developed to provide a nonlethal means for police departments to subdue violent prisoners or criminal suspects. Some stun guns require only three or four seconds of contact to deliver up to forty-seven thousand volts of electricity to the nerves and muscles of the person touched, disabling the individual in moments.

With his law enforcement and corrections background, Norwood knew about stun guns, and realized the danger. He moved fast, twisting and falling back, while swinging one of his feet upward in a hard kick. His foot caught Buckley in the ribs, and the big man fell backward onto a glass table, knocking it over as he expelled the air from his lungs with an agonizing "whumpf" and grabbed for his side. The stun gun flew from his hand and skidded across the floor.

Norwood was putting up a furious struggle. He wriggled loose from Buckley and was scrambling to his feet when the bigger man grabbed at his legs. But Norwood pulled free once more, and glanced around the room looking for the other intruder. DeLuca had just lifted the student's .22-caliber target-shooting rifle from the kitchen counter where it had been lying and was jacking a shell into the chamber. Buckley had pulled a pistol. Norwood leaped for the door, and was just about to scramble outside when the intruders began firing. One bullet slammed into his shoulder. It felt like fire as the metal slug tore through flesh and bone, but Norwood was running for his life. He was continuing his dash down the long balcony that rimmed the apartment complex when another bullet ripped through the fleshy calf of his leg. In moments, however, the fleeing law student had leaped a drainage ditch and was limping toward the parking lot.

August 30 was a bright, sunny morning on the campus at the edge of the Ozark foothills, and forty or more people had heard the gunshots and helplessly watched Norwood's frenzied dash for life. Their faces were blurs as he raced past them, before he at last collapsed on the asphalt. He couldn't run anymore. Sweat was stinging his eyes, he was trembling and gasping for breath, when he looked up and saw two people watching him. Understandably, they appeared startled. A tall, lanky man with near shoulder-length straight hair and a day-long stubble of beard was standing with a stubby, solidly built young woman near a car parked a few feet away. For a moment they stared curiously and silently at the frightened, gasping man wearing the blood-soaked shirt. He turned his head, alternately peering behind him to see if the gunman was following, then looking back to the man and woman, desperately pleaded with them to bring help. Without a word, however, they turned and climbed into the vehicle. Then Richard Michael Savage and Debra Mattingly drove away in the getaway car.

Savage and his girlfriend were stunned by the unexpected confrontation with Norwood. Savage wasn't prepared to finish carrying out the aborted contract himself. He was supposed to be the lookout on the job, not the triggerman.

By the time the startled couple began their drive away from the apartment complex, help was already being summoned. An employee of the nearby Hogwash Laundromat and bar, alarmed by the fracas, was already on the telephone calling campus police and an ambulance. There was a shooting at the apartment complex students referred to as the Law Quads. When officers arrived a few minutes later, the would-be killers were already gone.

The escape wasn't easy. The frightened law student had cracked four of Buckley's ribs with his terrified kick. Nevertheless, between Buckley snapping off a half dozen wild shots with the handgun, and DeLuca adding a shot from Norwood's rifle, the two would-be assassins had fired seven shots at their fleeing quarry. Norwood was struck by two bullets, but neither of the hits stopped him. And police were closing in. Just about everything that could go wrong had already gone wrong. And there was nothing to do but run for it. DeLuca tossed the rifle into a dumpster near one of the apartment buildings, and headed for the woods with his injured cohort. They were running the wrong way, away from their getaway car. But it had left anyway.

At that point, Buckley might have been almost as frightened as Norwood was. But he was heavier, slower, several years older, and his ribs were cracked. So he was nowhere near as good at jumping drainage ditches. And he was nowhere as swift or agile as his panicked teenage accomplice, DeLuca. When they approached a ditch a few yards from the apartment building, DeLuca cleared it easily with a smooth leap. The lumbering Buckley splashed down in the middle of the ditch. Water sloshed into his cowboy boots, quickly filling them to the top. There was no time to empty them, and Buckley slogged the rest of the way out of Fayetteville, painfully clutching his side and leaving a wet trail of ditch water behind him.

In the meantime Norwood was rushed to a nearby hospital and patched up. Almost miraculously, it seemed, although he had been attacked by two men and shot twice, his injuries were not critical. But the town police were about to add insult to injury.

The shaken law student wasn't the kind of man who made many enemies. So it wasn't much of a chore for him to figure out who was most likely behind the assault. The only person he could think of who might dislike him enough to send a couple of men to kill him was Larry Elgin Gray, the husband of his twenty-nine-year-old friend Kathy. The couple were in the process of getting a divorce. And thirty-nine-year-old Larry Gray, the chief financial officer of NIC, Inc., a Tulsa, Oklahoma, investment brokerage firm, was a nasty-tempered man and a poor loser. He collected guns, and told tall tales about his exploits as a soldier in Vietnam. And he was enraged over the breakup of his nine-year marriage to Kathy.

When Norwood passed on his suspicions to police investigators, however, they didn't show much interest in the theory. It didn't help when he agreed to take a lie detector test—and failed. Gray eventually submitted to a lie detector test, as well. The test was administered in Tulsa—and he passed. If the young law student was having trouble earlier getting Fayetteville police to take his suspicions seriously, the lie detector tests had shot even bigger holes in his credibility with investigators.

Norwood later told journalists he believed the lawmen suspected that he may have crossed someone in a drug deal and wound up as a target for assassination. Some police officers tend to be suspicious of people with beards who are inexplicably attacked by strangers. And there are few college campuses in the country, if any, where illegal drugs of some kind aren't traded or sold.

Consequently, when Norwood was released from the hospital, he didn't return to his apartment to stay. He hid out for a while at a friend's house. When he did return to his apartment, it was a disappointing experience. The stun gun the burly man had dropped was still lying on the floor. Two bullets fired by the younger man from Norwood's own rifle were still imbedded in the banister by the stairs. No one had even bothered to pick up, bag, and mark the stun gun as evidence, or to dig out the .22 rifle slugs for possible ballistics tests. The message was clear, and worrisome: Police weren't exactly busting their buns to solve the mystery of who had tried to murder a student in his off-campus apartment.

And Norwood was worried that the would-be killers would try again. It didn't take long before he had convincing reason to believe that his fears were justified. When he returned to his studies, he began to notice a stranger hanging around campus who seemed to be dogging his steps. And when he drove around Fayetteville, the stranger followed him as well. Paranoia? Norwood didn't think so.

If he had entertained any doubts at all that he was still marked for death by someone, they were dispelled by the terrifying events of September 30. It was almost exactly one month since he was attacked in his apartment and shot, and he was still recovering from the injuries.

Kathy Gray had moved to a new off-campus home a short distance away, and they were able to see more of each other than before. He was driving her 1982 Ford Escort, and had left it in the parking lot near the University of Arkansas's football stadium. There was no outward indication that anyone might have tampered with the vehicle when he returned from a class—not until he slid into the driver's seat and turned the key in the ignition. The engine didn't fire the first time. He tried again. A millisecond later, the vehicle exploded. Deadly shards of glass as lethal as any military shrapnel rained down on the parking lot. Windows in nearby cars were shattered. A couple of other students approaching their own vehicles a few yards away dove for the tarmac. And Norwood sat behind the steering wheel of the shattered Ford, with his face and body covered with a fine spray of broken glass, and his heart thumping. For long moments he sat there in dead silence, dazed and deafened by the terrible blast. But he hadn't been hurt seriously and his hearing quickly returned. Once more he had narrowly survived an attempt on his life.

It wasn't difficult for University of Arkansas campus police to figure out how he had managed to survive the devastating explosion. Whoever had tried to kill Norwood had wired the bomb to the ignition, under the hood of the car. Consequently when he turned the ignition and detonated the explosive, the engine and front end were badly damaged and burst into flames. If the bomb had been properly placed under the driver's seat, there would have been little chance that Norwood would have lived.

Norwood was even more convinced that Kathy's embittered husband was trying to have him killed. Campus police took the murder attempt seriously. They knew Norwood was a law-abiding citizen and serious student, and nothing had been uncovered in his background that would provide a conceivable motive for someone to try and have him killed. There was absolutely no one to put their finger on as a suspect, except Gray. But he had already breezed through a lie detector test that seemed to support his claims of innocence.

Some university law enforcement agencies act as little more than security guards. They do the best they can, but they don't share the same legal powers as their brethren with city, state, or federal law enforcement agencies. The University of Arkansas police, however, had the same authority to investigate and make arrests for offenses involving campus crimes as their colleagues did in the city or county. But like their colleagues in the city and county, they couldn't—and wouldn't—arrest one citizen merely on the suspicions of another citizen.

Norwood understood that, and as a law student, he respected it. But if the law couldn't guarantee him protection, he would have to protect himself. So he bought a .357 Magnum revolver and began to carry it around with him. He was no Dirty Harry, but someone was serious about trying to kill him. Norman Douglas Norwood was in more danger living and going to school on the normally quiet campus of the University of Arkansas than he had ever been in as a prison guard, working with some of Florida's most dangerous convicts. When he moved out of his apartment near the campus, to a new home in the nearby town of Springdale, he was living defensively.

During the following weeks, he repeatedly contacted campus police, Fayetteville city police, Springdale police, and the FBI to report suspicions that he was being shadowed or to talk about the attempts on his life that had already occurred. Campus police especially got used to his telephoning them or dropping into their offices to report sightings of suspicious strangers stalking him. Sometimes he talked with Lt. Jim Swearingen. More often he talked with John Herring, who coincidentally had once been a member of the police department in Tulsa, where Gray lived and worked. The officers may have been seeing and hearing more of the worried student than they would have wished for. Nevertheless, after each contact, one or the other—sometimes both—would climb into an unmarked university patrol car and follow up on the report. But there was never anyone to arrest.

While Norwood was attempting to juggle the job of looking through his law books while looking over his shoulder for paid assassins, Savage, Buckley, Jackson, and several of their cohorts who were linked to the loose-knit crew of want-ad killers were busy lining up and trying to carry out other contracts.

Late in October, Savage and Buckley accepted the most potentially devastating contract of all. They made a deal with a financially troubled Austin, Texas, salesman who had decided to murder his wife and children for their insurance money.

Albert Lee Thielman was a man who could have had it all. He was young, charming, had a gift for gab, and was successful at his job selling prefabricated homes.

And he had a loyal wife and three charming children, one a little boy still too young to attend school, at his own comfortable one-and-a-half-story stone and wood home a few miles outside San Marcos. San Marcos is a quiet central Texas town of about twenty-two thousand residents about halfway between Austin and San Antonio. Only about an hour's drive either way from the Texas state capital, or history-rich San Antonio with the famous Alamo, the San Marcos area was a nice place to live. And the Thielman home in the South Ridge Estates was especially attractive, situated on large lots overlooking a pond and wooded area. A children's slide was set up on the carefully tended lawn at the rear of the house. There was plenty of room for the youngsters and their neighborhood friends, who visited often, to play in the commodious yard.

Thielman was liked and respected by his unsuspecting neighbors, who considered him to be a devoted husband and father who was concerned about his family and enrolled his two oldest children, a boy and a girl, in a local Christian school. He was active in his church, and once played a lead role in bringing the Hill Country Faith Ministries, a religious crusade, to his house of worship.

Judging from everything that the neighbors knew about him, he was considerate and loving. On Sunday afternoons, when many men parked in front of the television set with a six-pack of Lone Star and the channel turned to sports, or sacked out for a long nap on the living room couch, he took his children for walks, or on impromptu picnics so that his wife could have some quiet hours and a brief respite from full-time parenting.

Some of the neighbors even considered him to be a bit too straitlaced. He didn't preach, but he was vocal about his faith and careful about his language. No one had heard him swear, and he never even used words like "damn" or "hell" around his friends. He seemed to get along well with his wife, Mary, and was an all-around good neighbor. So was she. No one ever worried when their children visited or played at the Thielman house. They were always carefully watched over, and fed if the occasion called for it.

Some of the neighbors chuckled about Thielman's awkwardness with tools, and his unfamiliarity with mechanical things. He would ask for advice from some of the more mechanically knowledgeable neighbor men before tackling even the simplest auto maintenance or repair problem. Thielman's admiring neighbors had no hint of his secret dark side, of a hidden sinister life he was leading that was rapidly dragging him along the road to self-destruction. Thielman was in the process of throwing everything away, because of his overpowering obsessions with reckless spending, gambling, illicit sex, and cocaine.

The thirty-four-year-old Thielman was more than twenty-two thousand dollars in debt, including ten thousand dollars to bookies for bad bets on basketball and football games. He sometimes bet as much as two thousand dollars on a single day of sports, and he lost more often than he won. He owed another twelve thousand dollars to credit card companies. And he had a stiff monthly mortgage payment, car payments, and bank loans to pay off as well. Yet, although he was already drowning in debt, he was secretly blowing up to five hundred dollars a month photographing naked girls in a South Austin nude modeling studio. For a while he tried to catch up on his burgeoning debts by dealing cocaine, investigators would later be told. Confidential sources told the FBI that he bought from eight to fifteen ounces at a time, for seventeen hundred dollars an ounce. But that only made things worse. The more cocaine he handled, the more he used.

At last he was forced to put his home up for sale. But not all the people he owed money to were the kind who would wait for a sale and settlement on the house, or appeal to the courts to help them collect. The troubled salesman's debtors were becoming increasingly insistent, and pressing him for payment, when he thumbed through a copy of *SOF* and found Savage's gun-for-hire ad in the back pages. He figured that he was looking at the solution to his money troubles. Thielman telephoned Savage and told him that he wanted to buy a bomb. Savage gave the assignment to his explosives expert.

Buckley assembled a crude time bomb from ball bearings, a six-volt battery, fuse, black powder, and clockworks—fitted neatly inside a small, military-type metal can. He made the bomb small, because the client had said he planned to use it on a light aircraft loaded with drug dealers. Then he traveled to Texas and turned it over to Thielman at a Houston hotel.

A few days later, Thielman surprised his wife with the news that he had gotten a good deal on some airline tickets for her and the children. It would be a good opportunity for them to visit with her parents in Des Moines, Iowa. He offered to stay at home and lead the quiet bachelor life until they returned.

The desperate husband had put together a scheme to ensure that his family never returned home. He already had $250,000 in life insurance policies on his family. And when he bought the round-trip airplane tickets, he took out another $2.4 million in new policies, $600,000 each on the lives of his wife and the three children. It was a fortune, and only a fraction of the money would be needed to clear up all his debts.

And if he stayed at home, it wouldn't be because he hadn't tried to schedule a more entertaining time for himself. He tried to talk his favorite nude model at the studio into taking off with him on a three- or four-day vacation. He told her that his wife and children would be out of state for a while, beginning October 30. The young woman rejected the invitation.

Thielman's family began the drive to the Robert Mueller Municipal Airport in Austin at 5:00 A.M., to catch an early American Airlines flight on the first leg of their trip to the Midwest. Thielman slipped the homemade bomb inside his wife's cosmetics case at the airport, after they preceded him inside the terminal. He transferred two pairs of children's boots into a suitcase, to make room. When Mrs. Thielman and the children were seated with 149 other passengers and crew aboard flight number 203 headed for a stop in Dallas, she had no idea that death was riding along in the baggage compartment.

She apparently hadn't even suspected anything was wrong earlier, when her husband got upset after learning that his family might not be able to make the 7:00 A.M., jet because the flight was overbooked. "You haven't seen the fit I'll throw unless they let you on this airplane," he threatened. The demonstration wasn't necessary, however. The Thielman family was finally allowed to board the flight.

No one learned for certain who bumbled the bombing, whether it was Thielman's clumsiness with mechanical things, or just one more example of the ineptitude that marked the crime career of Buckley. But the bomb didn't go off when it was supposed to.

The 153 unsuspecting passengers and crew members aboard flight 203 landed safely at the Dallas–Fort Worth Regional Airport at 8:06 A.M., a little more than an hour after the aircraft had lifted into the air in Austin. A few minutes after touching down, the Boeing 727 taxied up to its gate at the American Airlines terminal and was docking when the bomb that Buckley had so carefully assembled detonated in the jetliner's belly. The aircraft shuddered and lurched. Several crew members later reported that they heard a popping sound, and heard a thump. Some passengers thought the jetliner had collided with a ground vehicle.

As a thin wisp of smoke clung to the underside of the aircraft, and passengers began to unbuckle their seat belts and pull carry-on luggage from overhead compartments, a flight attendant appeared in the aisle near the front of the airplane. Calmly referring to the passengers as ladies and gentlemen, she asked them to leave their carry-on baggage and disembark as quickly as possible. But they had barely begun to move into the aisle before she was addressing them again—this time on an intercom. "Run! Run! Run!" she yelled.

An airport fire truck had already lurched to a stop beside the stricken aircraft, and fire fighters were checking it out as the alarmed passengers hurried outside. Crew members and ground workers quickly evacuated the passengers through the regular exit door and a seldom-used rear stairway in the terminal.

Damage from the blast was confined to the aluminum luggage pod in the belly of the jet. A portion of the bomb fizzled and popped a second time as workers were removing the pod from the luggage area, but there was no damage or injury. As talk of the bomb rippled through the airport, the worst possible scenarios were speculated on by frightened travelers and employes. They talked of a terrible midair explosion, and bodies and wreckage hurtling to the ground over the Texas countryside. It could have been a catastrophe. It seemed that a major disaster was avoided by no more than a few minutes. But as it was, except for a woman who slightly injured her leg as the passengers were being hurried from the aircraft, no one was hurt. About the most serious problems for the passengers were a bit of fright and a few missed flights.

They were incredibly lucky. Only the luggage pod itself and a few pieces of baggage were damaged. Several suitcases were scorched and burned. But the most serious damage was to a woman's overnight cosmetic case. It was shredded by the explosion, and the identification tags badly scorched. Several heat-blackened metal ball bearings were scattered around the compartment. Investigators with the Dallas–Fort Worth Regional Airport's Department of Public Safety (DOPS) and the FBI immediately focused their attention on tracking down the owner of the bag, which they were virtually certain had contained the bomb. And they began trying to piece together an idea of just exactly what components had gone into construction of the crude but potentially lethal fragmentation bomb.

The bombing attempt galvanized the FBI into action. And by the next day, Mrs. Thielman had been identified as the owner of the cosmetics case. FBI agents were waiting to talk with her when she arrived at the airport in Des Moines for the trip home with the children. She said she had packed the family's luggage the night before the flight. She hadn't seen a bomb. Other

FBI agents with the Austin office interviewed her husband and all airport employees there who might have had access to the luggage before it was loaded onto the jetliner. Thielman was nervous, and peevish when he was approached by the agents. When they told him that the explosive device had been in his family's luggage, he snapped: "You think I did it. I can see it in your eyes." He acted as if he had expected to be accused of having a hand in the bombing attempt, and his irrational testy behavior wasn't lost on the agents.

Eventually he calmed down, and conceded that he was having serious financial problems, and might have to declare bankruptcy. He listed some of his debts, and said he needed at least six thousand dollars in monthly income to survive. After the initial interview, the FBI men searched Thielman's office, his home, and his car. And they began investigating his background; checking out his associates, activities, and financial situation. They uncovered a lot of secrets he hadn't shared with them.

Surviving pieces of the explosive device, including the ball bearings, were packaged and sealed by the FBI and turned over to the BATF, which shipped them to a laboratory near Washington, D.C., for analysis. Close inspection of the scorched identification tag on the cosmetic bag had disclosed the name: Al Thielman.

Meanwhile the nervous flying public was told that even if the bomb had exploded while the Boeing 727 was airborne, it may not have caused a crash. An airline spokeswoman pointed out that sensitive areas of the jetliner such as fuel lines and electrical wiring were shielded from the cargo hold by an aluminum lining. Furthermore, much of the force of the explosion was absorbed by the packed luggage in the hold.

Nevertheless, not everyone was relieved or satisfied by the otherwise comforting supposition about the 727's probable survival. And other officials would later say that the aircraft could have indeed been destroyed and all the occupants killed if the bomb had exploded while it was airborne.

Unsurprisingly, news that a bomb had been detonated on the aircraft revived concern about safety measures. Authorities confirmed that bags were not normally screened on domestic flights. Despite the threat in recent years from aircraft terrorists and other assorted homicidal loonies, screening every bag that was checked through a ticket counter and carried on a flight was simply too expensive and impractical. Mobile scanners were available at some airports to airlines desiring to screen checked baggage, but were seldom used except for some international flights. And El Al, the Israeli airline, was known to check baggage in a compression chamber that simulated air pressure at fifty thousand feet. The device was devised to uncover bombs designed to explode at a certain altitude.

But there was no Federal Aviation Administration regulation requiring the widespread screening of bags if there was no special reason to believe they might contain something dangerous or otherwise illegal. The FAA did disseminate advisories on screening procedures that could be undertaken, but they were not required. The airlines, and the passengers, were basically on their own.

The FBI's primary concern had little to do, however, with regulations or practices governing the screening of baggage. That was the province of other agencies. Someone had attempted to blow up an airline full of people, and agents were determined to track down the person responsible as soon as possible. It didn't take the law enforcement agency long to learn about the prodigious amount of life insurance that had been taken out on the family of Albert Thielman, or about his secret vices and money troubles. The Austin salesman quickly emerged as a hot suspect.

Investigators learned that Thielman had filed an insurance claim after a suspicious fire damaged a house that was under construction in Georgetown, a city of some ten thousand people about midway between Austin and Temple. They learned about his love affair with nose candy—his extreme cocaine addiction. And he was unable to provide any kind of plausible explanation for the presence of the bomb in his wife's luggage.

Thielman's neighbors began to talk among themselves about the disturbing interest that the FBI and other law enforcement agencies were taking in him and his activities since the incident at the Dallas–Fort Worth Regional Airport. Most didn't want to believe that he was a serious suspect in the bombing attempt, and some argued that the FBI could have focused on anyone else's luggage just as easily as they had on the cosmetics case. Colleagues on the job were also caught up in the speculation. But almost no one wanted to believe that the man they knew would have tried to murder his own family, and more than one hundred other innocent people.

Thielman was also smarting under the unwanted attention he was receiving from the FBI. He told a neighbor who lived across the street from him that he didn't like being treated as a suspect in the bombing incident. The four most important people in the world to him were aboard the jetliner, he claimed. On November 18 he telephoned his boss at the Mile Homes Company, and told him that he wanted to step down from his job as senior sales representative in Austin. He explained that he wanted to spend more time with his family.

Three days later, on November 21, three weeks after the aborted bombing, he didn't come home from work. He had packed a bag, and vanished. His wife reported to police the next day that he was missing. The model Hays County husband and father, and mainstay of his church, was on the run. Two weeks later he was named in a one-count federal indictment in Austin charging him with conspiracy to place a destructive device on an aircraft. His description in the federal fugitive warrant that was issued noted that he wore a neatly trimmed beard and mustache.

FBI spokesmen pointed out that the state of Texas had jurisdiction over the filing of any charges of attempted murder. And state law enforcement authorities appeared to be in no hurry to pile up additional criminal counts against the fugitive. Nevertheless, it was becoming increasingly difficult for Thielman's friends to continue making excuses for him.

It took the lawmen two weeks to track him down. Unsurprisingly, perhaps, they caught up with him in Las Vegas. The Jekyll-and-Hyde husband had apparently had a last fling at the world of glitter, beautiful girls, the click of chips and busy clatter of slot machines. Shortly before daybreak on December 7, the FBI received a tip that the fugitive would be at the McCarrin International Airport in the gambling mecca. At 6:40 A.M. agents posing as ticket counter employees of the Muse Airlines arrested him there. Thielman was alone, unarmed, and did not put up a struggle. His distinctive beard had been shaved. He was locked up in a separate cell at the Clark County House of Detention.

The day before his arrest, FBI investigators had filed an affidavit in federal court in Austin stating that he was a heavy user of cocaine, had been selling large amounts of the narcotic since September 1984, and was heavily in debt.

At a five-minute arraignment before U.S. Magistrate Phillip Pro in Las Vegas, the suspect waived extradition and agreed to voluntarily return to Texas to face federal charges of placing a destructive device on an aircraft. The offense carried a possible penalty of up to twenty years in prison, and a $250,000 fine. Judge Pro refused to set bail, remarking that Thielman was a danger to the community and might again flee. As Thielman was led in handcuffs from the courtroom, he ignored a journalist's shouted question asking if he had planted the bomb. A short time later, he was flown back to Austin, accompanied by a team of U.S. marshals. As soon as he was back on Texas soil, the handcuffed prisoner was hurried by car to the Federal Correctional Institute at Bastrop. The federal prison, located about twenty-five miles southeast of Austin, was about a two-hour drive from his home.

The suspect's neighbors still found it difficult to understand how the life of the once-respected family man and church leader had undergone such a drastic and tragic transformation. Some blamed his troubles on personality changes caused by his drug abuse. Others were convinced that he was driven to desperation by the threats of gambling associates he owed money to.

Byron Sage, chief of the FBI office in Austin, told a reporter for the local newspaper, the *American-Statesman,* that he thought Thielman's desperate act was a culmination of a number of factors. "There was a steady downward spiral," he said. "This was sort of a last error."

Law enforcement authorities had tracked down and captured the man they were convinced had planted the bomb in the luggage. But they were still looking for the person who had assembled the parts and put it together.

While the law was closing in on the gang's former client, Savage, Jackson, and their cohorts had been busy with other pursuits. Jackson was keeping especially busy. He was not only continuing to take assignments from Savage, but he was also doing a little free-lancing.

A forty-two-year-old Houston man, John George Noppinger, Jr., had telephoned about Jackson's personal ad in the *SOF* classifieds. He had a ten-thousand-dollar job for Jackson to take care of. The ex–police chief had taken Savage's advice about the rewording, and stressing the claim of having served in Vietnam. It read:

GUN FOR HIRE: Nam Sniper, instructor; SWAT, pistol, rifle . . . All jobs considered. Privacy guaranteed.

The classified identified him as "Mike," and listed a telephone number in tiny Linden, Texas.

Noppinger was willing to pay big money to have Anthony Bennie Hunicke killed. Noppinger and Hunicke's wife, Janice, were close friends. Jackson took the job, but he was no more efficient at free-lancing than he was working for Savage. He tried three times to kill Hunicke, and botched up the attempted assassination every time.

Jackson's first try at earning the ten-thousand-dollar

murder contract fee occurred on November 22, when he hooked up a pipe bomb underneath Hunicke's truck. The bombing attempt was a miserable failure, so Jackson switched to guns. On December 13 he squeezed off a shot at Hunicke with a .45-caliber pistol that was fitted with a silencer. He missed. Six days later the bungling hit man tried again. This time he sprayed twelve to fifteen rounds at Hunicke from a silencer-equipped 9-mm semiautomatic rifle. Every one of them missed. Hunicke was every bit as difficult to kill as Norwood, Free, and Mrs. Brashear.

Three missed opportunities in four weeks had taken the wind out of Jackson's sails. He put the contract on hold, and returned to his home in Linden for the holidays. He could use the rest. Savage was lining up another important job for him. Savage was calling him in on the Norwood hit.

Chapter 7

Songbirds

Early in the new year, Jackson breezed into Fayetteville with murder on his mind. Savage was upset by the repeated failures of the gang's efforts to kill Norwood, and was determined to get the contract over with so that he and his cohorts could move on to other projects.

Jackson began shadowing the fidgety law student, checking out his schedule and movements in an effort to figure out the best time and place for the next assassination attempt. And Norwood continued to complain, to whatever law enforcement agency seemed to be most approachable at the time, that he was being stalked.

It was January 20, a crispy cool midwinter day in Fayetteville, when Norwood telephoned the University of Arkansas campus police department and complained again that someone was following him. This time the silent stranger was driving a late-model white Ford sedan. As an ex-policeman, Norwood knew a bit about being tailed, and he had swung around through a cam-

pus parking lot to get behind the Ford and jot own the
license plate number. Herring and Swearingen had
heard similar stories from the spooked law student before. Nevertheless, they climbed into their unmarked
squad car and drove off to check out the latest complaint.

They arrived at the law school just in time to see the
car that Norwood had described slowly exiting from the
parking lot. The experienced officers decided against
immediately pulling the driver over. It was between
classes, and the campus was filled with students walking from one building to another or simply idling. And
just in case the driver was up to no good as Norwood
feared, there could be trouble.

So Herring and Swearingen tailed the car for a couple
of miles until they reached a deserted area at the edge
of the school farm. Then they signaled the driver to
stop. The driver pulled over immediately, and as soon
as the vehicle rolled to a stop, he slid from the seat and
walked over to meet the two officers. Smiling broadly,
he introduced himself as Michael Wayne Jackson and
explained that he was also in the law enforcement business. Pulling a badge from his pocket, he said that he
had once been chief of police in Tatum, Texas, and was
at the university to check into a couple of classes in
criminal justice that he was thinking of signing up for.

As Swearingen talked to the friendly ex-lawman,
Herring wandered over to the white Ford and peeked
through the windows. On the front passenger seat, the
muzzle of a .223-caliber AR-15 military-style assault
rifle with an attached scope was peeping out from under
a sweater that had been thrown over it. Herring knew
that AR-15s aren't the weapon of choice of squirrel
hunters. The AR-15 is the civilian version of the M-16,

the automatic rifle issued to American troops during the war in Vietnam. AR-15s are for shooting people.

Herring glanced back at his partner and the stranger, and while keeping a wary eye on them, walked around to the other side of the car. Looking through the window, he could see a 9-mm MAC-11 machine pistol with a silencer on the floor beneath the steering wheel. They weren't the kind of armaments that a sportsman would use to hunt small game, any more than the AR-15 was. And the officers would later learn that the AR-15 had been tampered with to increase the already devastating firepower it had been outfitted with when it came off the production line. It had been converted from semi-automatic to fully automatic, and would continue firing as long as someone held his finger on the trigger, or until it ran out of ammunition. Fully automatic weapons were illegal without a special federal permit. The silencer-fitted machine pistol was illegal as well.

Herring caught his boss's eye, and signaled for him to be on the alert. Then he walked back to the two men, and advised Jackson that he was being taken into custody. Jackson appeared to be momentarily surprised, but didn't resist. Moments later he was handcuffed and inside the unmarked campus patrol car on his way back to the police headquarters for questioning. A later search of the car trunk a short time later turned up yet another weapon, a .38-caliber handgun. It was loaded with exploding bullets, which are illegal.

But the two officers barely had time to read Jackson his Miranda rights before he was reeling off an incredible story about a deadly dial-a-killer gang, murder contracts, bombings, and attempted bombings. The hired gun dropped a mother lode of information on the astonished campus cops. Lieutenant Swearingen and

Herring suddenly realized that all of Norwood's worst suspicions were true. There was indeed a murder contract out on his life, and it had nothing to do with drugs. Norwood had been set up by a jealous ex-husband for murder.

Of course, that's what Norwood had been saying all along. And he had never for a moment believed that the botched car bombing would be the last attempt on his life. After Jackson was stopped with the guns in his car, Norwood told an interviewer, "There is no doubt in my mind that Jackson was going to spray me with that machine gun." At last, police were agreeing with the jumpy law student.

Herring would later tell a newspaper reporter that the interview with Jackson was an eye-opener. "Jackson told us of other bombings and murders that he was aware of. I think I can say that the arrest of Michael Jackson led to the snowball effect," the veteran officer said. Jackson's arrest was the beginning of the end. And in fact, other hit men and guns for hire who had been drumming up trade through the classified pages of *SOF* were also about to go out of business.

With the advent of the new year, everything began to fall in on the killer gang at once. Jackson was barely locked up in the Washington County Jail in Fayetteville before Doutre got himself arrested again, this time in Athens, Georgia. Emert, the big, bearded teddy bear of a man who had worked for Savage as a Continental Club bouncer, and as a bagman for the contract killings, had also already wound up behind bars once more. And in Texas, Thielman was beginning to talk as well. The misfortune of Jackson, Doutre, Emert, and Thielman quickly began translating itself into bad luck for

Savage. Hardly anyone involved with the gang was being either discreet or private.

Savage had accepted a contract on the life of Bruce Lamey, a hardworking truck driver from rural Arnoldsville, a northeast Georgia community that is so small, it isn't on most road maps. Lamey's business partner, Kenneth Boswell Major, wanted him killed. Major was also from a small town, Winterville, which, like Arnoldsville, was only a few miles from Athens, the home of the University of Georgia.

Lamey and Major were both family men. Lamey was forty-five years old, married, and had a grown son. Major was thirty-seven years old, married, and the father of two children. The men had been friends for four or five years when they decided to go into business together just across the state line in Pineville, South Carolina, as partners in Harry's Fish Camp. The business was located at Santee Cooper, a busy area for hunting and fishing in the South Carolina Piedmont. Major borrowed seventy-five thousand dollars from a bank, and Lamey provided another thirty-six thousand dollars, and even though one partner had contributed almost twice as much money as the other, they began their business venture in February 1985 as a fifty-fifty partnership. It didn't take long before they realized that they had made a mistake.

The two longtime friends couldn't agree on business decisions. And as their business relationship slumped, their personal friendship also deteriorated. Major would later claim that he tried to buy his partner out, but Lamey wouldn't sell. By August, however, both partners gave up on the business and sold it to someone else. Major had taken a financial whipping, and didn't waste any time looking around for someone else to blame for the misadventure. He blamed Lamey. And when he found an advertisement in *SOF* by a "gun for hire" offering confidential services, he figured that he had found a solution to his problem. He called the telephone number listed in the classified and talked to a man in Knoxville, who said his name was "Terry." Terry was in the hired gun business.

Several weeks later, Major met with Terry at a small café in Knoxville. Major had already taken a financial beating, and he was shopping for a bargain. Terry agreed to see to it that Lamey was murdered for a measly four thousand dollars. Major paid him fifteen hundred dollars on the spot, and agreed to pay the other twenty-five hundred dollars later in two installments, as well as providing weapons for the hit. The mysterious Terry later disclosed to his client that his real name was Richard Savage.

Early in the new year, Major met one of Savage's men in an Athens shopping center and gave him one thousand dollars and a .38-caliber revolver, but the rent-a-killer ringleader still wasn't already to order the slaying. Savage drove to Athens, where he met with Major at the Family Inn, and the Georgia man gave him the final fifteen hundred dollars on the contract fee. At last Savage was ready to move. He returned to Knoxville and subcontracted the murder to Doutre, the only member of his gang who had been successful as a killer.

Doutre checked into the Family Inn on February 2, but quickly left again when Savage called him back to Knoxville to pick up a more powerful murder weapon. The gang leader gave him a .357 Magnum, and Doutre returned to Athens. Major met with him there and gave him a twelve-gauge shotgun. When Doutre returned to the motel, Savage telephoned him with more instructions. He told his hired gun to put on a ski mask and gloves, and to knock at Lamey's front door. When the truck driver answered the door, Savage ordered, Doutre was to shoot him. It appeared to be a fail-safe plan. The only detail remaining to be worked out was selecting a date for the slaying.

Savage decided that February 5, 1986, would be the last day of Lamey's life. Once more he telephoned Doutre at the motel, and told him to murder the trucker that evening. He also went over some suggested escape routes that Doutre could use to get away after the shooting. But he hadn't counted on his star hit man bungling the job with a small-time cheating caper.

When Doutre left the motel on his way to carry out the murder, he drove away without paying the telephone bill for long-distance calls he had made. That wasn't unusual. He didn't believe in paying his way if he had a choice. But this time his penny-ante chiseling got him in trouble. The motel operator notified Athens police that a guest had skipped out on his bill. The police department responded with a BOLO (be on the lookout) alert to their own officers and to neighboring law enforcement agencies, which included a description of the van and the license plate number.

A Morgan County sheriff's deputy spotted the van at the 76 Truck Stop along Interstate 20 about twenty miles south of Athens. The deputy took one quick glance inside the van, and realized that he had more business to discuss with the driver than his reported skipping out on a motel bill. He had been driving around with a loaded shotgun and a loaded .357 Magnum in the car. Doutre and another young man who was with him were taken into custody and driven to the Sheriff's Department headquarters. His twenty-eight-year-old companion was released. But Doutre was held for police in Athens on charges of theft of services, and for illegal possession of firearms by a convicted felon. A quick check with police computers had disclosed that he had a criminal record.

Doutre had a story ready to explain the presence of the guns in his van. He confided that he was working on an undercover project for the BATF. He also explained the presence of a large amount of men's and women's clothing that police took from the van by claiming that the wardrobes belonged to him and to his wife. Morgan County Sheriff Henry Burge had heard that other police agencies were looking for certain clothing that might be evidence in a murder investigation, so he decided to hang on to it for a while. And he refused to give it up when the man who had been with Doutre at the truck stop telephoned later from north Florida and asked if he could have the clothing back.

The women's clothing did indeed belong to Doutre's wife, and to a former neighbor girl who had taken off with them a few weeks earlier in a stolen Ford van for a wild spree in Florida. Except for the presence of their seventeen-year-old companion, the trip might have passed for the honeymoon that Doutre and his bride never had.

True to form, Doutre ripped off everyone he could during the impromptu vacation. The odd trio crisscrossed the state, living off money they stole by passing bad checks, camping overnight in cheap motels, and eating in diners or munching on fast food and snacks picked up from convenience stores. The good times ended when Doutre checked the girls into a condominium in the oceanside town of Punta Gorda, and left for

Georgia to take care of a job he said Savage had lined up for him. Then Sheriff Burge and Athens police cut his assignment short. Doutre never returned to his wife and their friend.

In Georgia, Sheriff Burge turned Doutre over to Athens police. And when the city police department detectives sat down to talk with him about the guns and skipping out on the motel bill, they learned that he had a surprising story to tell. When he was asked what he was doing with the weapons, he blithely explained that he was a professional hit man with a murder contract to take care of. And he began spinning outrageous tales to other dial-a-murder contracts that he and a loose-knit gang of cohorts had been involved in during the past several months.

It was a difficult story for police to believe. The quiet hill country of northeast Georgia is farmer-friendly. People grow soybeans and peanuts and raise dairy cows there. It is not a "Miami Vice" kind of community where drug dealers, bank robbers, and professional killers regularly blast away at police and at one another with Uzis and assault rifles. Furthermore, professional killers simply don't begin unloading all the details of their grim business to police when they are hauled in on reasonably minor charges such as theft of services and unlawful possession of weapons. If Doutre hadn't been so anxious to boast of his career as a hit man, Athens police would have had no reason to suspect that he had already been involved in homicide. From all appearances they had been dealing with a petty thief who was illegally in possession of a couple of guns— until he began to talk.

Western Circuit District Attorney Harry Gordon would later remark that when Doutre began spouting off his fantastic stories about being a killer for pay, his interrogators thought he was just a big-talking jerk. Some people will do just about anything for attention, even if it means talking themselves into serious trouble with the law. As Doutre began providing details about a planned hit on a local truck driver, however, investigators with the Athens Police Department's Drug and Vice Unit began revising their earlier opinions. They invited the DA and the Georgia Bureau of Investigation into the probe.

Soon they had Savage's name, as well as the names of other members of the ring. And Doutre had squealed on Major as well, fingering him as the disappointed businessman who paid for the contract on Lamey.

Four days after Doutre's apprehension, Savage was arrested in Knoxville on a Clarke County, Georgia, warrant charging him with conspiracy to commit murder. He agreed to voluntarily return to Athens with a city police officer, a Clarke County district attorney, and a DA's investigator. Once he reached Athens, he was lodged in the Clarke County Jail. He explained to reporters that he didn't force authorities to initiate extradition proceedings against him because he was anxious to tell his side of the story and clear himself of the conspiracy charges in the Lamey case.

Lamey and his family had been asleep earlier when Athens police, accompanied by Clarke County sheriff's deputies, knocked on his door. The officers advised the startled man that he had been marked for murder, and saw to it that the family was moved out of the house to a safer place for the night. Although they had one suspected would-be assassin in custody, police couldn't be sure that other hired killers weren't lurking around waiting to finish off his job. It was shocking news for the Lameys. Despite their business troubles, the trucker had known Major most of his life. Lamey's wife, Dee, had even worked as a secretary for Major for more than two years. The trucker later told a reporter that he was surprised. Contract murder plots between friends just didn't happen in rural Georgia. "It's like something you see in the movies about Chicago or New York," he marveled.

Lamey added that he couldn't imagine why Major was so angry. "I'm the one who lost money," he said. "Not him!"

Dee Lamey appeared to be equally mystified. Talking a few weeks later with a newspaper reporter, she said of the former family friend: "Ken's not that kind of person. Knowing him, if he did this, he had to snap. He had to crack. If I could just figure out why?" Then she added, "Thank God for the police."

The Lameys had good reason to be perplexed and worried. They eventually learned that Doutre had killed twice before. And he was only a few miles from the family's home when he was apprehended at the truck stop. A spokeswoman for the Athens Police Department would later say of Doutre that "he got pretty close" to the Lamey house before he was apprehended.

A few hours after the Lameys were moved out of their home, Major was arrested on a warrant charging him with conspiracy to commit murder and possession of a firearm. He was locked up in the Clarke County Jail, but was released on a six-thousand-dollar property bond later that morning after a hearing before Judge Pierre Boulogne. Investigators were outraged when they learned that the suspect had been released on such a low bond, and an assistant DA petitioned the court to reconsider. Judge Boulogne was convinced by argu-

ments at the subsequent hearing that the case was
stronger than he previously believed, and he responded
by upping the bond to one hundred thousand dollars.
Major was taken into police custody once more. But
shortly after nightfall, he was freed again after posting
the new bond.

Savage didn't share his hireling's disturbing penchant
for talking to police. In fact, he claimed that he barely
knew Doutre, and had nothing to do with murder-for-
hire enterprises. He said he knew his accused coconspirator only by the name "Pete," and insisted that the
young man had never worked for him. Pete had stopped
in the Continental Club a few times, but so had a lot
of other men, Savage said.

Regardless of the suspect's insistent denials, however, it was too late. Police were closing in on the ring
from several directions at once.

A few miles away, Fulton County Sheriff's Department homicide investigators had first run across Savage's name the previous September during their
investigation of the Braun murder. They had taken a
special interest in the timing of his classifieds in *SOF*
and the Sandy Springs businessman's ambush slaying and
were planning to follow up on their suspicions.

And in Austin, Thielman was being pressed by local
and federal authorities to tell them exactly how he had
come to acquire the bomb that was placed in his wife's
luggage before his family left on their flight to visit with
her parents in the Midwest. Police were closing in on
the gang in cities and towns ranging from Georgia to
Texas.

Most damaging of all, however, Emert, the hulking
red-bearded ex-convict who had worked for Savage as
a bouncer and onetime bagman, was in trouble again.

He had been sentenced to a ten-year prison term after being picked up for possession of stolen property and drug offenses, when he decided to see if he could work out a deal that would save him some time behind bars. He telephoned the BATF office in Knoxville, and said that he had valuable information that he would like to swap. BATF investigators in Knoxville had talked with Emert before, and agreed to listen to what he had to say. Emert didn't disappoint them.

He told the BATF investigators that he had collected a partial payoff from a man who had his wife murdered in Palm Beach County, Florida. According to Emert's reconstruction of events to the BATF men, and later to law enforcement officers in south Florida, Savage flew to Palm Beach International Airport on October 16 and collected a two-thousand-dollar retainer fee for the murder. The bar owner had learned at least some useful lessons from his earlier failures. He was doing his best to operate the murder ring on a sound business basis, and always insisted on a portion of his fee up front. The new client was Robert Spearman, Emert said. And the target of the hit was the client's ailing wife, Anita.

Emert said that Savage contacted him on the same day and instructed him to drive from Knoxville to Palm Beach County to collect several thousand dollars from Spearman. Savage ordered Doutre to ride along, and gave the men $50 for expense money. Savage told his crony to pick up the $18,000 still owed by Spearman on the contract, give $1,000 to Doutre, keep $250 for additional expenses, and to catch a flight at the airport back to Knoxville. Doutre would keep the car for transportation around the West Palm Beach area, and return to Tennessee alone, Savage explained.

The informant said the gang leader also gave him a

piece of notepaper with Spearman's name and address in Lake Park scribbled on it. Spearman's telephone number at the boatyard had been jotted down on another scrap of paper, which Savage passed on to him. Emert and Doutre left Knoxville four days later, on October 20, in the white Toyota. They traveled light, and neither of the men bothered to carry along a change of clothes. But they were equipped with a loaded MAC-10 machine pistol, and another handgun fitted with a silencer. They arrived in West Palm Beach the next day, and checked into an Econo Lodge. Emert claimed that he didn't know that his mysterious mission had anything to do with murder until Doutre broke the news to him on the drive south from Knoxville.

The two men had made the drive in less than twenty-four hours. There were no stops at Florida tourist information centers when they crossed the state line from Georgia. They weren't in the Sunshine State to see the sights. Although they wound up in the shadow of wealthy Palm Beach, there were no oceanside drives along scenic U.S. A1A to gawk at the Kennedy family compound, or at Donald and Ivana Trump's Mar-A-Lago. It was unlikely that either of the men had ever heard of the Trumps, or of such fun-loving denizens of Palm Beach as Roxanne Pulitzer and Zsa Zsa Gabor. They weren't celebrity watchers. They had come to South Florida's glittering Gold Coast to conduct the grim business of murder.

A few minutes after they settled into the motel, Emert telephoned Spearman at the boatyard. At Spearman's suggestion, Emert and Doutre met with him that afternoon in the parking lot of the Denny's Restaurant along U.S. Highway 1 in North Palm Beach. Doutre waited in the parked Toyota while his companion climbed into Spearman's Bronco for a private chat.

As Emert eased himself down onto the seat, he told Spearman who he was. The boatyard owner responded by telling him that he only had half the money with him. He explained that he would have to pick up the rest of the contract murder fee from his safety-deposit box at a bank and give it to Emert the next day.

The men talked for about twenty minutes about money and murder. Emert said that Spearman told them his wife would be in a wheelchair, and would likely be drowsy because she was taking strong medication. He said he wanted the murder to look either like an accident, or like it had been committed by a burglar. He promised to leave the sliding glass doors open. And he recommended that the killer ransack the house and take his wife's gold jewelry and some of the loose money that would be lying around in order to back up the burglary scenario.

He specified that he would like for them to make the killing quiet, clean, and quick. He would rather that his wife was smothered, or dispatched in a manner that would avoid any blood or mess in the house. Spearman knew exactly what he wanted, and said he would like the job taken care of within a few days, no more than a week. And he suggested that early morning, when he would be following his usual routine of sharing breakfast with friends, would be a good time to strike. It would give him an airtight alibi, he said.

According to the informant, Spearman insisted that he loved his wife. But he said she was dying of cancer, and was in terrible pain. Spearman reputedly added that she wanted to die, and he was merely making arrangements to put a stop to her suffering. But he also groused that he was fed up with her ill health. He complained that he couldn't have sex at all with his wife and sometimes had to resort to prostitutes and other women to take care of his sexual needs. But now, he said, he had found another woman to permanently take Anita's place. Spearman observed that he was thinking of taking a nice long vacation after the problem with his wife had been taken care of.

The rotund ex-convict took an instant dislike to Spearman. Emert had spent more of his life than he liked to think about behind bars, and he had met some nasty people. But although Spearman was on the outside, and presumably had never been part of the convict crowd, he wasn't the kind of person whom Emert wanted to waste time talking to. He told Spearman that he was just there to pick up money, and he didn't want to hear about his troubles or plans for the murder of his ailing wife.

"I didn't pay a whole lot of attention to him because I didn't care much for the man's attitude," Emert told his BATF interrogators. "I'm pretty good at judging character. I've got over the years to where I can tell what kind of a person you are by the way you talk."

Spearman at last gave him a large manila envelope and broke off his casual chatter about sex, vacations, and murder. Inside the package, two smaller business-sized envelopes were stuffed with about four thousand dollars in hundred-dollar bills. At Spearman's suggestion, after he pulled his Bronco out of the restaurant parking lot, they followed in the Toyota. Spearman drove to his home at 2367 Bay Circle. As he nosed his vehicle into the driveway, his coconspirators from Tennessee continued on by, made the turn around the circle at the end of the block, and returned to Idlewild Road. Spearman had promised to show them where he lived.

Emert and Doutre occupied the afternoon spending some of the money that Spearman had handed over to them. They drove to a business called the World of Sound, and paid $524 cash to have a stereo system installed in the Toyota. Then they drove to the Hollywood Palms, a motel in West Palm Beach, and rented a room for the night.

About ten o'clock the next morning, Emert again met Spearman in the Denny's parking lot, and the boat-yard operator gave him another large manila envelope. Inside, the final ten thousand dollars, in hundred-dollar bills, had been stuffed in two smaller envelopes. It was the final payment due for the contract on Anita Spearman's life. As her husband handed over the money, he casually mentioned that he had gotten in touch with Emert's boss through a classified in *SOF*.

Spearman was less casual about outlining just what he would do if Savage tried to rip him off. He warned that he had also been in the contract murder business for a while, and said that was why he had been familiar with *SOF* magazine. If Savage reneged on the contract, Spearman hissed, he would see to it that the bar operator was ''wasted.''

As far as Emert was concerned, that was Savage's problem. Without so much as grunting a good-bye, he stepped out of the Bronco, walked across the parking lot, and called a jitney from a public telephone to take him to the airport. A few hours later when Emert returned to Knoxville and the Continental Club, Debra Mattingly paid him five hundred dollars, according to the story he told investigators. It was only half the amount he had been promised.

Emert didn't learn until several days later that Doutre had left West Palm Beach without carrying out the contract. It would be weeks later before Emert learned that the murder was eventually carried out.

The burly ex–nightclub bouncer had more stories to tell BATF agents and other law enforcement officers about Savage and the Continental Club, as well. He said that the operator of the nudie bar had set himself up as the head of an entire ring of contract killers, who had already ranged over several states in the Midwest, South, and Southwest. And he described the seedy club as a noxious nest of thieves, whores, and hoodlums. Emert said that he got fed up with the hijinks and broke off his association with Savage and the club operator's hooligan pals soon after returning from the trip to Palm Beach County.

Emert obviously knew what he was talking about, and he was familiar with the interrogation routine and needs of law enforcement officers. He knew the kind of information they wanted, and he provided names, dates, and places as he spun out his tale of contract murder and bumbled assassination attempts. And he told the BATF men that if they wanted to find the weapon used to batter Mrs. Spearman to death, they should check with police in nearby Maryville for a twelve-gauge shotgun taken away from Doutre some four months earlier.

In fact, on the day after Anita Spearman was battered to death in her bed, BATF agents were having an earlier talk with Emert about the sinister extracurricular activities of the operator of the Continental Club and his handsome part-time bouncer Doutre. The Bureau had received a tip that the pair were involved in a plot on Lamey's life. They had already tapped the telephone line at the club, and they wanted to know if Emert had any information to share with them about the plot. Emert had severed his ties with Savage and his cut-throat cronies by that time, and couldn't offer much help.

The BATF contacted police in Maryville and passed on the tip about the shotgun. A short time later Mary-ville officers had retrieved the weapon from its shelf in the property room, and run the serial number through the NCIC computer once more. This time the printed report they received back listed the weapon as stolen from the scene of a homicide in Palm Beach County, Florida. The earlier computer check was made before Palm Beach County Sheriff's Department homicide in-vestigators had obtained the serial number and listed the shotgun as stolen.

BATF Agent McGarrity also telephoned the North Palm Beach Police Department and asked for infor-mation about Robert Spearman. McGarrity said he had the man's stolen shotgun. North Palm Beach Police of-ficers referred him to the Palm Beach County Sheriff's Department, which was investigating the homicide of Mrs. Spearman. McGarrity talked with Sergeant Kianka and advised the Florida lawman that he had information about the Spearman murder. He had located a shotgun believed to have been stolen from the crime scene. And he had a statement from an informant who claimed that he had traveled from Knoxville to Palm Beach County and collected eighteen thousand dollars from the vic-tim's husband for the contract murder. McGarrity wanted to check out some of the information that Emert had passed on to him.

Everything the BATF man told Kianka about his talks with the rugged convict fit in almost exactly with what the Palm Beach County homicide investigators had been able to dig up—or surmise—about the Spearman slaying. But the clincher came when McGarrity read off the serial number of the twelve-gauge pump-action shotgun. It was a match. Robert Spearman's missing scattergun had been found.

It was an exciting development for the Palm Beach County homicide investigators. They had been virtually certain for months that Spearman had played a big hand in the murder of his wife. Early in the investigation there seemed to be a good chance that he may have killed her himself. But now, at last, they were closing in on the real story. And they were developing the kind of evidence they needed to put the collar on Robert Spearman. Kianka and Springer talked over the new developments. And a few hours later, Springer boarded a flight at Palm Beach International Airport for Knoxville, and his partner left for Georgia. It was time that they had some talks with Ronald Emert, Richard "Doc" Savage, and Sean Trevor Doutre. In Knoxville Emert picked out a picture of Spearman from a collection of photographs of various men of similar age.

Suddenly police agencies in several states, as well as agents with the BATF and the FBI, found themselves up to their ears in a wide-ranging criminal investigation. Tom Stokes, agent in charge of the BATF office in Atlanta, called a conference there, and invited investigators from states as diverse as Georgia, Florida, Arkansas, Tennessee, Kentucky, Texas and Minnesota. It was time to begin exchanging information, and to launch a national investigation.

During their exchange of information, the task force officers began to develop a picture of a loose-knit gang of cross-country killers and would-be killers who were almost hopelessly careless and inept. They rented cars and didn't return them; ran out on motel bills; kept weapons that were stolen or used on hits; left illegal weapons, sometimes outfitted with equally illegal silencers, in plain sight in their cars; talked freely to acquaintances about contract killing; kept receipts; made long-distance calls from their own telephones; and took girlfriends or wives along on some assignments. They had even accepted personal checks as down payments for some hits. The dial-a-killers were virtually begging to be caught.

"They were like the gang that couldn't shoot straight or think straight," Stokes told a reporter a few days after the meeting. "Sometimes you had to wonder if this whole thing wasn't a comedy of errors."

But the BATF chief knew that they were killers, and there was nothing funny about murder. And despite the murder ring's sad record of reckless bungling and foul-ups, they did appear to be slowly learning from their mistakes. They were gradually becoming more proficient, and more dangerous.

Chapter 8

Arrest of a Merry Widower

Dressed casually in work-faded blue jeans and a white T-shirt, Robert Spearman was talking animatedly with the slender, attentive woman beside him as he walked out of the Bars & Stools furniture store on busy North Lake Boulevard in Lake Park, heading for his car parked nearby at the curb.

He was tanned and fit, and a satisfied smile split his rugged face, as it usually did when he was with a good-looking woman. He was so absorbed in his conversation with his companion that he wasn't even aware of the phalanx of grim-faced men watching him from a few feet away.

He was enthusiastic about the new condominium apartment he was preparing to move into in the seaside town of Jupiter, a few miles from Juno Beach, where Patricia Rozelle lived. He had just finalized the sale of his waterfront home on Bay Circle a few days before for two hundred thousand dollars. And he was looking forward to the delivery to his new bachelor apartment of four bar stools he had ordered from the furniture store. Spearman was tired of living on the forty-four-foot *Equalizer*.

It was a few minutes past noon on April 4, and the hot Florida sun was at its zenith, but Spearman was used to the heat. He was a longtime Floridian, and didn't bother to wear a hat, although his eyes were shaded by dark sunglasses.

It wasn't until one of the men who had been watching them broke away from the others, stepped up, and greeted him that Spearman became aware that he was in trouble.

"Hello, Bob," the man said.

"Hello, Sheriff. What are you doing here?"

"I've come to place you under arrest for first-degree murder," Sheriff Wille announced. Springer, Kianka, and two other detectives, who stepped up to flank the shaken murder suspect, had waited a long time to hear the sheriff speak those words. And neither they nor their boss were taking any chances.

Approximately three hours earlier on that bright, sunlit Friday morning, Palm Beach County Circuit Judge Daniel Hurley had carefully read thirteen pages of probable-cause affidavits prepared by sheriff's deputies and an assistant prosecutor. Then he had signed warrants for the arrest of Spearman, Savage, and Doutre as suspects in Anita's murder.

Outside the furniture store, Spearman's friend watched helplessly as the lawmen handcuffed their prisoner's hands behind his back, quickly and professionally patted him down, then hurried him to Sheriff Wille's parked 1985 yellow four-door Mercury Grand Marquee.

Two of the detectives made a rapid search of Spearman's car, peering into the glove compartment, under and between the seats, until they found a pistol, which they confiscated. Then they gave the shaken woman the keys to the car and told her she was free to drive it away. Before she left, she returned to the furniture store and canceled the order for the bar stools.

Accompanied by the detectives, Wille drove his prisoner directly to the Palm Beach County Sheriff's Office on Gun Club Road. The Sheriff's Office is part of a modern criminal justice complex that also includes courtrooms and the Palm Beach County Jail just outside the west edge of the sprawl of cities and towns that border the Intracoastal Waterway.

The sterile, secure county lockup was about to become the millionare's new home. A newspaper reporter was already waiting when the handcuffed prisoner was helped out of the sheriff's shiny Grand Marquee. Spearman's genial mood and attitude of only a few minutes before had quickly dissipated. Marching hurriedly between the sheriff and another detective, he kept his head down, with his eyes gloomily peering from behind the dark sunglasses at the asphalt cover of the parking lot, as a reporter followed along pestering him to give a statement. Spearman's only reply was a muttered "no" before he was led through a back door of the Sheriff's Department building away from the reporter and up a stairway to the second-floor Detective Division offices.

Inside, Spearman moved in a near daze, shuffling his feet and moving like a zombie, as he was led through the humiliating booking process. His face was grimly immobile and his jowls slumped as he stood in front of a horizontally lined backdrop while a police photographer snapped his mug shot. Another technician held his work-roughened hands, and with practiced moves he had performed thousands of times before, one by one pressed each of the prisoner's fingers and thumbs onto an ink pad, then rolled them into their proper spaces on a thin cardboard print sheet.

At last he was led out of the Sheriff's Department building, and walked a few yards to the Palm Beach County Jail. There, correctional officers issued him a pair of clean but rumpled blue jail coveralls, led him to a cell, and locked him inside with about a dozen other prisoners. He was being held without bond on charges of first-degree murder, conspiracy, and solicitation to commit murder. Guards placed him under suicide watch, and checked on him in his cell every fifteen minutes.

Other forces were at work while he was being booked, however. One of his employees, and a sheriff's deputy, had telephoned Spearman's attorney, David Roth. Roth learned of the arrest at about 12:30 P.M., approximately fifteen minutes after Spearman was taken into custody. He talked with his client for about two hours at the jail.

The experienced criminal defense attorney later told the press that his client was very upset by the arrest. He added that Spearman would plead not guilty to the charges at his arraignment.

News of the arrest spread through Palm Beach County like a flash fire. Spearman had barely been handcuffed and hustled into the sheriff's car before neighbors, acquaintances, employees at the boatyard, and Anita's friends in city government were excitedly exchanging stories and gossip about the incident. Many of the friends and former colleagues of the couple first learned of the arrest when they were approached for comments by newspaper or television reporters. The natural bureaucratic reluctance to be quoted that governmental officials and employees usually develop quickly asserted itself. And not everyone who agreed to talk would talk for the record.

One of Anita's friends at City Hall in West Palm Beach said it was simply unbelievable to think that Robert Spearman had deliberately caused harm to his wife. The woman said she was stunned by the senselessness and the brutality of the murder.

Simmons, who had left West Palm Beach and assumed new duties as city manager of Kissimmee near Orlando, was reluctant to talk about his former friends when he was contacted by the press. But he said that he would assume that his onetime assistant manager's husband was innocent until he was proven to be guilty.

Some neighbors and acquaintances were surprised and shocked. Others conceded that they had suspected for a long time that Spearman was behind his wife's slaying. At the E & H Boat Works, one of the company officers said he was surprised it took police so long to put Spearman behind bars. But another told reporters that it was absolutely out of character for Spearman to be involved in a murder scheme against his own wife. He said he still wanted to believe that it was all a mistake—and that Spearman was innocent.

One loyal friend insisted that Spearman wouldn't hurt Anita either for money or because he had a girlfriend. Even if Spearman admitted that he had deliberately hurt his wife or had her hurt, the woman stubbornly added, she still wouldn't believe it. Other friends talked of being in the Spearman home many times, and insisted that Robert and Anita were a loving couple. Neither would hurt the other.

At supermarket checkout lanes, conversation turned

Above: Sean Doutre (Courtesy Palm Beach County Sheriff's Department)
Left: Larry E. Gray (Charles Bickford, *Springdale News*)

Anita and Robert Spearman (John Pineda, *The Miami Herald*)

Prosecutor Moira Lasch holds a photo of Sean Doutre (Melisa Mimms, *The Miami Herald*)

Top: The funeral of Anita Spearman (John Pineda, *The Miami Herald*)
Bottom: Defense attorneys Richard Greene and Dean Willbur confer with Sean Doutre during the Spearman murder trial (AP/Wide World Photos)

Top: Patricia Rozelle points out Robert Spearman during the trial (C.J. Walker, *The Miami Herald*)
Bottom: Spearman being fingerprinted after his sentencing (Gary Bogdon, *The Miami Herald*)

Above: Richard Michael
"Doc" Savage on the first
day of his trial for the
murder of Anita
Spearman (Pat Farrell, *The
Miami Herald*)
Right: Doug and Kathy
Norwood in his law offices
(Courtesy of Charles
Bickford)

Above: Debra Ann
Banister and John Wayne
Hearn (Gary S. Wolfson,
Gainesville Sun)
Left: Mary Alice Wolf
(*Lexington Herald-Leader*)

Above left: Albert Lee
Thielman (David Kennedy,
Austin American-Statesman)
Above right: Robert
Vanoy Black, Jr., after
being sentenced to death
for the murder for hire of
his wife, Sandra Black
(AP/Wide World Photos)
Left: Robert K. Brown,
publisher of *Soldier of
Fortune* magazine (AP/
Wide World Photos)

from the garish headlines in weekly tabloid newspapers to the scandal and horror at home. This time the topic wasn't of marriages, divorces, cheating, and pregnancies of Hollywood celebrities, nor of the bored rich kicking up their heels just across the Intracoastal Waterway in Palm Beach. It was about people who, although a bit wealthier than most, had been very much like themselves. And it was about the ultimate betrayal—conjugal murder—the slaying of a spouse by or at the behest of the victim's life partner.

When the press contacted Anita's mother, Louise Jones, in South Carolina asking for her reaction to the arrest, she told a reporter for the *Miami Herald,* "I just can't believe it. They always seemed so fond of each other. He was good to her and he was good to us." Mrs. Jones told a reporter for the *Palm Beach Post* that she wasn't ready to commit herself about her belief in her son-in-law's guilt or innocence. She said that she and her surviving daughter had written to him, but they hadn't talked to him for a while, because it was too emotionally difficult. "What's going to become of him?" she asked.

Robert Spearman's mother, Alberta, was horrified and disbelieving. The deeply religious woman, who had attended a missionary school in her younger years, loved her son's wife. And she told a friend who was a county government official that she thought her son was being framed by someone else for the murder. The friend quoted the brokenhearted mother as saying that she believed the real killers would never be caught, and sheriff's detectives arrested her son because the pressure was on to make an arrest in the case.

But when Dr. Parker was asked by a reporter for his reaction, he said he hoped that Spearman would be convicted and receive the death penalty. "That's what he delivered to my cousin," the doctor declared.

Wille publicly credited Emert's cooperation with helping break the four-month-old case, and said the shotgun was an important key to tying together the various suspects. He refused to disclose where Emert was being held, in order to protect the witness. And he added that Emert hadn't been promised anything by authorities in Palm Beach County in return for his cooperation. But he conceded it was unlikely that the husky career criminal would be charged in connection with Mrs. Spearman's murder.

Springer and his Rent-A-Wreck colleagues had been busy. They had rounded up receipts from the Econo Lodge and from the Hollywood Palms Motor Lodge confirming Emert's statements about renting rooms in the motels during the October 21–22 visit to Palm Beach County to collect the bulk of the murder fee from Spearman.

And they had recovered receipts from the Holiday Inn on PGA Boulevard for a lone male guest who had checked in, apparently under an assumed name, on November 14. He stayed two nights, then skipped out on his bill. The receipts showed that the mystery guest had ordered two expensive dinners and charged them to room service. One of the meals, ordered November 15— on the night before Mrs. Spearman's murder—was a feast of prime rib, jumbo shrimp, broccoli, a salad, and a bottle of Grand Marnier. With tip, the sumptuous meal for one cost $91.29.

The investigators believed the high-living rip-off artist was Sean Doutre, up to his old tricks. It seemed that Doutre couldn't resist repeating his penny-ante cheating, no matter how sensitive or perilous his situation might be. Few real professional hit men bothered cheating on their food or hotel bills when they were working on a contract.

Just as the meticulous work of the Palm Beach County Sheriff's detectives going through the gun shop records had paid off, so, too, did their inspection of telephone bills. They tracked eighteen calls from Spearman's office to a Knoxville residential number listed to Debra Savage that were made between October 13 and November 11. The determined sleuths had traced yet another call made from a pay telephone along the Florida Turnpike near Orlando and charged to Spearman's office, to Patricia Rozelle's home in Juno Beach. The call was logged on November 27, more than a month after Anita Spearman's death, and long after Ms. Rozelle had claimed her romance with the city official's husband had cooled.

Detectives also pinned down seven long-distance calls from his business phone to numbers listed in three different gun-for-hire-type classifieds in *SOF* in addition to Savage's ad. Two of the calls were made to Patterson, New Jersey, and to Phoenix, Arizona, on October 9. The New Jersey call was traced to a classified that offered: "man for hire, intelligent and dependable, all jobs considered, call Dave." The call to Phoenix was tied by the investigators to an ad by a man who signed himself as Bill Stringfellow, and was soliciting clients seeking an "adjuster" who was "selective" and "effective."

The final call was made on October 13 to a Florida number, an advertiser who ominously announced that "the Wolf is taking new contracts. Will consider all situations." Spearman, it seemed, had done some shopping around before settling on a final deal with the Tennessee strip club manager.

The busy sleuths had also turned up a copy of a Delta Airlines round-trip ticket between Knoxville and West Palm Beach that Spearman had paid $511 for with his American Express card on October 15. The passenger listed on the ticket was Richard Savage.

The detectives tracked a copy of Emert's Delta Airlines ticket, confirming his flight on October 22 from West Palm Beach to Atlanta, where he changed airplanes, then continued on to Knoxville. They developed further confirmation through an interview with Robert Dix, a Blue Front jitney driver, who remembered picking up a lone white male near the Denny's restaurant. Dix said that he drove the man to a convenience store, where the passenger bought some envelopes, which he stuffed money into as they continued on to the airport.

And although the information could not be disclosed to a jury, the Rent-A-Wreck detective team had submitted Emert to a polygraph test that verified his statements about the contract murder of Anita Spearman were true.

Springer and his colleagues also checked out an intriguing lead from an anonymous telephone tipster who claimed that the murder suspect had asked a man from the exclusive community of Wellington in western Palm Beach County to kill Mrs. Spearman before contacting Savage. The informant claimed that the Wellington man referred Spearman to *Soldier of Fortune* magazine. The mysterious caller added that the man had a collection of automatic weapons, and that his wife provided the boatyard owner with prescription drugs shortly before he took the lie detector test.

When detectives talked with the Wellington businessman, he denied that Spearman had ever asked him to either murder the victim or to recommend someone who would do the job. He strongly denied referring Spearman to *SOF*, but told investigators that his brother had once worked for the magazine. And his wife conceded that she had mailed Spearman some prescription tranquilizers shortly after Anita's murder. She said that they talked on the telephone but never met.

Despite their own hard work on the case, the sheriff and his team of law enforcement officers were quick to give credit where credit was due. There was no evidence in their statements of the divisive jurisdictional squabbling that sometimes pits law enforcement agencies at each other's throats. Sheriff's spokesman Mike McNamee made sure that the press knew about the key role that the BATF had played in breaking the perplexing four-month-old homicide case.

"In reality, we would still be plodding along very slowly without the BATF contact," he said. "They were the critical link, and we want them to receive a great deal of credit."

Wille added that Spearman hadn't talked with investigators since the arrest. Consequently, the lawman said, he couldn't yet outline a firm motive for the slaying.

The *Post* reported in its main story that Spearman was accompanied by Patricia Rozelle when he was taken into custody. The next day the *Post* ran another story apologizing and explaining that the woman wasn't Ms. Rozelle after all. Sheriff's officers were blamed for the misidentification. This time the *Post* didn't bother to name Spearman's mystery companion, except to quote officials as saying she was a family friend of Spearman from Arizona.

Many south Florida residents were still reading about Spearman's arrest in their Saturday morning newspapers when he appeared for a hearing before Judge Daniel Hurley in Palm Beach County Circuit Court a few minutes before 9:00 A.M. Spearman may have been dressed in the uniform blue coveralls like the twenty-five or thirty fellow prisoners brought into court with him, but he wasn't just another face in the crowd.

He stood silently among the pitiful ragtag collection of accused burglars, rapists, robbers, drug dealers, and junkies, occasionally turning to glance at the members of the media while waiting for the judge to enter the courtroom. Roth was out of town, and attorney Tracy Sharpe was filling in for him on Spearman's behalf. Spearman was the first defendant called when Judge Hurley took his place at the bench. Responding to questions by the judge, Spearman spoke softly, confirming that he understood his constitutional rights and the charges against him. And he said he understood his attorney's request to postpone a bond hearing.

Approximately ten minutes after his name was called, Spearman was led to a private room where he was permitted to confer briefly with his attorney. Then he was returned to his cell in the jail. A few days later, Spearman entered formal pleas of not guilty to all the charges against him.

When Spearman finally talked again with detectives, he confided that he had figured out the real reason his wife was murdered. It was a terrible blunder. Spearman said the killers were really after a neighbor of his who was a drug dealer and had wound up as a murder target after a falling out with some of his criminal associates. The prisoner claimed the hit men had mistakenly gone to the wrong house, and the foul-up cost the life of his wife.

Springer, Kianka, and the state attorney's chief homicide prosecutor, Paul Moyle, had been doing their homework, however, and recognized Spearman's desperate effort to shift the focus of the investigation off himself for exactly what it was—a fairy tale. And it wasn't even a very good one. Nevertheless, simply because the accusation had been made, the detectives had to check the story out.

Investigators checked out the resident whom Spearman had named, probing his background and talking with other residents in the Lake Park neighborhood. Eventually Detective Springer talked with the man himself. The neighbor had never had any involvement with the illegal narcotics trade. And he wasn't happy about having his name and reputation dragged into the investigation.

He told the detective that he had already heard from different sources about Spearman's malicious accusation. "We all got a big snicker out of that," he said of the reaction when friends passed the story on to him. But whatever humor there may have been in the yarn quickly faded, and the neighbor wasn't smiling anymore. "I don't think it's particularly funny, because I'm being slandered," he said. Springer and his colleagues quickly confirmed their previous suspicions. Spearman's accusation against his neighbor was groundless. The neighbor was a law-abiding citizen with no links to the drug trade.

Although sheriff's investigators may have been satisfied with the results of their probe into Spearman's drug-dealing accusation, the neighbor wasn't. In July he filed a lawsuit in Palm Beach County Circuit Court against Spearman, charging him with slander.

Criminal charges and other troubles were also piling up against Savage and Doutre as they waited out the legal processes in their jail cells in Athens. And like Spearman, they had people who knew and loved them who didn't want to believe the charges.

At the Clarke County lockup in Athens, "Doc" Savage was trying his best to convince police and reporters that he simply wasn't the killer type. But he conceded during jailhouse interviews that he had made one incredibly bad mistake: placing a gun-for-hire ad in *Soldier of Fortune* magazine. Nervously chain-smoking Camels and with dark crescents under his red-rimmed eyes that betrayed his exhaustion and stress, Savage claimed that he was merely looking for a means of picking up some extra money through work as a courier or bodyguard.

He admitted that some forty to fifty people had telephoned him with murder on their minds, but insisted that he had refused to have anything to do with their schemes. He said he wasn't a killer and didn't believe in hurting people. Taking his time to think before speaking, and drawing out his words, Savage insisted, "I didn't want to go out and kill everybody in America. I don't know how it got this far."

In fact, Savage claimed, he contacted *SOF* and asked that the magazine discontinue his ad. He explained that he was afraid "some of these nuts" would respond by trying to murder him, his girlfriend, mother, or son.

When Savage was advised about Norwood's pending multimillion-dollar lawsuit against him, his cohorts, and *SOF* magazine, he responded that he had never heard of the Arkansas law student. Speaking in his soft Tennessee drawl, Savage insisted that causing pain to someone conflicted with everything he had learned from the Bible.

He pointed out that although he wasn't especially religious, he had been reading the Bible since he was locked up. And he said he firmly believed that no one should deliberately kill another human being. His mother was faithfully writing and sending him religious literature, and she urged him to pray.

Regardless of Savage's desperate denials of criminal involvement, and of Doutre's sudden uncharacteristic silence, the rapidly developing investigation was netting new suspects in several states. Federal and local investigators were collecting a blizzard of evidence that included telephone records, canceled checks, motel receipts, weapons, interviews, and confessions. And police agencies around the country were making arrests and filing charges against reputed members of the dial-a-killer gang, and their suspected clients.

And authorities were far from through with Savage. Utilizing information developed by the BATF and the investigation by Fulton County sheriff's officers authorities, a federal indictment was returned against Savage, Doutre, and Gastwirth in the ambush slaying of Braun just outside his Sandy Springs home. Doutre was charged as the triggerman in the cold-blooded execution. John H. Moore was named in a separate federal indictment, charging him with making a delivery of part of the contract murder fee to Savage.

Like authorities in Palm Beach County, Lt. E. E. Nixon, head of the major crimes unit of the Fulton County Police Department, was quick to publicly credit the BATF for its part in breaking the case. He told the press that BATF agents in Knoxville developed information that was instrumental in tracking down the killers.

Nixon couldn't resist adding a sarcastic remark about the tragicomic murder ring, however. He suggested that if a movie is ever made about the gang, comedian Don Knotts, who played the sheriff's old Mayberry sidekick on television's long-running "Andry Griffith Show," would be perfect for the role of the leader.

Early in May a federal indictment was unsealed in Atlanta naming Savage; his twenty-five-year-old girlfriend, Debra Mattingly; Buckley; and Jackson and Mrs. Brando in the two botched efforts in July and August to murder Free by blowing up his car with hand grenades. The indictment charged them with conspiracy and use of interstate commerce facilities in the commission of murder for hire, destruction of a vehicle by explosives and transportation of explosives across state lines with intent to kill. They were serious charges, and each of the defendants faced possible penalties of up to thirty years in prison and half-million-dollar fines if they were convicted.

The day the indictment was unsealed, Buckley was apprehended in Knoxville, and Mrs. Brado was arrested in Texas. A BATF spokesman said that officers were looking for Ms. Mattingly. And Jackson, of course, was already in custody in Fayetteville.

Several months later, Savage, Buckley, Lambeth, Mrs. Brado, and Ms. Breeden were named in a nine-court indictment returned by a federal grand jury in Houston accusing them of various offenses in the hand grenade attack on the home of Free's ex-wife in Pasadena. BATF agents arrested Ms. Breeden in Loudon County, and locked her in the Knox County Jail in nearby Knoxville. But she was quickly released on ten thousand dollars bail, and ordered by the court to live at her mother's home. She was also required to submit to random drug screenings.

BATF agents finally caught up with Lambeth in Denver and arrested the sixty-year-old trucker on charges of serving as a money courier for Mrs. Brado in the conspiracy.

Most members of Savage's pathetic gang of law enforcement washouts and dime-store adventurers crumpled and began to beg for a deal as soon as police started to question them. There was no honor among thieves shown by the gang, and they turned on one another like a school of hammerhead sharks at a blood feast.

Within thirty minutes after Jackson was driven to the UA campus police department headquarters, he was telling all about the plot on the law student's life. He not only provided Gray's name, address, and telephone number, but he agreed to help the lawmen reel in their Oklahoma quarry. As police recorded the conversation, Jackson telephoned Gray and told him that he was ready to do away with the elusive law student, but couldn't shoot him as previously planned. He said he needed another four hundred dollars to buy two hand grenades to blow up Norwood's car once more. Gray fell for the ruse, but recommended that he use three grenades instead of only two. Then he wired the money to Jackson in Fayetteville.

A few hours later, on a Tuesday evening less than forty-eight hours after Herring and Swearingen nabbed Jackson near the campus farm, Tulsa police arrested Gray at his brokerage company office. Earlier in the day Prosecutor Kim Smith of Fayetteville had filed charges against him in the Arkansas courts of criminal conspiracy to commit capital murder. According to information in the warrant, he was accused of hiring Jackson to murder Norwood. Gray did not resist arrest, and he was driven to the Tulsa police department, where he was booked on a local charge of being a fugitive from justice. Then he was locked up in the Tulsa City-County jail. After a few hours, however, he was released on $250,000 bail.

A few months later a twelve-count federal indictment was returned in U.S. district court in Fort Smith, Arkansas, against the Tulsa businessman, along with Savage, Buckley, DeLuca, and Ms. Mattingly for the murder attempts in Fayetteville. Jackson, who was already facing state charges linked to the scheme, was not named in the indictment. The crime was considered to be a federal offense because of the interstate telephone calls and interstate travel involved in the reputed scheme. Assistant U.S. Attorney Frank H. McCarthy, of Tulsa, presented two hours of arguments and testimony in court contending the jailed businessman would be a danger to the community if allowed to remain free, and opposing establishment of bail on the federal charges.

Sergeant Herring was McCarthy's key witness. Providing the first public glimpse at the details of the complicated death plot, the campus policeman recounted the statements of witnesses, and provided names, dates, and telephone records linked to the aborted murder scheme. He said the Tulsa businessman hatched the lethal plot against Norwood shortly after Gray's estranged wife, Kathy, told him that she wanted a divorce in early August 1985.

According to the officer's reconstruction, Gray spent considerable time shopping for a hit man and talked with several would-be killers before making a deal with

Savage. He said that the first attempt to carry out the contract in Fayetteville occurred after Savage and his companions drove to the college town and called Gray from a shopping center pay phone at 7:00 A.M. on August 30 to obtain Norwood's address. After the affair was bungled, he testified, a member of Savage's group made an anonymous telephone call to the hospital to inquire about Norwood's condition.

But the investigator had yet more shocking revelations to make. He said that Gray offered the murder contract to at least two other men, who were unconnected with Savage's ring. One Florida man made a tape recording of a telephone conversation during which Gray attempted to enlist him in the murder scheme, and turned it over to police. Herring said that Gray also contacted another man who rejected an offer of fifteen hundred dollars to murder the law student. And only a few weeks earlier, Herring added, the man who rejected the fifteen-hundred-dollar offer was threatened with death if he testified against Gray.

Eventually, after the bungled efforts by Savage's pathetic devil's brigade of losers to kill Norwood, and after others turned him down, Gray telephoned Jackson at his home in Texas and offered him the contract, the campus policeman said. The testimony was grim and frightening, and it exposed the defendant as a ruthless and vengeful man willing to go to any lengths to have his way.

Sergeant Herring also testified that Gray had arranged for the beating of the boyfriend of his first former wife in 1978.

The defendant's current wife, who was pregnant, testified for him and pleaded that he was needed to help operate their business.

At the conclusion of the hearing, U.S. Magistrate John Leo Wagner agreed with the prosecutor's argument that Gray was likely to be a danger to the community if freed. The magistrate issued an order denying bond, and ordering him to be placed in federal custody in Arkansas. Soon after that, Gray was transported to Fort Smith to face trial in U.S. district court there with Jackson and others accused as coconspirators. The Tulsa businessman was locked up in the Sebastian County Adult Detention Center.

Savage was still jailed in Athens, Buckley was behind bars in Kentucky, and authorities were searching for DeLuca, who had disappeared. The Canadian teenager was finally run down months later in Hamilton, Ontario, and arrested on a fugitive warrant. He was jailed at a Hamilton detention center and immediately began fighting extradition efforts by the U.S. Department of Justice. Meanwhile a public defender was appointed to represent Jackson, who said that he didn't have a job, and did not own any property. He remained in custody in Fayetteville, held on $250,000 bond. The charges filed against Gray in local state courts were dismissed.

In the meantime, while waiting for the trials of the men and the woman accused in the conspiracy to have him killed, Norwood continued to carry his .357 Magnum and to wear a bulletproof vest. And he set his sights on working as a prosecutor after graduation from law school.

The BATF and local Kentucky authorities were also busy in Louisville, closing their net on Mary Alice Wolf and members of the classified ad murder ring for their roles in the aborted assassination schemes against Victoria Morgan Brashear.

Ms. Wolf had already gotten into other legal troubles

and was in the women's jail in Louisville when BATF Agent Ed Verkin began asking her questions about a murder plot against her former love rival, and about a gang of professional hit men led by Richard Savage. On May 27, 1986, she gave Verkin a taped statement admitting that she had paid money to have the pretty schoolteacher killed.

Ms. Wolf, Savage, Buckley, Doutre, DeLuca, and the other two men Savage had dispatched to Kentucky were subsequently named in a federal indictment returned by a grand jury in Lexington charging them with involvement in the plot against the schoolteacher. Charges against the young Louisville woman included conspiracy to commit murder for hire, and three counts of traveling in interstate commerce to commit murder for hire. She was freed on ten thousand dollars bail, and put under court order not to leave Jefferson County (the Louisville area). The order also forbade her from contacting Alan or Victoria Brashear.

Doutre's wife and her teenage friend had finally learned that he wouldn't be returning to Florida to pick them up, and they made their way back to the Knoxville area. Linda had to sell the pearl necklace that her husband had given to her, to raise money for the trip home. Once she was back in Tennessee, she moved in with her parents for a while, and when she was located by reporters, remarked that if her husband had indeed killed anyone, it would probably be easy for her to get a divorce. She added that the young man who called himself Peter Tosh Marley worked for Savage. And she said his boss showed his employees how to handle weapons, and taught them how to kill.

Then she told her parents she was going to Knoxville to stay with friends, and dropped from sight. Her mother confided to reporters that she was afraid the young woman's life was in danger. She pointed out that strangers to her had been telephoning and asking for her daughter, and she was concerned for Linda's safety. Mrs. Smith recalled the bracelet and the pearl necklace that her son-in-law had given her daughter. And she said she was sure that he had murdered the woman in Florida.

Linda Smith Doutre was located by investigators, however, in time to provide them with a statement confirming that her husband drove to Florida a few days after their November 10 wedding in Tennessee.

In Florida, meanwhile, a Palm Beach County grand jury had returned criminal indictments against Spearman, Savage, and Doutre after a presentation by Assistant State Attorney Paul Moyle. Moyle was the county's chief homicide prosecutor. Spearman was charged with first-degree murder, conspiracy to commit first-degree murder, and two counts of solicitation to commit first-degree murder. The grand jury had tacked on an extra count of soliciting murder to the charges initially filed when Spearman was arrested. Savage and Doutre were each charged with first-degree murder and conspiracy to commit first-degree murder.

The Rent-A-Wreck squad and investigators with the State Attorney's Office had been busy. They had questioned eighty-five people as part of their intensive probe into Mrs. Spearman's slaying. And the more they probed the activities of her husband and the rent-a-killer gang, the more amazing the story that unfolded became. Springer had quietly transported Emert from the Knox County Jail in Knoxville to the Palm Beach County Jail on April 11, after Tennessee Governor Lamar Alexander signed a temporary custody order allowing the informant to be moved. Emert was serving a three-year sentence in Tennessee for violation of parole by receiving stolen property. And after being given limited immunity from prosecution, he was still providing information. Buckley was also chipping in valuable information from his jail cell in Douglas County, Georgia. And yet other intriguing details to help fill out the increasingly complex investigation were provided by Ms. Mattingly after she was at last taken into custody.

Between them, the two men and the woman outlined a fantastic tale of double crosses carried out or planned by the schemers in Tennessee and Florida when their own greed, failures, and fears began to catch up with them as the BATF was closing in. Doutre doublecrossed his boss, Savage. And Savage had planned an even more lethal double cross that could have cost Robert Spearman his life instead of that of his wife.

Both Buckley and the woman said that Doutre informed Savage that he had been arrested after Emert left Florida, in an effort to dupe his boss out of a big chunk of the Spearman payoff.

After being granted immunity from prosecution in the Spearman case, Ms. Mattingly, who was living in a halfway house in Atlanta, gave authorities a sixty-four-page statement. In the statement she said that Savage was immediately suspicious of Doutre's clumsy scam effort and made her check out the story.

"Richard had me calling the West Palm Beach Police Department and all the area police departments around there, and nobody had him," she told the investigators. Detectives later used telephone records to confirm that she had called the Palm Beach County Sheriff's Department, the North Palm Beach Police Department, and the West Palm Beach Police Department.

Doutre eventually returned to Knoxville and went back to work for Savage after telling him that he had escaped from jail, and recovered from a minor injury after being shot in the leg. By that time Spearman was furious and threatening. Buckley said that the boatyard owner was calling and telling Savage, "Hey, you better come down and do this job. I paid you for it, and by God, I want it done." He said that Spearman threatened to kill Savage if he didn't have Anita killed.

Ms. Mattingly also revealed that Spearman was outraged after Emert and Doutre left south Florida without carrying out the murder contract after their first meetings and he handed over the payoff. Spearman repeatedly telephoned Savage in Knoxville, and she answered many of the calls. She always said that Savage wasn't in. But the calls and the threats worried her.

"I knew I wasn't playing a game," she told the investigators. "When you take twenty thousand dollars from somebody, it's getting serious. It would be with me."

She said that, acting on her boyfriend's instructions, she once telephoned Spearman from a telephone booth in the neighborhood to pass on a message. Savage had given her a little black book with his client's name and two south Florida telephone numbers in it. She said she told Spearman that there would be "some people in Florida in the next three days."

The woman claimed that her boyfriend had never really planned to murder Anita Spearman. "He got into ripping the man off," she asserted. "He wanted the money, but he didn't want to do the job."

She said he talked to her before leaving on his trip

to Palm Beach County about his plans to bilk his client out of the cash. "Richard told me that the man wanted his wife killed; that she was dying with terminal cancer, and it was more or less a mercy killing, and he was going to take the man's money and not do the job, which I might add, Richard never did the job," she declared in her less than perfect sentence construction.

"Richard had went down there to get the retainer, and he was supposed to send two men down, and Mr. Spearman would finish paying him twenty thousand dollars . . . and he was just going to take the man's money," the woman stated. "He thought it was funny."

According to her statement, Spearman was furious, and threatening. "Just tell him I want the job done," she quoted him as saying. Then, she said, he threatened that if the contract wasn't carried out, he had friends who would "make sure that something happened to Richard's family." The calls then suddenly stopped, Ms. Mattingly said.

She explained that it was January, while another murder was being plotted, before she learned why the threatening telephone calls had suddenly ceased. She said that Savage was talking to Doutre about this when the young gunman provided the answer. "It's because he paid me five thousand dollars to do the job," she quoted him as saying. If Doutre was telling the truth, he had squeezed more out of Spearman than the total Savage had accepted for some of his other contracts.

Emert told BATF agents that he was present when Savage instructed Doutre about how to carry out the murder in Palm Beach County. "He was to kill the woman. He was to waste the man because the man could identify him as being the man down there and taking the contract," Emert declared.

According to a transcript of Emert's session with agent McGarrity of the BATF, he said that he and Savage were talking at the club one day near Thanksgiving when he asked his boss if the hit in Florida had been taken care of.

"Why do you ask?" Emert quoted Savage as responding.

"Cause Mr. Spearman said if you didn't do it right, he was going to blow your head off, and that he had done that kind of thing before, and it wouldn't be the first time," Emert replied.

"Is that the first time you told Savage that?" McGarrity asked.

"Yeah," Emert replied. "And he says, 'Well I had to send Pete [Doutre] back. He screwed it up and he went down and straightened it up.''

A couple of days later, Emert told a similar story to Palm Beach County detectives. He said that the strip club operator wanted his client "wasted" because he could identify him as being involved in the murder conspiracy against Mrs. Spearman. "And he was scared because the tobacco and firearms people were talking to him, and he was being investigated through his ads in the *Soldier of Fortune*, and he was getting sort of shaky, and he was really scared that he was caught. That's what it was."

In a statement to Moyle, Emert claimed that Savage once asked him to perform a contract killing for him. Emert said he told Savage that he was crazy. "I've bought some hot stuff, and then sold some hot goods, and things like that, and dealt in a little bit of dope," the informant declared. "But I don't go in for murder. That's against my better judgment."

Emert said that he was also personally threatened.

"They told me if I ever said anything, I'd be dead," he said. "They guaranteed he'd get me or my family wherever we were at. And I've got two young boys, and that's sort of scary, when they're threatening your kids' lives."

In a formal statement to investigators, Buckley backed up the basic facts of Emert's story about the plot on Robert Spearman's life. He said that Savage complained to him about threats from Spearman, and planned to have his hit man murder the boatyard owner after the payoff was received. According to Buckley, Mrs. Spearman was not supposed to be harmed unless she happened to stumble onto the hit man as he was dealing with her husband, or the double cross failed.

"At the time that I left Savage, he was desperately seeking for somebody to go down to Florida to actually do the work, and he says preferably get Spearman . . ." the Kentuckian declared. The hit man was to murder Mrs. Spearman only if her husband couldn't be killed. He said that Savage was determined that one of the Spearmans die, so that the vengeful boatyard owner wouldn't come gunning for him later.

Buckley also offered a few personal observations about the motives of some of the men, including himself, who were accused of being key members of the murder ring.

"Doutre, when you come right down to it, was the only one of the entire bunch . . . that enjoyed, or appeared to enjoy, the work," he said. He claimed that Savage was only involved for the money.

Of himself, he observed, "I was in it, one, because of money; two, because I really wasn't sure how the hell to get out of it."

Spearman was also pondering how he could get out

of the mess. And he wasn't putting all of his hopes on
beating the murder charges against him in court. He
was doing some fantasizing, and talking, about making
a dramatic prison escape. In the meantime, however,
his attorneys were working hard to win his permanent
release by legal means, through the courts. Both the
defense and the prosecution, in fact, were shaping up
their legal teams and plotting strategy for the approaching trial.

Roth had been joined by two young West Palm Beach
attorneys as cocounsel for Spearman. Thirty-three-year-
old Douglas Duncan, and Robert Adler, who was one
year younger, were picked for the defense team, to take
advantage of their skills in researching criminal law.
Their talents would be especially useful in researching
the conspiracy allegations.

On the side of the state, the lineup was headed by
Moira Lasch, an assistant state attorney for seven years.
At first glance, the slender thirty-five-year-old prosecutor might seem to have had an unlikely educational
background for someone with the job of prosecuting a
high-profile murder case. A few years later however,
she would attract international attention as chief prosecutor in the William Kennedy Smith rape trial.

After completing classes at a Catholic high school
for girls, she graduated magna cum laude from Vassar
College, with a degree in art history. After leaving the
exclusive women's college in Poughkeepsie, New York,
she continued her education with graduate work in art
history at Boston College. Then she obtained her law
degree at the University of Maryland. She did her in-
ternship at the West Palm Beach City Attorney's Office,
and was a prosecutor with the county attorney before
moving to the job as an assistant state's attorney in 1979.

At a willowy five feet five inches, 110 pounds, and with delicate fine features, she was physically unimposing. But she knew her way around in the courtroom and could be counted on to hold her own, no matter how wild, free swinging, and vicious the legal bickering became. Both colleagues and opponents described her in terms such as "tenacious," "unflappable," "dedicated," and "prepared." Especially "prepared."

She was always prepared. A tireless, methodical worker, she had paid her legal dues, working everything from traffic court to disgusting sexual offenses and grisly homicides. And she had undergone some hairy courtroom experiences, including a trial when an angry serial rapist she was prosecuting rushed at her and had to be subdued by bailiffs. Another time when she had been prosecuting a particularly foulmouthed defendant, he spit on her and called her a name. Later, as she recounted the incident with an amused grin, she repeated the name: "Miss Pointy Face."

After hearing the story, one courtroom wag remarked that for the defendant to have used such a remarkable epithet on the prosecutor, he, too, must have studied at Vassar.

Kerry St. James, another experienced and able member of the state attorney's staff, joined her on the prosecution team.

Ms. Lasch said that she would seek the death penalty against Spearman.

The man selected to preside over all the legal fireworks was one of Palm Beach County's most colorful, experienced, and respected jurists, fifty-eight-year-old Carl Harper. During a nine-year career on the bench, the judge had presided over a host of famous and infamous cases, and no one in the local legal community expressed doubts that he would be fully capable of dealing with the Spearman trial. Judge Harper knew how to handle defendants, lawyers, and the press. And although he had a refreshing country wit that emerged when the occasion permitted, he ran a tight ship. In his courtroom, he was the captain. He was a big man who could be gruff and cranky if things weren't running smoothly. In private, outside the judge's hearing, lawyers sometimes guardedly referred to him as "The Bear."

There was little question that the most titillatingly salacious and widely reported trial The Bear had presided at was the bitter divorce battle between Palm Beach's Roxanne and Peter Pulitzer over custody of the couple's twins, Mack and Zack. At one point while the case was progressing, the judge wisecracked that Palm Beach was an "island off the coast of the United States." At the conclusion of the scandalous proceeding, Judge Harper awarded custody of the boys to their father. And he made no secret of his distaste for the flamboyant mother of the boys, remarking that he doubted she was "capable of human emotion and concern."

Judge Harper scheduled the murder trial in the slaying of Anita Spearman for August 25.

The prosecutor's ability to put her nose to the grindstone and handle expeditiously the job of assembling legal jigsaw puzzles such as the Spearman murder case served her well after Roth filed a petition early in June demanding a speedy trial for his client. U.S. law and Florida rules of law were very specific about protecting the rights of defendants in criminal cases to speedy trials. And Spearman was well within his rights to demand trial within 180 days of his arrest, even though the move represented a surprising turnaround of the usual defense strategy in major criminal cases. Most often it is the prosecution that pushes for an early and expeditious trial, while defense attorneys petition the court for repeated delays.

The demand was as troubling a development for the prosecution and the court as it was unexpected. If Judge Harper approved the motion, Spearman's trial would have to begin within fifty days, and cut weeks off the time for preparation. It was time that could be vital to the state's chances of success or failure in its efforts to win guilty verdicts. The Spearman slaying was a complicated case that couldn't be put together by the prosecution overnight. And the state had other serious considerations in addition to preparation to deal with, as well.

If Spearman was put on trial before his accused co-conspirators, both Savage and Doutre could plead their Fifth Amendment constitutional right against self-incrimination, and refuse to testify. And state attorney's officers were still seriously considering the possibility of putting all three of the major defendants in the Palm Beach Gardens homicide on trial together.

At a hearing on the request for speedy trial, Judge Harper noted that the defense had previously filed several discovery motions that the court hadn't yet ruled on. Roth responded by stating that he was withdrawing the other motions, and said that he was ready to go to trial. In legal terminology, discovery gives the defense access to information developed by the prosecution. Consequently, it appeared that Roth was offering to give up an important advantage—an opportunity to get a peek at part of the prosecution's case prior to the trial—

for another obvious advantage—forcing the state to go to trial early before all the loose ends had been tied up.

The prosecutor opposed the motion. She needed more time for preparation, and pointed out that investigators were still working on the case. It would be difficult on such short notice to bring out-of-state witnesses to Palm Beach County in time for the trial, she said. And the prosecution added that if the case went to trial early, Doutre and Savage would probably have to be tried separately.

The judge announced that he would schedule another hearing to question Spearman under oath to determine if the defendant had a clear understanding of his attorney's request for speedy trial. Judge Harper said that in the meantime he was taking the petition under advisement and would study case history relating to the issue of speedy trials. "I'm not about to put this first-degree murder trial in jeopardy," he declared.

Court authorities in a half dozen states were clamoring for a crack at Savage, Doutre, and other accused members of the slay-for-pay ring, in fact. No one wanted to line up, pick a number, and wait his turn. BATF agents and other law enforcement officers who put together the interlocking multistate investigation had done a credible job. But in doing so, they had left the courts with an intricate tangle of charges and jurisdictional and scheduling problems that were as confusing as any Gordian knot. Experienced defense attorneys knew how to use those difficulties to their advantage.

After researching the request, and questioning Spearman, Judge Harper reluctantly granted Roth's petition for speedy trial. The proceeding was scheduled to begin with jury selection on July 14, cutting approximately six weeks of the preparation time for the prosecution, defense, and the court. The judge re-marked that he complied with the request in part because he was worried that if he refused, the denial might provide grounds for an appeals court reversal of a possible conviction in the case. "I am not willing to gamble on an error," he said.

But the jurist sternly cautioned Spearman and his attorneys that he would not permit any postponements if they later came to him complaining they were having trouble preparing the case in time. The surprise legal tactic had been successful, and the prosecution was forced into a furious scramble to wrap up details of the case and get witnesses lined up in time for the courtroom battle.

A petition for court permission to take blood, saliva, and hair samples from Spearman, Savage, and Doutre was one of the prosecution's more intriguing moves. The state explained that prosecutors wanted to compare laboratory tests on the samples to hair and semen found near or within the body of the victim.

Judge Harper agreed to permit the samples to be taken from Spearman, with the condition that information about the laboratory tests be shared with the defense. But he rejected the request to do the same with Savage and Doutre. The jurist pointed out that he thought it would be too difficult to force their compliance with a Palm Beach County court order while they were still being held in Georgia.

The courtroom cast for the Spearman trial already promised to be intriguing, when the defense team introduced a dramatic new player in the joust.

Late in June, less than three weeks before the trial was scheduled to begin, Roth and Duncan advised the court that they wanted out. They argued that irreconcilable differences had developed between them and their client. Roth insisted that the move to sever their legal relationship with Spearman was not a stalling tactic.

The prosecution had recently disclosed that they had uncovered the evidence showing that Spearman had paid for Savage's round-trip airline ticket between Knoxville and West Palm Beach, and had contacted other *SOF* advertisers offering personal services. Roth said the disclosure had produced difficult ethical considerations that made it necessary for him and his cocounsel to withdraw. He declined to be more specific in open court about the differences, citing the confidentiality between attorney and client. And the judge refused to allow him, his cocounsel, and Spearman to go into details privately in chambers after a media attorney indicated he might launch a legal challenge to a closed hearing.

But Roth reported that Spearman had already contacted two other lawyers about handling his defense. Roth suggested that Jerry Milano, a nationally known defense lawyer from Cleveland, take over the defense. And Milano told the judge that he was ready and willing to take the job, if he could have a two-week delay to prepare. The judge refused. Then Milano said that he would be ready to try the case by the July 14 date already set if the court would allow him to take two more depositions. The prosecution opposed the request to take the depositions, and the judge upheld the objection. Judge Harper pointed out that Spearman had relinquished his right of discovery when he petitioned through his defense for the early trial and his request was granted.

"If the defendant's not ready for trial, that's the defendant's problem," he said. "I know I might be putting the thing in jeopardy, but I'm sorry. That's the way the ball's going to bounce.''

Harper wasn't buying the last-minute move to switch attorneys, and castigated the defense effort as a ''thinly disguised ploy'' to slow down the beginning of the trial. ''If you want to call a spade a spade, I think this is a ploy by the defense to avoid the speedy trial that they sought and got. The defendant wants a speedy trial as far away as possible,'' the crusty judge grumped.

Judge Harper declared that the trial would begin at 9:30 A.M. on July 14, as scheduled. And addressing the prosecutor, he remarked that he was certain she would be ready to go to trial at that time. ''I know you've been working very hard,'' he complimented her in his best backwoods country manner. ''You've been busy as a cat in a litter box.''

Dressed in his loose-fitting jail jumpsuit, Spearman sat silently at the defense table, showing no emotion as the debate swirled around him. Occasionally he would peer down as if he were studying his work-hardened hands, fiddle with the case for his glasses, or shift uncomfortably in his chair. He appeared to have lost some weight.

A few days later, Roth made it official. He announced that Milano was joining the defense. The acerbic, hard-hitting attorney would, in fact, become the lead defense lawyer. And Roth, a former U.S. magistrate who was recognized as one of the top criminal defense lawyers in south Florida, would take the secondary position.

Milano and Roth had teamed up before in major Palm Beach County criminal trials. Just two years earlier they had won an acquittal for Nick Tufaro, a Florida truck driver accused of first-degree murder in the shooting death of a Palm Beach County sheriff's deputy during a siege by a SWAT team on the defendant's town house in Greenacres City. The lawyers capitalized during the trial on what they pictured as slipshod police procedures.

And just a year before teaming up on the Spearman case, they defended John Stuart Trent, a West Palm Beach businessman accused, with a prominent Ivy League–educated cancer specialist, of murdering Ralph Walter, an employee of his who was a reputed drug courier, during a wild Palm Beach drug and sex party. The victim's decomposing body was discovered stuffed into a steamer trunk in a van parked outside Trent's shop, the House of Draperies, after the owner of an escort service tipped off the police.

The doctor, John S. Freund, was convicted of first-degree murder after pleading not guilty by reason of insanity, and sentenced to life in prison, with no parole for twenty-five years. The jury in Trent's first-degree murder trial was deadlocked on a verdict when he pleaded guilty to second-degree murder. Trent, who was accused of setting up the grisly killing, was sentenced to a twelve-year prison term but was eventually released.

Milano had a nimble legal mind, and the ability to switch gears rapidly during the courtroom skirmishes of a headline-grabbing murder trial. But he was biting and caustic, as well. The fifty-eight-year-old courtroom veteran hadn't earned an endorsement from the National Association of Criminal Defense Lawyers as one of the nation's six best attorneys in the business by retreating or playing nice guy. Local reporters in south Florida referred to him as the defense team's hatchet man for cross-examination. Milano was a tough, formidable opponent, a ruthless courtroom commando who asked for no mercy and took no prisoners.

While the defense and prosecution teams jockeyed for position during the last few days before the trial's scheduled beginning, and Spearman's healthy suntan was slowly fading to a pallid prison gray in the Palm Beach County Jail, he was busy doing some scheming. Doutre and Savage weren't the only ones capable of dreaming up a dirty deal. However, the target of his latest plot wasn't any of the men who had double-crossed or planned to double-cross him. It was Springer, one of the Palm Beach County sheriff's detectives who had played such a key role in putting him behind bars. Late in June, less than three months after Spearman was jailed and with the beginning of the trial about a week away, a cellmate told authorities that the boatyard operator had offered him between seventeen hundred and two thousand dollars to "set up" Springer for a phony drug arrest.

On June 27 twenty-four-year-old Randy Turner told State Attorney's Office investigator W. J. Patterson, and two detectives with the Florida Department of Law Enforcement, that Spearman had approached him that morning about the plan. Turner was jailed on charges of burglary and grand theft, and had just returned to his cell from court after pleading guilty and being sentenced to a five-year prison term, he said. The judge had ordered that he be given one week of freedom to spend with his family before beginning to serve his sentence.

Spearman wanted him to frame the detective during that week of freedom, Turner told the investigators. Turner said that Spearman promised to have the payment put in the mail in time for a Saturday or Monday delivery, and he wanted the job carried out on the Sunday between those days.

"I asked him about, you know, well, if the money ain't there on time, you know, how am I going to do it Sunday?" Turner said in his statement. "And he said, well, he'll work that out, and that was about it."

Turner recounted a similar story to Detective Springer a few minutes after talking with Patterson and the state police investigators. He told Springer that Spearman had claimed the detective lied in his deposition, but didn't pin down any specific statement that he contended was untrue. Spearman was quoted by the jailhouse informant as saying that the detective was out to get him.

The confessed thief said Spearman wanted him to plant marijuana in Springer's house, then tip off federal drug agents that the sheriff's detective was a dealer. Spearman was reputedly reasoning that if Springer was in trouble, accused of dealing pot, he would be unlikely to testify in the trial. And his investigative work and deposition involving the Spearman case would be tainted, as well. Turner claimed that he never intended to frame the detective, but instead planned to double-cross Spearman and keep the money.

Then Turner dropped another bombshell. Spearman had admitted conspiring with Savage and Doutre to arrange his wife's murder, Turner declared. He said that his cell mate claimed that he had later tried to back out of the devil's pact, but it was too late because he had already revealed the location of his home and the fact that he kept a large amount of money in the house. Turner quoted Spearman as saying he thought his wife was murdered when she blundered in on some of the Savage gang during a burglary.

Spearman claimed Savage had tried to get him to sell him a tugboat to use running drugs, Turner said. The vessel was advertised for sale in a Tennessee-based magazine.

Turner made four formal statements in all, switching from murder plots to proposed frame-ups, legal maneuvers, and escape. According to one account, Spearman shared information from his attorneys with his cell mate. Turner said that Spearman showed him sworn statements lawyers had given to him, and told him their motion to withdraw from the case was merely a stall for more time. Turner said the accused wife killer was spending a big part of his time behind bars daydreaming about fleeing to Venezuela or some other country and hiding out. The informant said Spearman had a girlfriend in Colorado, whom he would sometimes call from a jail telephone.

Prosecutors publicly disclosed details of Turner's startling allegations on Friday, July 11, three days before the trial was scheduled to begin. Several details of the investigation were also publicly released at the same time, including a report that bloodstains were found in the defendant's car three days after the slaying, and the disclosure that a hammer was given some consideration as the possible murder weapon.

Detectives who inspected Spearman's car after the murder reported they found bloodstains on the floor of the passenger's side of the front seat, on the seat itself, in the front of the vehicle, and in the trunk area. And laboratory tests were conducted on two hammers taken from a pegboard in the suspect's garage on the morning of the slaying. The laboratory examination provided strong, although not conclusive, indication that there was blood on one of the hammers.

It was an intriguing development. Police and prosecutors had been favoring the theory that Anita Spearman was beaten to death with the butt of her husband's
shotgun. But laboratory tests by technicians with the
Florida Department of Law Enforcement had failed to
turn up any traces of blood, human body tissue, or hair
on either the butt or the muzzle of the gun to back up
the suspicion that it was the murder weapon.

Nevertheless, the state had marshaled a total of 240
separate pieces of evidence, and more than eighty potential witnesses. Despite the pressure of the stepped-
up trial date, and the staggering complexities of the
case, prosecutors Lasch and St. James were prepared.
The trial was about to begin.

Chapter 9

The Two Faces
of Robert Spearman

Criminal trials are not only debates about innocence
or guilt, right or wrong, good or evil. They are also
contests between opposing attorneys, ruthless tugs-of-
war in which justice can become less important to the
outcome than rules and interpretations of law. The terms
justice and *law* are by no means synonymous.

The personalities and personal styles of opposing attorneys can be vitally important to the outcome. And
in the case of the *State v. Spearman,* the personal styles
of the prosecution and defense were about as different
as they could be.

The lead defense attorneys could be flamboyant, dramatic, emotional, and intimidating. Milano, especially,
was known for courtroom bellicosity and irascibility.
After thirty-one years in the business, he had acquired
a reputation for verbally chopping prosecution witnesses to pieces during ruthless cross-examination. And

opposing attorneys were as likely to be the targets of his acerbic wit and piercing jibes as prosecution witnesses.

On the other side of the playing field, the lead prosecutor's presentations were unemotional, low-key, and devoid of frills. Moira Lasch was precise, concentrating at times on almost dreary recitations that focused on minute details, delivered in the patient manner of a schoolteacher. She relied heavily on records and charts, and introduced dry technical reports and laboratory analyses as building blocks to construct and illustrate her case. In court, her dress was austere, businesslike, almost prim. Some courtroom observers referred to her as the "ice maiden."

Despite the pressure of Judge Harper's decision to step up the trial date, the prosecution had assembled an impressive list of more than eighty potential witnesses, and collected a staggering number of pieces of evidence to introduce. There were crime scene photographs, diagrams, bloody bedclothing, the victim's nightgown and robe, jewelry, the shotgun, motel receipts, charge slips, telephone records, and copies of *Soldier of Fortune* magazine.

Emert and other associates of Savage were expected to be key witnesses for the prosecution. But Savage himself, and his accused star hit man, Sean Doutre, would not appear. They were still jailed in Georgia, where they were opposing extradition, and exercising their constitutional rights against self-incrimination by refusing to testify.

On the opening day of the trial, Courtroom 413 was filled with news reporters, friends and acquaintances of the victim and the defendant, and idle curiosity seekers—many of them retirees on hand for the entertainment. The proceeding was a major media event that promised a juicy tale of betrayal, wealth, murder, and sex, as titillating as any soap opera.

Television newscasters had occupied a utility closet a few feet down the hall from the courtroom, where they could watch the activities inside 413 on a monitor. A few days into the trial, a crew from the popular ABC television program "20/20" would show up to film scenes for a segment of the show. *People* magazine had already published a story focusing on the gang, that prominently featured the Spearman slaying.

Anita's mother and sister reportedly flew to Palm Beach County on the weekend before the trial opened, and stayed at the Helen Wilkes Hotel. But neither they nor other close relatives of the defendant and his late wife were noticed by observers in the fourth-floor courtroom on Monday morning.

If the spectators who did show up to fill the seats the first day were expecting immediate excitement, they were disappointed. Instead of explosive fireworks, the proceedings opened with a fizzle. Spearman's lawyers made a last-ditch effort to have the trial delayed. They advised the court that they needed time to examine laboratory tests tied to examination of the victim's body, and to review and evaluate Turner's statement about their client's reputed proposal to frame Springer for a narcotics arrest.

Judge Harper turned down the requests. The decision for speedy trial had freed prosecutors of their obligation to share evidence with Spearman's defense, he pointed out. "He painted himself in this corner," the judge observed. "He'll have to paint himself out as far as I'm concerned.

Nevertheless, Prosecutor Lasch said that she would give a copy of Turner's statement relating to the plot against Springer to the attorneys as soon as it was transcribed. But she refused to share the laboratory tests, pointing out that Roth had known about them before his request for a speedy trial.

Rebuffed in the effort to delay proceedings to permit review of the laboratory test results and Turner's statement, the defense lawyers sought to block introduction of some of the evidence. Duncan asked for suppression of statements by Turner to the effect that Spearman had admitted taking out a murder contract on his wife but claimed he later tried to back out of the deal.

And Roth argued against use of telephone records showing that Spearman had contacted other classified advertisers in *SOF* in addition to Savage. Roth contended that the prosecution had concealed the information until after his request for speedy trial.

The lead prosecutor reminded the judge that she had advised the defense attorney at the time the motion was made for speedy trial that her investigation was continuing. When Roth responded by claiming that he was totally surprised when he learned of the evidence, she exhibited signs of shock herself.

"I can't believe his recollection is so weak," she asserted. "I'd stake my life on that, Judge Harper."

Roth pounced: "My client's life is the one at stake," he declared. Judge Harper denied the motion for suppression of either Turner's statements or of the telephone records.

The puckish exchange between the attorneys was only a small example of the passionate jousting to come. But the opening salvos had been fired, and spectators had gotten their first glimpses of the acrimonious sniping and bitter exchanges that would mark the course of the trial.

Spearman's defense lawyers had commissioned a telephone survey a few days earlier which disclosed that about 90 percent of the one hundred people who responded had heard of the case, and 70 percent said they already believed he was guilty of paying for his wife's murder. The lawyers cited the survey to back up a motion for individual examination of prospective jurors, away from the presence of other men and women in the jury pool. They claimed that publicity was so heavy that would-be jurors could be tainted or prejudiced if they overheard the questioning of others preceding them.

Jeffery B. Smith, a jury selection consultant hired to make the survey, testified that about one in every six people contacted responded to questions. "We had some people say, 'Yes, I could give him a fair trial as long as he got the death penalty,' " the witness declared. Despite the survey and Smith's testimony, the motion was rejected.

But the defense attorneys had yet other last-minute motions for Judge Harper to deal with, before they could even begin to move on to jury selection. Roth and Duncan again brought up their request to bow out of the case, and said they planned to file written reasons for the move. Judge Harper had already advised them to set down their reasons and to submit them in a sealed affidavit at the conclusion of the trial.

When jury selection at last got under way, the lawyers spent the entire first day without selecting a single member for the panel. Several jurors were rejected because they stated they had already formed opinions based on news stories they had either heard or read about the case.

Attorneys were no more successful in agreeing on

jurors the second day. But prosecutors had a surprise at its conclusion. They proposed that Harper review the request for withdrawal before the affidavits were sealed.

"I wish you would have made that request before we went through two days of voir dire" [jury selection], Judge Harper admonished the prosecutors. Roth pointed out that he and Duncan were prepared three weeks earlier to submit sworn statements in support of the motion.

The defense attorneys' flurry of motions and persistent arguments were clearly irritating the judge. At one point he compared their insistence in continuing to pursue a point after he had made a ruling to the practice of former baseball manager Billy Martin kicking sand on an umpire's shoes. He pointed out that kicking sand still didn't change the call on the play. Judge Harper was a quick man with a simile, and he would draw on all the homespun humor and patience he had learned during his earlier years in the U.S. Navy town of Pensacola to preserve the fragile decorum of the courtroom.

Milano didn't waste any time in upholding his reputation for stinging personal jibes, sharp-tongued criticism, and courtroom petulance. When prosecutor Lasch asked the judge to order attorneys to address one another with the formal titles of Mr. or Ms., Milano scoffed that the move "borders on the ridiculous." After the judge granted the motion, the Cleveland lawyer responded by snidely referring to the prosecuting team as "Mr. and Mrs."

The puckish Cleveland lawyer also jarred prosecutors by accusing them of refusing to provide him with documents they had promised earlier. "I've asked every way I can," he complained. "I'm not going to continue licking their boots."

There was no reply from the state's prosecution team. But Judge Harper had heard more than enough fussing between the opposing attorneys, and responded instead. Peering down from the bench, he sternly admonished them as if they were naughty children. "I'm not asking you all to like each other," he declared. "I'm asking you as officers of the court to confer with each other and resolve these issues. We're going to try this case in a dignified, orderly fashion."

In the spectator section, where the audience had thinned considerably during the tedious infighting over jury selection, a middle-aged woman in a sundress turned to her gray-haired companion, and muttered in a sarcastic stage whisper: "Good luck!"

Despite the judge's cautious optimism, it seemed that the court was caught in a situation where anything that could go wrong, would go wrong. Defense attorneys approached him with a new problem. They complained that a television reporter for Channel 12 in West Palm Beach had tried to interview their client in front of jurors.

Spearman was called to the stand and testified that reporter Gary Tuchman had asked him, in front of at least ten jurors while they were all outside the courtroom, if he thought he could get a fair trial. But when the reporter testified, he claimed that although he did ask the question, the bailiff had already recalled the jurors to the courtroom. "If there were any jurors out there, they were jurors who were not supposed to be in the room," he asserted.

Judge Harper pointed out that he had given strict orders Spearman was not to be moved through the hallway unless all jurors were in the courtroom, and refused to dismiss the jury panel. "I believe Mr. Tuchman," the judge told Roth. "I do not believe your client."

At last, a few minutes before 5:00 P.M., six exhausting days after questioning of prospective jurors was begun, a panel of seven men and five women, along with two alternates, was sworn in for the trial. Only one juror was a retiree.

Early the next morning the prosecution began presenting its case. Lasch told the jury that the state would prove that Spearman schemed with professional hit men to have his wife murdered. He wanted to devote his attentions to his girlfriend, and was tired of his ailing spouse, who knew about his long-term love affair, but didn't want to risk financial ruin in a messy divorce. He had her murdered in what the prosecutor described as "a crime of affluence."

As she presented her opening statement, Milano leaned back with his eyes closed and his glasses pushed up on his forehead. He rested his head on the back of his chair and then shifted in his chair and leaned his head to the side, supporting it with one hand, still with his eyes closed.

The prosecution team appeared oblivious to Milano's show of boredom. And they moved quickly to steal the fire from defense attorneys, by anticipating their moves and attempting to frustrate their strategy. In a move to block the possibility of the defense arguing that investigators overlooked or failed to consider all potential evidence in the slaying, they sought a court order to require the defendant to provide a sample of his semen. The motion was especially important to the prosecution, because Milano had indicated that the defense would attack Emert's credibility by seeking to show that he was in the Spearman house and raped the victim. It appeared that Spearman's lawyers were about to try to pin the murder on the big Tennessee convict.

The question of the semen sample was a sensitive, unpleasant subject to bring up in an already unpleasant case, and would eventually be argued outside the presence of the jury. And despite all the fuss, a laboratory analysis of the sample wouldn't even help prosecutors prove their case. The sole advantage was blocking an anticipated defense move by showing that the homicide investigation was efficiently and properly carried out, and that laboratory tests were performed to show that the semen found in the victim's body most likely came from her husband.

In a hearing, a serologist testified that there was no sperm in the semen from the victim. Court officers were already aware that the defendant had undergone a vasectomy fifteen years earlier, and would be unlikely to produce sperm.

Spearman's former urologist told the judge that he had treated the defendant three years earlier for flagging sex drive and trouble maintaining satisfactory erections. The inference was clear: Spearman might not be able to provide the sample, even if there was a court order, and he wished to comply. In order to provide the sample, the fifty-six-year-old murder defendant would have to masturbate. And Milano said that his client was still bothered by the problem of maintaining erections.

"I'm going to tell you, he can't do it," Milano said, in arguing against an order to produce the semen sample.

Judge Harper nevertheless reluctantly upheld the prosecution's request, and after conceding the intrusion of privacy and the "demeaning nature" of the act that would be required, he issued an order for Spearman to produce the controversial sample.

"How do I enforce this order?" he asked. "Somebody would have to be there to make sure he makes a good-faith effort."

But the embarrassing question of the semen sample wasn't yet disposed of. A few days later, Milano repeated his claim to the judge that Spearman was physically unable to comply with the order.

Prosecutors had been busy with other matters, however, and quickly moved through introduction of evidence and questioning of witnesses to show that Spearman was a man of wealth, whose riches increased substantially after the slaying of his wife.

Attorney Robert Marshall testified that the defendant sold the business property along the Intracoastal Waterway for $3,150,000 in June, more than two months after his arrest. Marshall, who handled th sale, said that Spearman would not have been able to sell the property while his wife was alive, without her signature. And proceeds of the sale would have been divided between the husband and wife.

Another witness, Robert Lawson, Jr., testified that he bought Spearman's house for $200,000 just before the boatyard owner's arrest. A pension officer for the city of West Palm Beach told the court that Spearman was a lifetime beneficiary on Anita's pension, and was still drawing $688 a month from the plan. Another witness reported that the victim had invested $55,085 in a deferred compensation plan, which was paid out to her widower in a lump sum.

Spearman subsequently picked up another $55,000 for his Beechcraft Bonanza airplane, and $271,000 for his sport-fishing boat. Anita had also carried a $10,500 life insurance policy that named her husband as beneficiary and included a double indemnity clause. He was a rich man, who was quite able to afford his blue-ribbon defense team.

Anita's will, filed in Palm Beach County circuit court after her death, left 80 percent of her estate, excepting jewelry, cars, and household goods, to her husband. The other 20 percent of the estate was left to her mother.

Other witnesses were called to confirm the telephone calls made from the boatyard to the Debra Savage residence in Knoxville. Testimony was also provided pointing to seven other long-distance calls from the boatyard during the previous October. The jury, however, wasn't advised that police had traced the calls to classifieds in *SOF* magazine, including some that were made only two days after Anita returned home from the hospital to recover from her double mastectomy and breast reconstruction. And yet another witness and telephone records were produced to show the widower's repeated calls to Patricia Rozelle after his wife was bludgeoned to death.

When Ms. Rozelle was called as a witness, her testimony provided one of the dramatic highlights of the trial. Spectators lined up outside the courtroom for seats, and people who couldn't find a place inside hurried down the corridor to the hall closet to watch on the TV monitor. Some people brought brown-bag lunches, bolted them down while seated on hallway benches during the noon break, then rushed back inside to reclaim seats. Even county government employees inched into the courtroom on their breaks to watch and listen. No one wanted to miss the appearance of the slender witness who had been named as "the other woman" in the sensational murder case.

Ms. Rozelle hardly looked the role of femme fatale when she walked to the front of the courtroom and quietly took her place on the witness stand. Slender, middle-aged, and dressed in a modest suit with a scooped blouse, she calmly traced her relationship with the former boatyard owner. She talked about their rendezvous, the intimate lunches and dinners they shared, and their trips together. They took one overnight trip to a resort owned by actress-singer Frances Langford in nearby Jensen Beach only two months before her lover's wife was beaten to death, she said. And they were considering another trip to the Caribbean islands, although they hadn't made definite plans. "This summer perhaps," she speculated.

Under questioning by Ms. Lasch, she recalled the telephone call from Spearman on the morning of his wife's murder. She said he sounded composed, and they talked casually of routine matters. To another of the prosecutor's questions about her continued contacts with the defendant after the terrible morning of November 16, she responded with her own query, then answered herself.

"Have I had dinner with him?" she asked. "Is that the question? Yes!"

And she admitted that she had been in Spearman's new condominium apartment after his wife's murder. Yet she also claimed that by 1985 their romance had cooled into a relationship that was no more than that of two good friends. She said she had begun to date another man.

She said that she stuck by him because he was a friend who needed her. He had only her and his mother to lean on, the witness claimed. Except for his mother, Ms. Rozelle said, there were no close relatives whom he could go to for comfort.

During cross-examination by Spearman's defense, she confided that the relationship hadn't been without cost to her. It was difficult for her to admit the affair, she said. And she added that she lost her job after her relationship with the defendant was publicly revealed.

The witness said that she didn't talk with Spearman after the slaying until about a week after the funeral. "He came back into town and called me. I was concerned about him," she testified. "He wanted me to come over and tell me face-to-face exactly what happened." She said that she was confronted with a man who was grief-stricken, and cried over his wife's shocking murder.

Ms. Rozelle kept her eyes trained on the attorneys questioning her, avoiding looking at her former lover. But she pointed him out for the court when she was asked. She glanced quickly at him only one other time.

Despite the drama tied to Ms. Rozelle's appearance, several other witnesses provided more damaging testimony against Spearman. Debra Mattingly was one. She talked of the telephone calls from Spearman, and his pique at the gang's failure to carry out the killing he had paid for. And she told how his anger built. "He would continue to threaten me and Richard's fourteen-year-old son," she said.

Prosecutor Lasch asked, "Did he ever indicate that he changed his mind about the contract?"

"No, ma'am," the witness replied.

"Did he ever indicate he wasn't one hundred percent serious?" the prosecutor persisted.

"No, ma'am," Ms. Mattingly repeated.

The plump, composed young woman was the kind of witness ready-made for a Milano cross-examination. He quickly turned to her story about telephone threats from Spearman, and demanded to know if she had made a written record of the conversations.

"Why should I?" she shot back. "I'd remember something like that."

The feisty defense attorney also brought up the witness's own troubles with the law, and she conceded that she was facing a five-year prison sentence in Georgia after pleading guilty to a charge of conspiracy to commit murder. But she rejected the defense attorney's insinuation that she was also charged with criminal offenses in Texas, Arkansas, and Tennessee.

"The only thing Arkansas said to me was they don't want me," she asserted. "They want the triggerman."

And although she conceded that she had been granted immunity from possible prosecution for anything based on her testimony, she insisted that she had made no deals to testify in the trial. When Milano referred to her longtime live-in lover as a "high-class con man," she agreed. She also agreed with Ms. Lasch's reference to him as a "devious individual."

Nevertheless, when the defense attorney asked if she still loved Savage, she said that she did. Following up, Milano asked, "You'd do anything to help him, wouldn't you?"

"Not if it meant perjuring myself," she said.

As the trial moved into its fourth week, the prosecution called its key witness, Ronald Emert. He was a convict, an admitted thief who had dealt in drugs and stolen goods, and he was in court to tell the judge and the jury that he had served as a bagman for a contract murder. But he was a man who had been under pressure in courtrooms and police interrogation rooms before. And he was unflappable on the stand.

The jury and other players in the complex legal drama had just returned from a half day off to permit the judge to undergo minor surgery, and the courtroom filled once more with spectators looking forward to the big man's testimony. Emert was spiffed up in a plaid work shirt and a new pair of tan trousers for his appearance in the limelight. He explained that the state bought his new pants because prosecutors didn't want him to testify in his Levi's.

Most of the people in the courtroom were hearing the burly witness's account of his trip to Florida with Doutre for the first time. For all the emotion that Emert showed, he could have been an accountant discussing gross income and net profits. He was calm and polite. When he replied to questions by prosecutor Lasch, he addressed her, without sarcasm, as "ma'am."

He pointed out almost casually that he and the accused triggerman weren't even sure as they sped south in the Toyota, loaded down with firearms, just who the target of the hit would be. Emert said that Doutre told him that Savage had sent him to Florida to kill someone. "They couldn't make up their minds whether they were going to kill Mr. Spearman or Mrs. Spearman at the time."

Several jurors turned their heads to look away from the witness, and peer at the defendant. But Spearman, dressed in a neat brown suit, continued to sit quietly by his attorneys and look straight ahead without showing any visible reaction other than a bunching of the wrinkles in his forehead.

The defendant continued to watch without comment or emotion as Emert explained that Savage was upset about the threats from the boatyard owner, and also worried that Spearman might someday identify him as a hired gun.

Emert talked about his conversations with Spearman, and of his remarks that he wanted the murder to be carried out quickly, without a mess. "He said she wanted to die," Emert declared.

At last prosecutors completed their direct examination of the witness, and it was the defense's turn to cross-examine. It was an opportunity for Milano to perform at his best.

Word quickly spread through the courthouse, and county employees who could get away from their work for a while inched inside Room 413 to squeeze into tiny spaces still left on the benches or to stand along the wall at the back. A bench behind the defense table filled with young lawyers and a smattering of their older counterparts, whom Judge Harper allowed to occupy the preferential vantage point so that they could watch and listen to the anticipated fireworks. Sitting in on choice segments of the case was a learning experience for attorneys who practiced criminal law.

Milano came out slugging. He attacked the witness's credibility by hitting at his criminal record; he questioned him about his motives for dealing with federal agents; he made insulting remarks about the nightclub where Emert had worked; and he even made nasty insinuations about his sexuality.

Responding calmly to Milano's scathing attack, Emert revealed that he pleaded guilty in 1984 to a charge of receiving stolen goods and was sentenced to a three-year prison term. He said he was released after serving about five months.

The previous January, three months before he told

BATF Agent McGarrity about the murder conspiracy, he pleaded guilty to other felony offenses dealing with drugs and stolen property and was sentenced to a ten-year prison term, he said.

Milano reminded him that the March meeting didn't mark the first time that he had met with McGarrity. And the lawyer asked if, in fact, it wasn't true that he was a snitch for the BATF. Emert replied that he wasn't completely a snitch, and had never accepted money for information. Irregardless of the emotion, sarcasm, or apparent anger with which Milano's questions were hurled at him, Emert consistently and calmly replied to the defense attorney by respectfully addressing him as "sir."

Milano demanded to know if he had made a deal to swap information to McGarrity about the Spearman murder and other cases in return for the agent's help in obtaining lenient treatment.

"I asked about a work-release program," the witness responded. "He told me he couldn't make any promises. He said he'd check on it. He never gave me an answer."

Milano seemed disbelieving. "You didn't talk about a deal?" he asked again, as if he couldn't believe what he had just heard.

Emert stared calmly at the lawyer, never blinking his eyes. "No, sir," he said.

"But you got a deal?" Milano persisted.

"Yes, sir," the witness conceded.

Milano asked if it wasn't true that Emert wasn't even charged with involvement in the murder of Mrs. Spearman. Emert agreed that he wasn't.

"How much did you get paid for snitching?" the lawyer demanded.

"I haven't got paid nothing, sir," Emert replied. He said the only thing he was given for agreeing to testify in the case was a few cigarettes.

Milano wasn't able to shake the thirty-nine-year-old convict. Trying to browbeat the man was like attacking a bowl of jelly. If he was poked with a verbal finger, the gelatinous mass shimmered and resumed its original shape as soon as the offending digit was withdrawn.

Milano brought up Emert's job at the Continental Club as a bouncer, or doorman. "It was a big whorehouse, wasn't it?" the attorney scolded.

Emert responded with a one-word reply, and a slight nod of his head. "Basically," he agreed.

Spectators appeared to be enjoying Emert's performance at least as much as Milano's. The convict was easily holding his own against the best that the big-name lawyer could throw at him. He simply refused to become rattled or ruffled. Several of his deadpan replies brought amused smiles and giggles from spectators, and occasionally from the jury.

When the defense attorney asked him if it wasn't true that one of the women in Savage's alleged gang of hired killers was a prostitute, Emert's answer was a simple "No! She's gay." That brought one round of laughter.

Emert knew what he was doing. He kept his replies short and to the point. He answered the questions without hesitation or stammering. He didn't volunteer information he wasn't asked. He responded at times to the attorney's rapid-fire accusations, framed into questions, as if he were a straight man in a comedy act. And he knew how to stop a lawyer who was grilling him in his tracks.

Milano wanted to know if the witness was aware that Bradley Tipton, the former teenage disk jockey who worked briefly at the club, was reportedly paid $1,480 for helping investigators, and was a federal informant. "Was Bradley an ATF snitch? How'd you find that out?" he commanded of the witness.

"You told me at the last hearing," Emert laconically replied.

When Milano asked if another informant who had worked with investigators was "a good honest man or a liar," the unflappable witness replied: "A little of both."

Milano asked if he was like that, as well.

"To a certain extent," Emert conceded. "Everyone is."

Emert testified over parts of two days, without significantly changing the story he had originally told to investigators. The closest he came to becoming rattled occurred when Milano pointed to contradictions in statements the witness had made about the exact amount of Spearman's money turned over to Savage, and what he knew about Savage's reputed involvement with drug trafficking. The soft-spoken witness claimed that he had simply been a bit mixed-up.

The prosecution called more than seventy other witnesses to the stand, but none who had the dramatic or storytelling impact of Emert, Ms. Mattingly, or Ms. Rozelle.

Spearman's longtime employe, Jean Tetta, testified about her boss's nervousness in the days leading up to the murder. But she blamed his change of behavior on his project selling off the marine construction company equipment and conversion of his business to a do-it-yourself boatyard. She also told about taking a telephone call at work one day from a man who said he was Sean Doutre. She said she transferred the call to her boss.

Sergeant Johnson told the court about stopping the black Camaro in Maryville the day after Mrs. Spearman's murder, and finding the stolen shotgun, the other weapons, and six thousand dollars in cash and jewelry. "I thought all I had was a good stolen car arrest with some of the other stuff thrown in for good measure," he recalled. The state used Johnson's testimony to introduce the shotgun into evidence.

Rent-A-Wreck squad detective Gregory Richter testified that when he investigated the crime scene shortly after Mrs. Spearman's body was discovered, he could not find any indications that the house had been broken into. "The only way someone could have entered this residence is if the door was left open or they had a key," the detective declared. His testimony was important to the prosecution's efforts to show the killer was helped to gain entry into the house by the victim's husband.

Eileen Henney, a close friend of Mrs. Spearman, who styled the victim's hair for the funeral, was an effective witness for the prosecution. She testified that the defendant telephoned her a few days before his arrest to brag about the new condominium apartment he had just bought that overlooked Jupiter Inlet, and a trip he was planning to the Bahamas. She quoted him as boasting, "I might as well tell you now, I'm not going alone."

The witness, who at one point emotionally covered her face with her hands, remarked, "I was real shocked. He said, 'I'd want the same for Anita if she was still here. I've got to start spending this money.'"

Doutre's mother-in-law testified briefly, and told the court about his trip to Florida shortly after the wedding and a few days before the murder. And she told about the tricolor gold bracelet that he gave to her daughter when he returned. The victim's former secretary, Meg Jones, took the stand and identified the bracelet as belonging to Mrs. Spearman. The woman said that when she saw the bracelet after her boss's death, she felt as if she had been kicked in the stomach.

Detective Springer was the prosecution's final witness. And paradoxically, Springer's own key account of his investigation would take second place to tape recordings he played for the court at the opening of his testimony. The courtroom lapsed into an eerie quiet as Springer activated the recordings of the statements he took from the defendant on the day of Mrs. Spearman's death, and two days later.

Spearman's heavily lined face seemed to slump and collapse as he sat at the defense table listening to his voice describe finding his dead wife on that terrible morning. "She was laying there, and there was blood on her and she was white and she was cold," the choked-up voice on the tape recounted.

Spearman's previous calm demeanor deserted him. He pulled a white handkerchief from his pocket and wiped his eyes. Before the tape was turned off, Spearman's voice had retraced his steps that day, and in the second interview, reluctantly admitted his relationship with Patricia Rozelle and described it as a short affair.

Many of the spectators in the courtroom seemed to be as relieved as Spearman when the dismal recitation was ended. But their attention was quickly riveted on Springer, as he recounted the details of his investigation.

It was Springer's turn to face Milano. The defense attorney quickly turned to the statement that Springer had taken from Tipton on the same day the detective first questioned Emert. The detective said that until a few weeks ago, shortly before the trial was scheduled to begin, he had simply forgotten about the statement. But the defense was determined to show that withholding the statement wasn't an oversight at all, but a deliberate act to cover up things Tipton had said that conflicted with Emert's story.

"Why did you withhold that tape?" Milano demanded.

"I didn't withhold it. I inadvertently left it out of my report," the detective explained.

"Would you agree that tape shows Emert is nothing but a liar in many ways?" Milano roared. "You buried it, didn't you?"

Not so, insisted the detective. Springer was as composed and unflappable on the stand as Emert had been.

It was late Friday afternoon when the police sergeant at last stepped from the witness stand. The state rested its case. Seventy-seven witnesses had been called.

Spearman's former cell mate, Turner, was never asked by the prosecution to testify. Earlier in the trial, the convicted thief wrote to Circuit Judge Marvin Mounts asking for suspension of his five-year prison sentence. Turner said he was a key witness in the murder case and claimed that Spearman had threatened to kill or injure him if he testified in court. "I know for a fact that Mr. Spearman has the power and the money to carry out such a threat," Turner wrote in his plea for freedom.

Turner said that after receiving the death threat, authorities transferred him to the Palm Beach County Jail in the town of Belle Glade, where he was being held in protective custody. But the twenty-four-year-old man said he was still frightened.

"Your Honor, the prison system's grapevine is worse than a Peyton Place," he wrote. "I am scared to death that I will be hurt or killed, which I do not deserve. I'm just helping the officials." He added that he hadn't been promised any deals for testifying, and claimed he wasn't looking for any.

No one ordered the convict's release. And Judge Harper advised prosecutors and defense attorneys that Turner was worried that Spearman was plotting his death. Giving copies of the letter to both the prosecution and the defense, he remarked, "I thought you would want to know he's looking for something for his testimony."

Spearman's lawyers had waited until almost the last minute to reveal whether or not they planned to call witnesses in their client's defense. As defense attorneys sometimes do when there is a preponderance of prosecution evidence, they could choose to focus their efforts to win their client's freedom through cross-examination of the state's witnesses, and with their own opening and closing arguments. One advantage of the tactic was that it would allow the defense the opportunity to give the first and last presentation in closing arguments. If the defense called witnesses, however, it relinquished that privilege.

Neither Roth nor any of his colleagues had yet revealed whether they would call Spearman to testify. It is common courtroom belief that except for very special instances, it is bad strategy for a defendant in a major felony case to testify in his or her own behalf. A defendant may indeed be able to help his or her own case during the friendly questioning of a defense attorney.

But once he or she has opted to take the stand, the prosecution has been given the opportunity for cross-examination and can bring up many subjects previously prohibited from the testimony.

The United States Constitution prevents defendants from being compelled to testify against themselves. And waiving that protection can be risky business.

But when it was at last the defense's turn at bat, they were caught off guard. Spearman's attorneys hadn't expected the state to rest its case so quickly, and they weren't ready with their witnesses. And their surprise led to a sharp confrontation with Judge Harper. Milano said that he thought the judge had already agreed that the trial would be recessed after the state completed its case. Harper disagreed.

"We're going to get on with this trial," he declared. And he suggested that the defense call Tipton, who was waiting outside the courtroom in the corridor.

Judge Harper knew the teenager was available because he had ordered the state to have the young man flown from Tennessee to West Palm Beach, after Spearman's lawyers said that they wanted him there so he could testify. But Milano explained that there had been a change of plans, and the defense wasn't going to call Tipton as a witness after all. The surprise information left Harper fuming. And his pique escalated when Milano said the defense wouldn't pay for Tipton's food and lodging.

"I don't mind telling you I'm a little upset by the fact that you've been telling me all along you had to have Tipton here," the judge grumped. "When the stakes are that high, I don't like to see either side play games with someone's life—either Anita's life or Robert's life—because they're both precious to me." Judge

Harper ordered Spearman's lawyers to have a witness in court to testify within twenty minutes.

The defense attorneys complied with his demand by calling two employes of the Palm Beach County Sheriff's Department. The defense continued to snipe at Emert's testimony by casting him in the role of the victim's rapist. The witnesses testified about blood and semen samples. Then court was adjourned for the weekend break.

When the trial resumed, the defense quickly ended speculation about whether their client would testify in his own defense. Spearman was one of the first witnesses called. It was an occasion, once more, for the fourth-floor courtroom to fill up with courthouse employees and other spectators. It was an opportunity to hear Spearman's story in person, from his own lips. It was an opportunity, as well, for Spearman and his lawyers to cement the tugboat defense—their argument that Savage might have killed Anita over a potential tugboat purchase gone sour.

Dressed in a neat charcoal-colored suit, and looking every bit the serious businessman, Spearman eased into the witness chair with a barely perceptible wobble. Peering at the court reporter, he apologetically remarked that he was a bit jittery. Then, after turning to look at the impassive jury and flashing a nervous smile, he began to talk about his life with Anita, his work, his infidelities, a tugboat, would-be drug smugglers, a gang of Knoxville ruffians, and murder.

Retracing his life with his wife, he created a picture of a relationship that, except for a few minor flaws and missteps, was almost idyllic. He choked up, wiped his work-callused and nicotine-stained fingers at his eyes, and sometimes sobbed openly as he talked of the woman he had married more than a quarter of a century earlier and spent so much of his life with.

"She was my whole world," he cried. "She was not only my wife, she was my buddy."

Turning to the subject of reputed contract killers, Spearman conceded that he had met Savage and his roughneck hirelings. But he insisted that the meetings had nothing to do with any desire by him to harm his wife, or with *Soldier of Fortune* magazine. "I never knew that magazine existed until the day I was arrested and read about it in the *Post-Times*," he declared.

The witness claimed that Savage had initiated the contact, because he wanted to buy a tugboat that was formerly used in the marine construction business. Spearman said Savage became interested in buying the craft named the *Robert Henry* for his father, after seeing it advertised for sale in a trade magazine published in Tennessee.

The witness said that Savage telephoned him early in October about buying the tug, and a few days later showed up at the boatyard. Spearman said that Savage brought a middle-aged man he introduced as "Dick" and a seventeen-year-old boy. He recalled that he thought at the time that Savage looked like a businessman type. "He struck me as being pretty smart," he said.

"I told them the boat was only four years old, that I was going out of business," he said of his talk with the trio. "I'm not sure if I told them my wife was sick or not. I told most people that."

Continuing his account with few interruptions from either his own attorneys or from prosecutors, the defendant said that he struck a deal with Savage and Dick to sell the boat to them for one hundred thousand dollars.

They handed him a twenty-thousand-dollar cash down payment, and agreed to pay the balance in about two weeks, he added.

"I remember making a comment to him, there's nothing as good as money," Spearman observed. He said that after they made their bargain and he accepted the down payment, he let them use his office telephone. A few days later, the witness said, Dick stopped again at the boatyard to talk with him and was once more permitted to use the office telephone.

Spearman seemed to be telling his story with all the feigned sincerity of a used-car salesman during a national economic downturn, but the implication was clear: It could have been Savage and his mysterious friend Dick who made the calls from the boatyard office phone to the other *SOF* advertisers. Or it could have been someone else. Spearman's lawyers had established that there were three telephones at the boatyard. And there were yet other revelations to explain his suspicious dealings with the Knoxville-based murder broker suspect still to come.

One of his employees even witnessed the negotiations for the tugboat, Spearman claimed. Unfortunately, she couldn't testify for him at the trial because she was hospitalized in a coma, following a tragic motorcycle accident.

Spearman said that when he telephoned Knoxville to ask when he could collect the balance of the agreed-on purchase price for the *Robert Henry*, Savage explained that he planned to fly to West Palm Beach the next day. Unfortunately, Spearman quoted him as saying, someone had stolen his billfold. So he asked the boatyard owner to buy his round-trip ticket for him. Spearman said that he agreed and paid for the ticket with a credit card, even though he thought the request was a bit strange.

Spearman told the court that it was only after he picked Savage up at the airport, and they stopped in a restaurant for a snack and a chat, that he learned what the crafty Tennesseean was really looking for. Savage wanted him to turn the tugboat over to him so that he could use it to push a barge south to the Florida Keys. In the Keys they would meet a freighter or shrimp boat and transfer six tons of marijuana onto the barge, which would then be moved on to Tennessee, he told the hushed courtroom. He said that Savage planned to weld the hatches shut to hide the telltale odor of the marijuana. In return for the use of the tugboat, Spearman claimed, Savage offered to reward him with $1 million in cash within six weeks.

But Spearman was a legitimate businessman, nearing his sixtieth birthday and looking forward to retirement. It was no time to be going into the drug-running business. He said he turned down the proposal, and offered to return the deposit after deducting five hundred dollars for Savage's airfare. But Savage asked him to think the proposal over, and returned to Nashville.

"Richard Savage is the best con man I ever met," the witness marveled.

According to Spearman, soon after their restaurant chat, he telephoned Savage in Knoxville and offered to mail him a check for the fifteen hundred dollars or return the money by bank transfer. But Savage said that he preferred to send someone to Palm Beach County to pick up the money.

Emert telephoned him the next day, Spearman said, and they made the money exchange. But Savage's messenger refused to give him a receipt. Furthermore,

Spearman testified, Emert made a last-ditch plea to get him involved in the drug-smuggling scheme. "He even said he might sweeten the pot a little," Spearman asserted.

Roth asked his client, "Did you want your wife killed?"

Spearman looked his lawyer straight in the eye. "Certainly not," he replied.

Spearman pointed out that even though he wanted nothing to do with drug running, he stayed in touch with Savage because he was hopeful that the Tennessee man would still buy the tugboat. And he claimed that the previous January he had informed narcotics officers with the Palm Beach County Sheriff's Department about the drug-running scheme involving the *Robert Henry*.

Records of his talk with the local drug agents, however, indicated that he told a slightly different story at that time. He said that three or four Cuban men had approached him with a proposal to use the tugboat to transport a barge loaded with cocaine. He claimed then that he couldn't remember the names of the Cubans. He still hadn't recovered emotionally from his wife's murder.

For someone with Spearman's long years of experience and impressive record of success in business, the account of his dealings with Savage seemed to be riddled with examples of incredible naïveté. Successful businessmen and women just can't afford to be so trusting. Nevertheless, his ability to get the jury to believe his explanation for his relationship with Savage could mean the difference between freedom or imprisonment, or life and death. He also had to survive what was certain to be an agonizingly detailed and cutting cross-examination by the prosecution.

Prosecutor Lasch launched a flurry of questions and accusations at the defendant that painted him as an insensitive, abusive husband, a philanderer, liar, and engineer of a brutal murder scheme.

She reminded him that his first wife had cited "extreme cruelty" as grounds for divorce when their marriage broke up. She accused him of being insensitively cruel to Anita while she was hospitalized following her double mastectomy.

"Didn't you send her flowers shaped as two breasts with a card that said, 'Now you have two'?" the prosecutor demanded.

Spearman shifted in his seat, and stared at the prosecutor as if he were surprised she should bring the subject up. "She thought it was pretty great," he said of his wife's reaction. The prosecutor wrinkled her brows, and shook her head from side to side as if she were disgusted at the mere idea of the crude prank.

Continuing her attack, Ms. Lasch brought up his long-term affair with Patricia Rozelle once more. "You didn't think you were hurting Anita by cheating on her?" the prosecutor asked.

The defendant's reply was barely audible, and he didn't look at the prosecutor when he spoke, but seemed to be studying his knees. "Yes, I'm sure I was," he answered.

Framing her remark in the form of a question, she asked if it wasn't true that he didn't want a divorce, and all the problems that would be involved. "She just wasn't going to roll over in a divorce action," Ms. Lasch said.

"I didn't want a divorce, period," Spearman insisted.

Continuing to construct her accusations as questions,

the prosecutor asserted that he had carefully thought out and planned his breakfast at Denny's with a customer who was well-known there, then met with a longtime employee at the boatyard so he would have an airtight alibi when his wife was killed.

And she questioned him about the killer's deliberate act of leaving the telephone off the receiver, claiming that it was a prearranged signal to the victim's husband that his wife was dead. She pointed out that paramedics had noted that Anita's head was covered by a pillow when they arrived. And she accused him of figuring out ahead of time exactly what to say when he called paramedics from his home.

"If you had gone in to check your wife, wouldn't you have taken that pillow off her head?" she inquired. Spearman said he didn't remember that there was a pillow covering her head.

"You told 911, 'I can't wake her up,' " the prosecutor asserted. "But what you did, Mr. Spearman, was stick to the script, didn't you?" she declared.

"Mrs. Lasch, that's untrue," Spearman objected. The witness was courteous, and less emotional than he had been when his wife's health and personal aspects of their relationship were being explored in the questioning. But some of his replies were still couched in words so soft that they could barely be heard. He had a hangdog look about him, and the ordeal was clearly draining his vitality. Sometimes he seemed to be struggling to hold his temper. At other times he sniffled, and wiped with his fingers at unseen tears. But he was hanging on.

The prosecutor was undeterred and inflexibly pitiless. She kept the pressure on. She picked at the tugboat story, and suggested that there were other faster,

more efficient ways for big-time drug dealers to move
their illicit cargo than by using a tugboat.

"It would have been smarter to buy the airplane,
wouldn't it?" she asked, in a reference to his Beechcraft. Spearman replied that it was more important to
the drug smugglers to outsmart law enforcement agencies than to outrun them.

Undiscouraged by the reply, she moved on and
scoffed at his explanation for his payment of Savage's
airfare for the round-trip flight between Knoxville and
West Palm Beach. She criticized Savage's reputed story
about the lost billfold as flimsy.

"Wouldn't you think that a man who was about to
buy a hundred-thousand-dollar tugboat would have more
assets than what was in his billfold?" she asked, dis-
believingly.

"I would have bought him a half dozen plane tickets
if he had bought that boat," the witness replied.

The prosecutor pointed out that the defendant had
used his personal American Express card to pay for the
ticket, instead of another card that he routinely used for
his business expenses. "When you purchased that airplane ticket for Mr. Savage, you were pretty sure Anita
was going to be dead by the time that bill came in?"
she accused.

"That's a lie, Mrs. Lasch," the witness shot back.
The prosecutor had good reason to spend so much time
and effort verbally fencing with the defendant over the
ticket. It was a key piece of evidence in her case, which
she was determined to use to establish a direct link
between Spearman and the accused Knoxville murder
broker.

"It didn't take you long to get over Mrs. Spearman's

death and start planning on spending that money," she charged as she continued her attack.

In a soft, choked-up voice that was filled with apparent emotion, Spearman replied: "Mrs. Lasch, I'm still not over it."

It was nearly five hours, extending over a two-day period, after Spearman first seated himself in the witness stand before the prosecution had enough. Spearman was finally allowed to step down and return to the defense table. The prosecutor had submitted him to two grueling hours of harsh cross-examination. It had been an ordeal that Spearman wouldn't easily forget—or forgive.

Two of his former employes were among the witnesses who followed him to the stand, and they provided testimony that served to back up his claims that the unsavory characters he was rubbing shoulders with wanted his tugboat to use transporting illegal drugs.

Eddie Evans, who worked for Spearman for nine years, told the court that his boss had advised him in October that he was going to the airport to pick up a customer who was interested in buying the tugboat. And he recalled seeing two men in a car with Tennessee license tags, who stopped at the boatyard to look over the *Robert Henry*.

Havlick also testified that he recalled Spearman mentioning that someone had approached him about using the tug to move illegal drugs.

Spearman's contention that Savage wanted to use his tugboat in a drug-smuggling scheme seemed to provide a strongly credible explanation for his association with members and associates of the Knoxville rent-a-killer gang. It could also raise the question of a motive for the slaying other than a husband's selfish desire to rid himself of an unwanted wife, or murder during a burglary. If drug traffickers were putting the pressure on the boatyard operator to use the tug in one of their smuggling schemes, Anita's murder could have represented a grisly warning to cooperate if he didn't want to be next.

The prosecution had anticipated the tugboat defense, and during Ms. Mattingly's earlier testimony, Savage's live-in girlfriend asserted he never discussed buying a tugboat. Even if he had been interested in such a purchase, she added, he couldn't have afforded it. She claimed, however, that it was true that Savage had done some drug dealing. She said his supplier was in Athens, Georgia.

And Chris Day, another Spearman employee, testifying as a prosecution witness, said that he didn't know of anyone from Tennessee ever stopping at the business to look at boats that were for sale. Although he conceded during cross-examination by Milano that it would have been possible to use the tugboat to move drugs, he pointed out that it would have been a slow process. He said the *Robert Henry*'s top speed was eight and a half miles per hour. And if the tug were pushing a barge, the top speed would be cut to only seven miles an hour.

As the defense neared the conclusion of its case, Spearman's attorneys called eight character witnesses, who included friends, business associates—and the defendant's divorced first wife, Beverly "Brandy" Spearman.

The defendant's lawyers quickly moved to dispel the idea that their client had been a cruel husband by asking his former wife about his treatment of her, and the divorce that ended their five-year marriage. She was asked why she had cited "extreme cruelty" as grounds for the 1963 parting.

"Those were the only grounds at the time that you could get a divorce," she explained. "I think it's embellished to serve the situation, the purpose." The divorce, she asserted, was friendly. And she said she didn't remember claiming in her divorce complaint that her husband had threatened her. "Violence was a no-no with us," she insisted.

St. James handled the cross-examination, and he had prepared for the job by obtaining a copy of her divorce complaint. He pointed out statements in the document that referred to a "violent argument" between the couple, accusations that her husband was mean to her three children, and claims that her marriage to the defendant had been a "dangerous and oppressive burden." The woman glanced at the document, then at the lawyer.

"This is ludicrous," she said. "I don't know how to explain this. Really, I don't."

But the prosecutor had some suggested explanations of his own, which he brought up for Spearman's first wife and the jury to mull over. He pointed out that the defendant was earning only two hundred dollars per week when they were married, but had become a rich man after the divorce. And he brought up an overnight trip to the Florida Keys that he said the witness and her former husband had taken together on his yacht after Anita's murder.

"Your information is incorrect," the woman snapped. "We didn't go in the boat."

Other character witnesses had an easier time of it on the stand. A former neighbor recalled that at a dinner she once shared with the couple, Robert Spearman had provided a touching demonstration of his love for Anita.

"You know, this is a fine old broad," she quoted him as saying. "You don't mind if I kiss my sweetheart in front of you? I love my wife very much."

Another acquaintance of twenty-five years testified that she had dinner with the defendant a few weeks before his arrest, and he was still grieving at that time over Anita's death. "I told him that all the crying in the world would not bring her back," the woman testified.

Defense attorneys took one final jab at the credibility of Emert, the state's star witness, before resting their case. Terry Zaiko, a probation officer from Tennessee who had investigated Emert's background, was called as the last witness of the trial. He said he considered Emert to be a liar. It was nearly 4:00 P.M. when Zaiko left the witness stand. A total of ninety-one witnesses had been called to testify since the beginning of the trial. Closing arguments were scheduled for the next day.

During their statements, both the defense and the prosecution carefully retraced the testimony of key witnesses and pointed to evidence—and suspicions—that each side insisted proved its case.

The state insisted that Spearman's account of the dealings over his tugboat was neither reasonable nor believable. The prosecution charged that Spearman was guilty of arranging his wife's slaying, in "a shockingly evil murder conspiracy."

Referring to Spearman as cold and devious, Ms. Lasch advised the jury that "your imagination cannot take you to the depth of degradation of the human spirit in this case." He sought out and paid criminals to carry out the brutal murder, she said, then sought to cover up his tracks with a carefully planned alibi.

"He calculated and chose his hit men, his killing machine," she declared. "You cannot escape culpability for first-degree murder by hiring henchmen."

Defense attorneys, of course, claimed just the opposite. They insisted that members of the Knoxville-based gang wanted the *Robert Henry*, and had made some of the suspicious long-distance calls from the boatyard telephones. Both Roth and Milano made closing statements.

Roth labeled the prosecution's claim that Spearman ordered his wife's murder in order to avoid a messy and costly divorce a smoke screen. He conceded that Spearman had cheated on Anita, but contended that it was possible for a man to carry on an affair and still love his wife.

"He loved his wife and had nothing to do with killing her," the lawyer declared. "He made a mistake with Pat Rozelle and shouldn't pay for it with his life."

Milano's closing was predictably biting, bombastic, and nasty. Police who investigated the murder came in for some of his ripest criticism, but most of his ire was directed at the state's star witness, Emert. The hard-hitting lawyer labeled Emert as a "snitch," a "scumbag," and a "liar."

"That guy lies when he says good morning to you," he roared.

The defense lawyer hit at the burly convict for making a deal with authorities to save his own skin. "Emert will be walking the streets in no time murdering, robbing, raping, pillaging, and anything else he can do," Milano predicted. "Thanks to people like Springer . . ."

The jury deliberated eight hours the first day before they were sequestered and driven to a local hotel to spend the night. During their deliberations they listened again to the tape recordings of Spearman's two statements to sheriff's detectives, and to the tape of his 911 emergency call.

When they reconvened at nine o'clock the next morning, they began work by listening to court reporters read testimony to them from Spearman, Debra Mattingly, and Robert Dix—the jitney driver who transported Emert from the Denny's restaurant parking lot to the West Palm Beach airport. Then they resumed deliberations. They continued through the noon hour while snacking on brown-bag lunches, and skipped dinner before reporting to the court bailiff at 7:15 on Friday evening, August 15, that they had reached a verdict. They had deliberated a total of eighteen hours.

One month and a day after the errant husband's first-degree murder and conspiracy trial opened, the jury announced that they had found him guilty on all counts.

As the court clerk read the chilling verdicts aloud—guilty of first-degree murder; guilty of conspiracy to commit murder, and two counts of solicitation to commit murder—Spearman slumped back into his chair. His face flushed crimson, his eyes blinked rapidly. "I can't believe it," he whispered. As Spearman rubbed at his forehead with a shaky right hand, attorney Duncan leaned forward, with his head bowed. His fellow members of the defense team showed no visible reaction.

Across from them at the prosecution table, Ms. Lasch swiveled in her seat and smiled at Springer, who was sitting a few feet away in the front rows of the spectator area. St. James's face was also creased in a satisfied grin. Later, in remarks to news reporters, the lead prosecutor cited Springer and his colleagues for much of the credit for making the conviction possible through their exhaustive and professional investigation.

In the courtroom, Judge Harper dismissed the jury for a long weekend and instructed them to return three days later on Tuesday morning to begin considering their recommendation for the penalty. Then he permitted Spearman to talk for a few minutes with his lawyers, before sheriff's deputies hurried him past a scramble of waiting reporters into a holding cell. Spearman wobbled between the lawmen unsteadily and silently as if he were in a daze.

When the jury resumed deliberations, they would have two choices they could recommend to the judge for sentencing on the most serious of the charges, first-degree murder: a life sentence in prison, with no possibility of parole for twenty-five years; or execution in Florida's electric chair. The jury's recommendation is an important part of the penalty-fixing process, but Florida's criminal code permits judges in capital murder cases to overrule the panel if he wishes. Consequently, Judge Harper would be empowered to lessen a recommendation for the death penalty to life in prison, or to upgrade a recommendation for a life sentence to death in the electric chair.

Neither possibility left much to look forward to for the convicted wife killer's future. At fifty-seven, even if he was given a life sentence and paroled in twenty-five years, he would be eighty-two years old when he was released from prison.

And execution in Florida's electric chair, which convicts and many correctional officers have given the outrageous nickname "Old Sparky," was a horror to contemplate. Death row inmates at the Florida State Prison at Starke refer to the once-in-a-lifetime experi-

ence as "riding the lightning" or "the electric en-
ema."

When the first powerful four-thousand-volt surge of
electricity slices through a body strapped to the solid
old wood and metal chair, the bowels and bladder are
violently and suddenly emptied. Sometimes the intes-
tines burst. Smoke curls from electrodes attached to the
shaved spot on the skull. And the convicted killer
lurches inches into the air, then drops back onto the
seat. Official electrocution is a messy, nasty business,
but death row killers who have raped, robbed, and murdered are nasty people. A wife killer would be among
his own on Florida's death row.

Spearman knew, as his lawyers and others did, that
Florida, with Texas, had become one of the two leading
states in the number of executions carried out since a
1976 U.S. Supreme Court ruling permitting reinstitu-
tion of the death penalty based on guidelines established by the federal jurists. The possibility of a death
sentence was a sobering prospect.

And Prosecutor Moira Lasch was all set to argue that
it was the proper punishment for Robert Spearman. She
said from the beginning of the trial that she would seek
the ultimate penalty, and during jury selection had
carefully questioned all prospective panel members
about their opinions concerning the death sentence.

Prior to jury selection, Spearman's defense team had
also anticipated a worst-possible-scenario conclusion to
the trial when Duncan filed motions challenging both
the constitutionality of the state's death penalty law,
and the right of the prosecutor to dismiss prospective
jurors who were opposed to execution. At the time,
Duncan described the motions as standard procedure in
first-degree murder cases. In the event of a conviction,

the motions could be useful in appeals. And now Spearman had been convicted.

When the jury reassembled in Courtroom 413 on Tuesday morning, attorneys had one more opportunity to influence their life-or-death decision.

The lead prosecutor retraced much of her earlier presentation, reminding them that Spearman had paid to have his wife killed because of greed. She showed photographs to the jury of the victim's devastating, gory injuries, pointing out that Anita's husband had placed more value on his riches than on the life of his wife, or on her suffering. And she cited evidence that the ailing woman had put up a desperate fight for her life.

"If anyone had a right to live . . . it was Anita Spearman," the prosecutor asserted. "She spent the last year of her life facing death, and believed she had conquered it."

Spearman's lawyers called three more witnesses. The convicted wife killer's heartbroken mother presented a poignant plea for mercy for her only child. The eighty-three-year-old woman had been too frail to sit through the agonizing trial or to visit him in jail. "As long as there's life, as long as there's breath, there's opportunity," the woman implored. "I just want him to have his opportunity."

Roth asked the jury to be merciful, observing that their lengthy deliberation indicated there must have been a few members of the panel who had some reasonable doubts about his client's guilt. There was no coming back from a death sentence, he reminded them.

The jury deliberated three hours before returning to the courtroom with a recommendation for a life prison sentence with no parole for at least twenty-five years on the most serious of the two charges. Eight of the jurors had agreed on the prison term for the first-degree murder conviction. The other four had favored execution.

Spearman reacted calmly, but Roth turned to him and embraced him in a relieved bear hug. Both men were aware, of course, that the final decision would still be up to the judge. And it would seem that the split decision by the jury would make it easier for him to overrule the panel if he was inclined to invoke the ultimate penalty.

But Spearman, his attorneys, the prosecutors, and the public would have a long time to wait before the question of life and death could be answered. Judge Harper said he expected to withhold sentencing until after the trials of the convicted man's accused coconspirators were concluded. And the progress of extradition proceedings and other pretrial moves indicated that was likely to be several months in the future.

Chapter 10

Justice for a Hit Man

Police and prosecutors know better than to take anything for granted. Nevertheless, about a week after Spearman's conviction of the murder of his wife, they were mildly surprised to learn that his accused coconspirators were dropping their struggle against extradition. First Doutre agreed to return to Florida to face the murder charges against him in Mrs. Spearman's death, then a day later, Savage also waived his extradition rights.

On a typical blistering late August afternoon, Springer and Det. Rick Oetinger stepped off a twin-engine Cessna 421 at Palm Beach International Airport, escorting their two prisoners in handcuffs and waist chains. Another Sheriff's Department detective, Lt. Edward Hurley, piloted the charter aircraft.

Bareheaded, with his shock of straight brown hair flopping over his forehead, Savage danced off the airplane and chatted with news reporters gathered on the tarmac at the Sheriff's Office Aviation Division headquarters as if they were old friends. During the mini press appearance, and later as he was transported to the county jail, he complimented Springer and Oetinger for their great company, said a few good words about Hurley's skill as a pilot, and revealed that he was glad to be back in Palm Beach County. He explained that he was looking forward to the opportunity to prove his innocence.

Doutre's behavior was just the opposite. He was morosely silent and wanted nothing to do with the clamoring reporters. With Springer's steadying hand on his arm, the accused bludgeon murderer stalked across the tarmac with his shoulders hunched and his eyebrows furrowed in a nasty scowl. Dressed in blue jeans and a striped dress shirt, he ignored the shouted questions from the media and hurried into the Sheriff's Department car waiting to transport him to the county justice complex. He had maintained similar silence on the flight from Georgia, speaking up only one time to growl that he hated to fly.

A few days later Savage and Doutre entered pleas before Judge Harper in Palm Beach County Circuit Court of not guilty to matching charges of first-degree murder and conspiracy to commit first-degree murder in the slaying of Mrs. Spearman. Doutre was already represented by an assistant public defender, Dean L. Willbur, Jr., who entered the not-guilty plea at the hearing. Willbur was assisted by attorneys Richard Greene and Barry Weinstein, who would do much of the legal research.

When Savage advised the judge that he couldn't afford to hire his own lawyer, Harper appointed West Palm Beach attorney Peter Birch to represent him. Birch filed a written plea of not guilty for his new client.

"He's a good lawyer, by the way," Harper advised the accused murder broker as he announced the appointment of counsel. "I appreciate it," Savage replied.

Judge Harper was aware of Savage's petulant complaints, while he was jailed in Georgia fighting extradition, that one of the reasons he didn't want to return to Palm Beach County was that he was afraid he would be appointed "trash" for a lawyer.

A few days before pleading not guilty in the Spearman slaying, Doutre and Savage were named along with five others on federal charges of interstate conspiracy to commit murder and interstate travel to commit murder in the foiled plot against the life of Victoria Morgan Brashear. But federal authorities would have to wait their turn for a crack at the murder-for-hire ringleader and his ace triggerman. Judge Harper set their trial in the Spearman case for January 20, 1987. Palm Beach county authorities weren't about to relinquish their custody until they had a final answer to the charges against the pair for Anita Spearman's brutal death.

But there were still some unwelcome surprises in store. In October, almost eight weeks after the accused killers were returned to Palm Beach County, the prosecution team was confronted with their old bugaboo from the Spearman pretrial jockeying. Doutre's lawyer filed a motion demanding a speedy trial for his client. Willbur had been representing Doutre in the case since May. But because of Savage's own reluctance to permit earlier appointment of an attorney in the case, Birch had represented his client only since the arraignment on September 5—a little more than six weeks earlier. The defense strategy was obvious, however.

There would be the advantage of again forcing the

prosecution to hurry its preparation of a complex and challenging major felony case. But there was an additional and important advantage, as well. If the court was forced to schedule Doutre for trial within sixty days, it would mean that he and Savage, his codefendant in the Spearman slaying, could not be tried together. And if they weren't put on trial together, their attorneys could avoid the nasty probability of the accused crime associates turning on each other in order to save their own skin.

Prosecutor Lasch objected, pointing out that the Spearman trial was concluded only a few weeks before. And as she did when Spearman's lawyers demanded a speedy trial, she cited the difficulties of arranging for out-of-state witnesses to travel to Palm Beach County in time for the proceedings. She reminded the judge that some of the witnesses were not expected to voluntarily comply with a summons to travel to South Florida and testify.

The lead prosecutor also argued that it was important to put the two men on trial together because they were accused in the indictment against them of joining in a conspiracy. And she complained that Doutre's defenders had asked for the speedy trial because there was no legitimate legal basis for severing the cases against the two reputed murder-for-hire partners. In response to a query from the judge, however, she had to concede that she could not cite any legal reason to refuse the request.

Willbur countered that the case wouldn't be as difficult for the prosecution as Ms. Lasch had indicated, because the witnesses and other aspects of the case would so closely resemble those of the Spearman trial. And he noted that there seemed to be a question about whether or not Savage would even be ready for trial on the January 20 date already stipulated by the court.

Birch agreed, remarking that he couldn't guarantee he and his client would be ready for trial by that time. He said he was making his best efforts to prepare in time. But he conceded, "At this point it's fifty-fifty at best."

The lead prosecutor also questioned Doutre, to make sure that he understood the seriousness of the demand for speedy trial, knew about the advantages he would be giving up in the discovery process, and was aware that the state was seeking the death penalty. He said he understood and supported the petition. Finally she asked if he knew that he would also be giving up the right to use an insanity defense.

"I'm not crazy," he snapped.

Three days later, after taking the petition under advisement, Judge Harper issued an order granting a speedy trial to Doutre. He set the new trial date for December 1, less than six weeks away. And he reserved four weeks on his calendar for the proceeding. Savage's trial continued to be set for January 20. The cases had been effectively severed.

In his written order, Judge Harper pointed out that prosecutors had successfully proven the charges of conspiracy against Spearman, who was tried separately. And he added, as he had when ruling on the similar motion on Spearman's behalf, that he was reluctant to rule against a speedy trial, in part because of the danger of a higher court reversal during the appeals process, based on denial of the motion.

Willbur had also submitted a petition weeks earlier for change of venue, a request to move his client's trial to another county because of the extensive publicity

surrounding the Spearman murder case. Shortly after-
ward, Judge Harper rejected a defense request for as
much as seventeen thousand dollars in taxpayers' money
to pay for a study of the impact of pretrial publicity on
the case. But after ruling on the speedy trial motion,
he scheduled a hearing on the change-of-venue request
for the next day.

After listening to the attorneys' presentations at the
hearing, the judge announced that he was withholding
a final decision. He said that he wanted to begin the
jury selection process first. Then if it became apparent
during the first week of voir dire that an impartial and
fair jury couldn't be found in Palm Beach County, he
promised, he would order a change of venue. Several
days later, he stepped out of the case and turned it over
to a retired jurist, Judge J. Gwynn Parker. Judge Harper
explained that he needed a vacation.

Attorneys had barely begun their efforts to select a
jury for the opening of the December trial before proceedings bogged down in a legal brouhaha tied to the
presence of television cameras and crews. When Judge
Parker ruled against allowing TV camera crews into the
deliberation room where prospective jurors were being
interviewed because it was too crowded, he ran into a
flurry of objections from the electronic media.

Lawyers for WPEC Channel 12 in West Palm Beach
immediately appealed the judge's ruling to the Fourth
District Court of Appeal, as an infringement of the
press's constitutional freedoms. They also claimed that
the ruling violated an administrative order governing
media access to the local courts. When the appeals court
ordered a halt to the proceedings for twenty-four hours
so the judge could explain his order, Parker relented.
He ordered the cramped jury room opened to the tele-

vision crew and camera, but stipulated that the operators and equipment were not to interfere with the interviews.

Then Doutre's attorneys complained, and filed a formal request to have the television cameras barred. "This is not a sitcom," Willbur groused.

But Parker had already heard from the appeals court, and had enough. He ruled that the camera crew members and their equipment could stay, as long as they weren't disruptive. And he rejected another suggestion by Willbur that the camera crewmen dress up more. "All these cameramen look like mechanics," the jurist conceded. "But I'm not going to force them to wear a bow tie." Doutre's trial was getting off to an exasperatingly shaky start.

And the situation didn't immediately improve. If anything, it became worse. Just about everyone the lawyers talked to during their efforts to select an impartial jury admitted having heard lots about the case. It had been in local newspapers, on local and national television, and featured in newspaper and magazine stories in the national press. One potential juror reported that her boss had remarked to her, "He's already been convicted. Go ahead and fry him."

Greene cited her remark when he argued during yet another hearing on a renewed defense request for change of venue. "It is intolerable for a fellow citizen to be tried for his life in this atmosphere," he declared.

Ms. Lasch protested. A change of venue would mean a delay, and after the order a few weeks earlier for speedy trial, she had already set up a hurry-up schedule for out-of-state witnesses. Setting everything back again would mean recontacting nearly one hundred people and establishing new transportation and hotel plans. The question of a final trial date for Doutre was becoming a legal yo-yo.

Greene observed that the prosecutor was complaining about an inconvenience. "But we're dealing with the most fundamental concepts of fairness," he asserted.

Judge Parker agreed, and ordered the trial held off for at least ninety days until a better location could be found. He said that Judge Harper, who would return from vacation in January, would make the final decision on the new trial site. Judge Harper moved the trial to Pensacola, and set the new date for proceedings to begin as February 4, 1986. His vacation was behind him, and he had once more taken over the reins. He would preside at the trial.

Judge Harper had not only returned to the case as the trial judge, but he was also going back home. He grew up in the Panhandle city on the Gulf of Mexico, and his elderly parents still lived there. He knew the kind of people who lived in the Panhandle, and respected them for their work ethic and blunt honesty. And he liked their down-home friendliness, taste in food, and countrified manner.

When people there said they were from "L.A.," they generally meant lower Alabama instead of Los Angeles, and they had the accents to prove it. Most shared a conservative honesty, and many were from military families with links to the giant Pensacola Naval Air Station. They were people who took their citizenship seriously.

Judge Harper told reporters that he didn't expect publicity to be a problem picking a jury in the Escambia County city in North Florida. He said that people there had never heard of Doutre, Savage, or Robert

Spearman, and weren't interested. The jurist was already familiar with the legal ins and outs of the area because he had worked as an Escambia County prosecutor for approximately fifteen years. Pensacola appeared to be an excellent city to look for an impartial jury that hadn't heard about Sean Doutre or formed an opinion about the Spearman murder case.

But that had already begun to change when Panhandle residents, along with other viewers all over America, watched a national television news program about the case late the previous year. The cake was put on the icing when the story was front-paged in the *Pensacola News Journal* on the Sunday before Doutre, Judge Harper, and his legal retinue came to town to begin picking a jury. By the time the prosecution and defense gathered in a fifth-floor room at the Escambia County Judicial Center to began their second effort at selecting a jury, the story was already big news in the Gulf coast city. They could run from the publicity, but they couldn't escape. It had followed them six hundred miles, catty-corner across the state.

Doutre's defense lawyers had help with jury selection. They had hired Margaret Covington, a Houston lawyer and psychologist who was considered to be an expert in the field, to help them select a jury likely to rule favorably for their client. Ms. Covington was not licensed to practice in Florida but could advise the three lawyers who were teaming up for his defense. She told a reporter that the defense was looking for intelligent jurors who were open-minded and would listen to both sides of the story before making their decisions.

But jury selection was barely under way when Ms. Lasch informed the court that Doutre's jury expert had gotten in trouble herself for reputedly making a deal with a hired gun. The prosecutor revealed that the Texas lawyer was once accused of violating federal law by using Western Union to send money to Terry Noah, an Arizona man, to "sexually incapacitate" her former boyfriend.

Noah subsequently testified that he shot Cage Wavell five times in the Corpus Christi, Texas, attorney's law office on November 2, 1981. Wavell, who was the father of Ms. Covington's child, survived the shooting. Ms. Covington was convicted in a Texas district court of burglary with intent to commit aggravated assault. But District Judge Michael Westergren ruled that there was insufficient evidence for the jury's verdict, and ordered her acquitted.

Noah had testified at her trial that she promised him thirteen hundred dollars and a Mexican vacation to "sexually incapacitate" the Corpus Christi lawyer because he wouldn't acknowledge he had fathered her baby.

Prosecutor Lasch told the judge that the propriety of the Houston lawyer participating in the case was questionable. The judge decided that Ms. Covington could continue to act as a "passive participant" and whisper advice to the Florida attorneys. But Ms. Covington was outraged and accused the lead prosecutor of bringing the Texas troubles up as a means of discrediting Doutre's defense.

An already weird case was becoming more bizarre by the day. Court watchers began to joke about moving the trial to Disney World. Orlando, after all, was only a couple of hundred miles away.

Nevertheless, seven work days after jury selection began in the Escambia County Judicial Center, a panel of nine women and three men, with two male alternates, was seated. A few minutes later, attorneys began presentation of their opening arguments in Courtroom 502.

Doutre's defense attorneys claimed that Spearman murdered his wife himself, without help from Doutre.

Willbur advised the jury that the defense expected to prove that Spearman beat his wife to death with a hammer he took from the pegboard in his garage because hired hit men had twice welched on murder contracts.

"There has rarely been a case more misconstrued than this one," Willbur declared. "Robert Spearman killed his own wife. He didn't hire anyone to do it. There's not one scintilla of evidence that Sean Doutre was ever in Spearman's house."

It was a shocking and intriguing theory. Doutre's lawyers were setting out to convince the jury that their client worked with Savage and Emert to rip off the boatyard owner for the twenty-thousand-dollar murder contract fee, then welched on the deal. They made fun of Spearman, ridiculing him as a "bozo" for believing they would actually kill his wife, Willbur said. Then the twenty-one-year-old Doutre bilked the businessman for a second time.

"It was a very wacky way to get twenty thousand dollars. But they followed it, and they got twenty thousand dollars," Willbur observed. And he argued that neither his client nor Savage was guilty of Mrs. Spearman's murder. They were a pair of con men, he insisted.

The defense lawyer explained that Doutre had been impressed with how easily his boss had conned Spearman out of the twenty thousand dollars and decided to pick up another eight thousand dollars in easy money for himself from the gullible boatyard operator. So he took advantage of Spearman's frustration and rage over the unfulfilled contract with Savage, and contacted the philandering husband with an offer to make a deal between just the two of them and do the job himself.

He asserted that Spearman met with Doutre at the Denny's restaurant and turned over the shotgun, pieces of Anita's jewelry, and eight thousand dollars in cash after the young con artist agreed to carry out the slaying.

The lawyer told the jury that his client double-crossed Spearman, however, and left with the payoff without carrying out his part of the devil's bargain. But on the day the murder was supposed to be carried out, Spearman carefully built up his alibi with his early morning activities before returning home, where he expected to find his wife dead. Instead, he found that she was still alive. He had been double-crossed twice. Willbur said that the boatyard owner flew into a rage, and caved in his wife's skull with the hammer.

Willbur pointed out that examination of the crime scene had turned up a trail of blood leading to a garbage can, and blood in Spearman's Blazer. He concurred with the prosecutor about the motive for the murder. "Robert Spearman wanted his wife dead for one reason: He was greedy."

In the effort to convict Doutre, the prosecution was counting on the same kind of evidence they had used to win their case in Palm Beach County: a load of circumstantial evidence including motel receipts and telephone records detailing calls from Spearman's office phones to Savage's numbers in Knoxville, as well as to other advertisers in the *SOF* classified pages. And, of course, the prosecutors would rely heavily on the damning testimony of Emert and Ms. Mattingly.

The prosecutor promised to use the paper trail left in Palm Beach County at the time of the murder, in addition to evidence gathered when he was arrested in Maryville, to prove his direct link to the crime scene in the Spearman home. She cited the twelve-gauge shotgun and the jewelry as being among the evidence she would use to prove her case. And she pointed out that Spearman wasn't the only accused conspirator who was motivated by greed.

"This case is about money: people who murder for pay and people who pay for murder," Prosecutor Lasch told the rapt jury. She said that Doutre needed money to get his recent bride out of jail.

The prosecution wasted no time before launching an attack on the credibility of the defense claim that Spearman hammered his wife to death in frustration, after realizing the men he had paid weren't going to kill her for him. Dr. Frederick Hobin, an associate medical examiner for Palm Beach County, was the first witness called, and he indicated that it was unlikely that Anita Spearman was beaten to death with either a claw hammer or a smaller drywall hammer like those investigators found on the garage pegboard.

If a claw hammer was swung with heavy force, the round head of the tool would have caused a different type of injury than the triangular and moon-shaped wounds found on the right side of Anita Spearman's head, he testified. And the drywall hammer was too small to have caused the injuries to the woman's skull.

"It was the nature of the wounds that indicated that a conventional hammer used in the conventional way was not the instrument," he declared. He said any one of three major head injuries could have caused the victim's death.

Yet during cross-examination he conceded that he couldn't absolutely eliminate a hammer as the possible murder weapon if it was used in an unconventional manner. And he wasn't sure what had caused the injuries.

The woman was struck on the head with six or seven blows, with what the pathologist described as a "moderately heavy, somewhat elongated instrument." Although not specifically referring to a shotgun barrel, Dr. Hobin said he believed the fatal injuries were inflicted with what he described as a pipelike object. There was no evidence that she had been smothered with a pillow or anything else.

The jury inspected several grisly slides and photographs of the head injuries, and others showing a bruise on her right hand. Dr. Hobin said the hand injury probably occurred when she attempted to defend herself.

Detective Richter also testified during cross-examination by Willbur that laboratory tests had shown a positive reaction to blood on the head of one of the hammers.

Prosecutors ran into strong defense objections and a demand for a mistrial early in the proceeding when they produced three-foot-high blowups of the 1985 cover of *SOF* and three pages of classified ad exhibits. Greene argued that the enlarged magazine pages contained material that was inflammatory and unrelated to the case. Ms. Lasch responded that it was necessary to show the full-page layouts so the jurors would understand the type of magazine the ads were placed in.

"He wasn't consulting *McCall's* when he made these calls," she said of Spearman's hit-man shopping.

Judge Harper permitted use of the blown-up cover and the three pages of advertisements. But he ruled in favor of the defense on an objection against using the entire magazine as evidence. He explained that it would be duplicative, and contained information that was irrelevant.

Many of the witnesses called by the prosecutor had appeared during the earlier trial. Patricia Rozelle once more had to publicly trace her affair with the convicted wife killer, and recounted the confrontation with her boyfriend's wife in the Jupiter restaurant. Spearman employes testified, and Rent-A-Wreck squad detectives outlined their investigation, and the prosecution used their testimony to introduce evidence. Sergeant Johnston returned to Florida once more to tell about Doutre's arrest in Maryville, which some courthouse gossips mistakenly referred to as Mayberry.

There were a few new witnesses as well, however. Merchants from the Gateway Mall in Jacksonville testified to show that Doutre had gone on a shopping binge on the day of the murder. Receipts were produced showing that he spent one hundred dollars for new cowboy boots, and six hundred dollars on other articles of clothing that day.

The prosecution also introduced evidence about Doutre's feast of prime rib and Grand Marnier at the Holiday Inn on PGA Boulevard the evening before Mrs. Spearman was killed. He had claimed to work for Gulf Oil and signed for the meal with one of his favorite aliases, Robert Dawson, before skipping out on the bill.

During questioning of an Atlanta insurance company executive, the prosecution came within what Judge Harper termed "a gnat's hair" of creating a mistrial. Robert Kaye, a benefits manager with the Trans-America Occidental Life Insurance Co., testified that Spearman filed a claim for his wife's double indemnity

$10,500 accidental death coverage, but the company didn't pay off.

St. James appeared to be just about to inquire why the company refused payment when he stopped short and asked to talk privately with Judge Harper outside the presence of the jury. After the brief conference, Kaye was excused from the witness stand. Judge Harper had confirmed during the brief tête-à-tête that if the witness had been allowed to explain that the payment was witheld because of Spearman's conviction in the murder of his wife, a mistrial would have had to be called. The jury was not permitted to know about Spearman's conviction, because of his alleged contract with Savage—and ultimately with the defendant, Doutre—to carry out the killing. The information would have been considered prejudicial against the defendant.

But once again, Emert and Ms. Mattingly, the two former employes at the Continental Club strip joint, were the star witnesses. As they had at the trial in West Palm Beach, both testified under immunity.

Citing a conversation she overheard while riding in the backseat of a van her boyfriend was driving from Sweetwater, Tennessee, to Knoxville about two months before Mrs. Spearman's death, Ms. Mattingly laid the responsibility for the murder solidly on the defendant. She said Savage couldn't figure out why Spearman had stopped harassing him over the unfulfilled contract on his wife's life until Doutre spoke up and solved the mystery.

"He said he had cut his own deal with Mr. Spearman and that he had killed Anita Spearman," she testified. Peering straight ahead and speaking with studied conviction as she replied to a question from the prosecutor, she said that Doutre didn't behave as if he were joking.

"He really showed no emotion. He wasn't bragging. He just said it. He was very serious," she declared.

During cross-examination from Willbur, she conceded that she didn't hear the entire conversation, and she didn't know how Doutre had carried out the killing. When Willbur pointed out that she had said in a sworn statement that Doutre claimed he smothered Mrs. Spearman, the witness denied making the remark.

The defense lawyer hit hard at the witness's credibility, bringing up her own troubles with the criminal justice system and her abuse of drugs. She admitted that she was serving a prison sentence in Georgia at that time. And she was awaiting sentencing in another case in Arkansas, she said.

Speaking evenly and audibly, she also conceded that she had used marijuana and had experienced trouble with cocaine, but claimed that her drug abuse had nothing to do with the conversation she overheard during the drive between Sweetwater and Knoxville.

"I had not done any cocaine that day," she told Willbur. "I heard him tell Richard that he got five thousand dollars for the job. I believe that's what I heard." Then she corrected herself: "I know that's what I heard."

The prosecution, however, had saved their heaviest hitter for the windup. Even then, when Ronald Emert at last walked once more to the witness stand, it was a day later than previously planned. Ms. Lasch, who planned to handle the direct examination, had temporarily lost her voice the previous day, so his testimony was delayed.

The admitted bagman said that neither the defendant nor his boss, Savage, indicated they were merely bilking a gullible businessman out of his money, and weren't really serious about seeing to it that someone was killed in Palm Beach County. Emert claimed that when he left Knoxville, he didn't even know why he was being sent to collect money from a man in Florida.

"I was on parole, so I was a little leery about it because I know most of his business is illegal," he said of the mission Savage had sent him on.

The only question on Doutre's mind during the wild dash from Tennessee to Palm Beach County was just exactly who was to be killed, the burly witness said.

"At the time he wasn't sure whether he was going to kill Mr. Spearman or Mrs. Spearman," Emert recounted.

The witness said that his companion "drove like a madman" on the way to Palm Beach County, and kept a loaded gun on the seat beside him throughout the trip.

"He said his girlfriend was in jail and he wanted to get her out because he wanted to get married," the big man testified. "He needed the money to get her out."

Willbur called on a former chief medical examiner from New York City to bolster the defense contention that Spearman beat his wife to death with a hammer. Dr. Dominick DiMaio testified that the four triangular wounds on the right side of the victim's skull could have been made by the octagonal head of one of the hammers found by police in the Spearman garage.

"Unless you come up with something better, the hammer is the one that inflicted the injuries," the nationally known forensic pathologist and consultant in homicide cases declared.

When the prosecution charged that he had based his conclusions solely on his review of an autopsy report and photographs of the hammer and the victim's injuries, he remained unshaken. "Whether I'm present at

the autopsy or not makes no difference. Believe me!''
he responded.

Doutre's defense attorneys also called Palm Beach
County Sheriff's Deputy William P. Harris, Jr., who
testified that he saw blood all over Mrs. Spearman's
bedroom when he arrived at the crime scene. The prosecution had previously questioned a paramedic, who
said he didn't notice blood when he first arrived in the
bedroom and thought the victim may have suffered a
heart attack before turning her head and discovering the
injuries.

Terry Zaiko, the Tennessee probation officer who
testified during the Spearman trial, was also called again
to discuss his knowledge and perception of Emert.
Zaiko repeated his previous testimony, branding the
state's star witness as a liar and a druggie. ''Mr. Emert
is well-known to the police,'' the witness observed.

Unlike the defense in Spearman's trial, Doutre's lawyers chose not to have their client testify. They closed
their case after calling nine witnesses. There would be
no chance of Doutre accidentally sabotaging his own
case by making a damaging statement on the stand
either through direct or cross-examination.

On Monday morning, February 23, the trial in
Courtroom 502 was reconvened to hear closing statements.

St. James told the jury that Doutre stalked into Anita
Spearman's home at 5:30 in the morning, after her husband left a door open for him, with plans to suffocate
her. The woman's husband had told him that she was
still so weak from her surgery and bout with breast
cancer that she was wheelchair-bound, the assistant state
attorney declared.

But when Doutre pressed a feather pillow against her

face, the ailing woman fought desperately for her life, St. James said in the closing argument. So Doutre beat her to death. St. James suggested that the butt of the .45-caliber pistol Doutre was reputedly armed with may have been the instrument of death. The prosecutor told the jury that the defendant stripped the rings from the victim's limp fingers, scooped up some of her jewelry, and grabbed the shotgun before he fled from the house. Finally he met Anita Spearman's husband at the restaurant, gave him the rings as proof Anita was dead, collected the last of the blood money, and headed for Tennessee. It was a chilling and grim scenario for the jury to ponder.

Doutre's lawyers, however, had another explanation for what happened that was predictably far different. Willbur insisted that his client was guilty of nothing more than a scam, and that he only posed as a contract killer to bilk a gullible businessman out of his money. Neither Doutre nor Savage ever intended to murder the former West Palm Beach assistant city manager, the lawyer insisted.

Robert Spearman, Willbur contended, beat his wife to death himself. The lawyer branded the philandering businessman as such a ''cold fish'' that he had sexual relations with his wife the night before her murder so that homicide investigators would believe that he still loved her. Presumably it would help eliminate him as a suspect in her slaying.

The jury deliberated more than six hours over two days before reaching a verdict. Seated next to Willbur at the defense table, Doutre appeared uncomfortable in a necktie he was wearing for the occasion. He trembled as he waited for the jury to file into the courtroom. Aware of the defendant's obvious distress, the judge asked him to do his best to control his emotions when the verdict was read—whichever way the decision went. "Can you do that?" the jurist kindly inquired.

"I'll try," the shaky defendant muttered.

A few minutes later the panel members seated themselves in the jury box. Doutre was ashen-faced, and appeared to be holding his breath. When Judge Harper spoke, however, it wasn't to ask the jury for its verdict, but to direct the panelists to change their seats. On the order of a well-meaning bailiff, the jury members had switched from the seats they had occupied during the three-week-long trial so that forewoman Joyce Ann Penton could be closest to the judge to announce the verdict. But Judge Harper wanted them in their regular places.

Doutre looked as if he wanted to run, but was afraid his legs wouldn't support him. At last, however, the jurists were seated properly and the foreman read the verdict aloud. The jury had found the defendant guilty on both charges. Doutre lurched in his seat, then bowed his head and put one hand over his eyes as the verdict was read. Willbur and Greene took the verdict stoically. But Willbur, who had already left the public defender's office to go into private practice, put his hand on Doutre's shoulder to comfort him. Weinstein was not at the defense table.

Doutre had slumped almost horizontal in his chair and was holding his head in both hands as photographers crowded around to snap photographs. Finally Willbur looked up from the distraught youth and angrily demanded, "Would you like him to bleed for you?"

The question of Doutre's guilt or innocence had been settled, although it hadn't been easy. The jury forewoman later revealed that the panel members voted three times before reaching a unanimous verdict of guilty on each of the two charges. The first poll of jurors resulted in an eight-to-four vote for acquittal, she said. The next vote was seven-to-five for conviction.

Judge Harper, who had sequestered the jury at a local motel the previous evening, sent the panelists to their homes with instructions to return the next morning for the penalty hearing. Like Spearman, Doutre faced possible penalties on the first-degree murder conviction of life in prison with no parole for a minimum of twenty-five years, or death in the electric chair.

The prosecution didn't call additional witnesses for the penalty hearing. But the defense had assembled an impressive array of relatives, social workers, former foster parents, and others as character witnesses to plead for their young client's life. Some of the most poignant testimony was delivered by the first witness, the defendant's father, Lloyd Lee Perry. The Phoenix salesman traced his son's tragic childhood, and told of his repeated neglect and rejection as a baby and little boy.

After his testimony, Perry told reporters that if his son was allowed to live, he himself would move to a town near the prison so that they could visit regularly. Father and son had been separated for nineteen years before Doutre's arrest.

Doutre's stepfather, Robert Swetich, also pleaded with the jury for the young man's life. ''Sean might very well be the weapon in this case, but society pulled the trigger,'' he said. When his stepfather talked of the anguish of turning six-year-old Sean over to welfare authorities in Nevada, Doutre broke down in tears.

Some jurors also reached into purses or pockets for handkerchiefs and dabbed at teary eyes or suddenly runny noses as witness after witness retraced the convicted killer's miserable childhood. They told how the once quiet and loving little boy who was a good and attentive student gradually transposed into a morose and distrustful child with few friends after he was repeatedly rejected by those he loved and trusted most.

Louis Sexton and his wife, June, were the first foster parents to take the boy into their home, the jury was told by another witness. Mrs. Sexton explained that they wanted to adopt him. But they had to give him up because Nevada law forbade foster parents to adopt children they had been caring for. "He must have figured, 'Here I go again,' " she said.

Dr. Keith Hayes, a psychiatrist from Delray Beach, Florida, testified about the devastating emotional effect on the defendant resulting from his repeated abandonment as a child, and the damage it wreaked on his ability to behave in a law-abiding manner. Abandonment was the most dominant force in the youngster's life, the witness claimed. And he added that Doutre was a sitting duck for a father figure like Savage. Hayes said that Doutre's wretched record of childhood abandonment made him susceptible to manipulation by older men.

Hayes described Doutre as a textbook case of maternal deprivation.

A private investigator who worked for the defense testified that Doutre's mother, who had remarried and had two daughters, was contacted but refused to leave her Phoenix home to testify for her son. "She told me she wanted to have nothing to do with Sean," Gerald Justine testified.

Defense attorney Weinstein drew heavily on the testimony about Doutre's wretched younger years in pleading to spare the killer's life. "Sean Doutre was a throwaway all his life. He was the throwaway child," Weinstein declared. "Sean Doutre is pathetic. Sean Doutre is sad. But Sean Doutre does not deserve to die in the electric chair."

Despite the heart-wrenching picture drawn of Doutre's awful childhood, the prosecution was determined to convince the jury that the death penalty was the only proper punishment for the savage murder of Mrs. Spearman. In her argument for the death sentence, Ms. Lasch labeled the convicted killer as a "paid machine of death." And he could not be rehabilitated in prison, she asserted.

The jury opted for mercy, and recommended a life prison sentence. This time Doutre had better control of his emotions. He squinted his eyes shut as the jury forewoman made the announcement. But there were no tears, and there was no visible trembling. He was clearly relieved.

Again the forewoman gave the press a glimpse at what had gone on behind the closed doors of the deliberation room. She said the jury had split in favor of sparing Doutre the death penalty. The naval air base employee said the panelists had felt that Doutre was roped into the scheme by the older men, Savage and Spearman. "He needs another chance in life," she said. "He didn't really have a chance in life."

Judge Harper reluctantly agreed. More than three months after taking the jury's recommendation under advisement, he officially concurred with the panel's wishes. Back in his own courtroom in West Palm Beach, he sentenced Doutre to life in prison with no possibility of parole for twenty-five-years on the first-degree murder conviction. He tacked on another thirty-year prison term on the conspiracy count. Judge Harper put great stock in jury recommendations, and took them seriously.

"Doutre should be eternally grateful to the ten jurors who recommended life imprisonment," the judge read from a nine-page sentencing order. "Had the vote gone the other way, the court would have given Doutre the shock of his life."

Doutre was pale and grim-faced as he quietly listened to the sentence. His colorful dress shirt and necktie were gone, replaced by a wrinkled jail jumpsuit, cuffs, and chains. He had already been convicted, and there was no danger of prejudicing jury members by allowing them to see him shackled and in prison garb. According to the judge's sentence, the life term and the conspiracy sentence would be served consecutively, not concurrently. Consequently Doutre would have to complete the minimum twenty-five-years of his murder sentence before beginning to eat away at the thirty-year conspiracy term.

Even if Doutre was able to shave fifteen years off the conspiracy sentence with credit for good behavior, there still appeared to be little chance that he would be freed from prison before he was sixty-two years old. It was a distressing prospect. And serious charges were pending against him in other jurisdictions as well.

Despite Doutre's conviction, sentencing, and the judge's disclosure of retirement plans, there were still a few curious twists and turns to be followed before the case would reach a final conclusion. Defense attorneys had made fifty motions for mistrial during the proceedings. All were denied, but the motions and denials could provide diverse and fertile material for possible appeals.

One of their first moves was to appeal his conviction, on grounds that jurors had improperly consulted a pocket dictionary during deliberations. In a written motion filed by Greene prior to sentencing, the defense argued that the jury had committed a reversible error by looking up the word *reasonable* during deliberations. That act might have been responsible for changing the jury's original vote from eight-to-four favoring a not-guilty finding, to the final verdict of guilty of murder in the first degree, the defense lawyers contended.

The forewoman and another panelist had told reporters that the panel was grappling with the exact meaning of the judge's charge to the jury that to convict the defendant, they must believe him to be guilty beyond a "reasonable doubt." Once they agreed that *reasonable* was defined as *logical,* they quickly reached their verdict. The jurors said they used the dictionary to look up several legal terms, an act that the defense claimed was improper and prejudicial.

Surprisingly, Ms. Lasch filed court papers indicating she agreed with the defense that Doutre was entitled to a new trial. She said that she and her colleagues had decided that they couldn't win an appeal, and that it would be better to retry the case quickly rather than wait a couple of years. She asked the judge to reschedule Doutre's trial so that he could be tried at the same time as his codefendant, Savage.

But Doutre's lawyers responded to the assistant state attorney's flabbergasting stand by indicating they were suspicious of their unexpected ally's motive. Defense attorneys accused the prosecution of supporting the new trial bid because they wanted another crack at winning the death penalty for Doutre. The prosecution was accused of trying to use the maneuver by Doutre's lawyers to bushwhack their client. Ms. Lasch denied that was her motive.

After studying depositions from the jurors, Judge Harper ruled against the motion. None of the jurors indicated in the statements that the dictionary had any effect on the verdict. The judge remarked that another trial would make a mockery of justice, and said he had found no evidence that use of the dictionary had influenced the jury's verdict. ''The error was harmless beyond a reasonable doubt, considering the overwhelming proof of his guilt,'' the judge wrote.

Even if Judge Harper's decision was later reversed in higher courts, he would not be presiding at a new trial. He planned to retire on June 30, in about four weeks, and was looking forward to returning to Pensacola to stay. After the sentencing he remarked, ''That severs the umbilical cord I have with this case. But I'll remember this case until my dying day.''

Nearly two years after Judge Harper's ruling on the motion to overturn the conviction, the First District Court of Appeal in Tallahassee upheld his decision.

Chapter 11

A Desperate Man

While preparing to wait out Judge Harper's sentencing decision, authorities began making plans to transfer Spearman as soon as possible into the Florida state correctional system, where he would spend the rest of his life. Roth requested the move, explaining that living conditions for his client would be better in a state prison than in the Palm Beach County lockup.

Before the transfer from the jail, Spearman consented to two interviews with reporters for the *Palm Beach Post* and the *Miami Herald*. As he talked and smoked in the bare interview room, he continued to insist that he loved his wife very much and was innocent of involvement in her murder. And he moaned that even if he escaped the death penalty, his life was over because he would never be able to serve twenty-five years behind bars.

He was outspokenly bitter and blamed just about everybody but himself for his conviction. He castigated the media, police, the sheriff, prosecutor, and what he asserted were the political ambitions of Palm Beach County State Attorney David Bludworth. He even claimed that his own wealth had worked against him, disclosing that he had spent four hundred thousand dollars on his defense. He said that the multimillion-dollar fortune that he accumulated before and after his wife's death was gone.

Actually, much of the wealth was tied up in claims by his mother-in-law against her slain daughter's estate. Although Anita's husband was named as the principal beneficiary in her will, his conviction in her murder had made the document invalid. Florida state statutes stipulated that anyone who unlawfully and intentionally killed someone could not benefit under the victim's will.

Assistant State Attorney Moira Lasch had even intruded into the money scramble by filing a motion asking the court to make him repay $33,876 to the taxpayers for money the prosecution spent to help put him in prison. Expenses the prosecutor wanted charged to the disgraced and imprisoned millionaire included everything from $22,310 for airfare and motel bills for witnesses, to $30 paid to a babysitter for Doutre's mother-in-law.

The hearing on the matter before Judge Harper in Palm Beach County Circuit Court brought out several other interesting tidbits of information about the convicted killer's financial affairs and dealings. Timothy Whalen, the lawyer who handled the sale of Spearman's boatyard, testified at the hearing that his client cleared about $1.13 million from the transaction. But a stipulation included in the closing agreement set aside $150,000 for Roth, and another $30,000 payment to Robert Marshall, Spearman's civil attorney.

Roth didn't disclose in the court hearing whether the

$150,000 represented total payment for his fee and expenses. But when Harper remarked that he presumed the money wasn't a charitable contribution, the lawyer good-naturedly replied, "I'll stipulate to that, Your Honor."

More interesting, perhaps, Gene Fenno, a close friend of the imprisoned man, testified that approximately $900,000 had been transferred from Spearman to his ex-wife, Beverly. Fenno claimed that his friend only had about $8,000 left from his former riches.

Although the motion to force Spearman to help pay for his own prosecution was based on firm legal grounds, it was extremely unusual. Prosecutors weren't known for attempting to recover trial expenses from convicted defendants. More often, defendants who were found not guilty or otherwise cleared of charges sought to recover their legal expenses from the state. Judge Harper took the request under advisement and said he would rule on it when he pronounced sentence.

And there were new pressures on the judge to backtrack on his stated reluctance to quickly sentence Spearman. The Florida Department of Corrections notified him that the convicted wife killer wouldn't be accepted as a prisoner until he was sentenced.

Spearman had been an active outdoorsman all his life, but there was little to keep him busy as he waited out the judge's sentencing decision at the jail. He talked about his troubles with loyal friends who visited, conferred with his lawyers, and occasionally read. But he wasn't a chess or checkers player. And he didn't watch much television. He said it rotted the mind. Most of the time he slept—or spent his time quietly examining and turning over his problems in his mind.

A few weeks into the new year, Judge Harper relented and agreed to sentence Spearman on all charges. Doutre had been convicted, but was still awaiting sentencing. And Savage wasn't expected to be put on trial in the Palm Beach Gardens slaying until July. The judge wanted to sentence Spearman before retiring from the bench in June.

Early in April in a Palm Beach County Circuit Courtroom jam-packed with lawyers, courthouse employes, investigators, journalists, and friends of the victim and her killer, Judge Harper ordered Spearman to serve a life prison sentence with no parole for at least twenty-five years, on the first-degree murder charge. He tacked on another total twenty-year term on the lesser charges of solicitation for murder, and murder conspiracy, to be served after the first-degree murder sentence was completed.

In total, Spearman's sentence was ten years less than Doutre would receive a couple of weeks later from the same judge, for his role in the same slaying. But there was no question that the onetime respected businessman was doomed to live out the rest of his life behind bars, even though the sentence permitted him to die a natural death. Spearman had already been in jail a few days more than a year.

The decision hadn't been easy for Judge Harper. He had seen too many ruthless killers, and the shocked and grieving relatives of too many victims, walk through his courtroom during his career on the bench. In a seven-page written statement, Harper made it clear that it wasn't a decision that he was completely at ease with. He hadn't spared the convicted killer because of sympathy for him.

"Out of his financial greed, he became a monster whose bestiality is utterly revolting in a law-abiding society,'' the judge declared. Judge Harper said he wanted to be certain that Spearman never walked the streets as a free man again.

The judge also took the opportunity to settle the question of billing Spearman for his own prosecution. He ordered him to pay $22,569 in court costs, to include some of the expenses listed by the prosecutor. He rejected another $6,000 bill the prosecution had added up for travel expenses.

Spearman's former wife, Beverly, whom court testimony indicated had received nearly $1 million of his money, watched the proceedings from the spectator section. Spearman had also paid his attorney fees, and given another $125,000 to his ailing mother. And Anita's seventy-three-year-old mother had finally accepted $1.2 million in an out-of-court settlement that avoided a lengthy probate battle. It would be almost a year before the slander suit filed by Spearman's former neighbor, Peter Fisher, would be settled in the complainant's favor. The court-ordered award would add another $110,000 claim against him, although few people expected the money to be paid. The convicted wife killer was no longer a rich man.

Manacled and dressed in his dark blue jail jumpsuit, Spearman stood quietly by his squad of attorneys as the sentencing order was read. Roth patted him reassuringly on the shoulder. There was also a new face among the defense lawyers, Jeffery Smith, who would be handling Spearman's appeals and had already filed a motion for a new trial. Judge Harper advised the Fort Lauderdale lawyer that he had stricken the motion, which he criticized as poorly prepared.

On October 1 Smith filed a similar motion for review of his client's conviction, claiming that startling new

evidence had been uncovered that could prove Spearman was innocent. The lawyer asserted that police and
prosecutors had known about the evidence but withheld
it from the defense before and during the trial.

According to claims in the eight-page document, the
new evidence included a statement from Doutre that
supported Spearman's claims that Savage was in the
drug business; accusations that Springer may have attempted to conceal a possible information source; and
mistakes or deliberate lies in testimony about the locks
on the garage door of the Spearman house.

Spearman was still in the Palm Beach County Correctional Center when authorities heard rumors through
the institution grapevine that the convicted wife killer
had put contracts out to "hit" Sheriff Wille and Ms.
Lasch. The informant said he wasn't sure if the hit was
for murders, or if Spearman wanted to get back at the
sheriff and the prosecutor in some other way. But according to the story, he had already sent seven thousand
dollars to a friend in Palm Beach.

Rent-A-Wreck squad detectives quickly opened an
investigation into the unsettling report and confirmed
that Spearman did indeed have seven thousand dollars
delivered to his friend. But the jailed wife killer insisted
that the money was intended as extortion payoffs to buy
protection from other violent inmates who had threatened him. He explained that he sent the cash to his
chum so that it could be forwarded to relatives or friends
of the inmate he was afraid of. The Palm Beach County
Jail was a nasty, dangerous place, he said.

Spearman's friend confirmed that he had received the
money and passed it on to a West Palm Beach woman
who was a stranger to him. And he said that his im-

prisoned pal told him that it was for protection inside the jail.

As soon as Spearman told corrections officers and other investigators the story about the reputed threats to his safety, he was transferred to another area of the jail. No charges were filed against anyone in the incident.

By the time the new motion was filed, Spearman had long ago been moved from the Palm Beach County Jail across the state to the Zephyrhills Correctional Center a few miles northeast of the Tampa–Saint Petersburg metropolitan sprawl on Florida's Gulf coast. Spearman kept busy in prison: hiring and firing lawyers as his efforts to get out became increasingly desperate; and threatening to wreak a terrible revenge against the people whom he blamed most for putting him inside the institution walls. He was still mad at reporters, police, and prosecutors. Lead prosecutor Moira Lasch was at the top of his hate list.

Spearman wasn't much different from most of the other convicts he was locked up with. He complained about the food; he talked about being railroaded for a crime he didn't commit; he talked about getting out; and he got into minor troubles. Once he was written up for a violation of prison rules for possession of negotiables. Prison regulations prohibited inmates from accumulating excessive amounts of cash or anything else, such as cigarettes, coffee, or candy, that could be used for barter. Thirty days of good-behavior time was deducted from his personal file for the violation.

But for the most part he did nothing to attract the special attention of his fellow inmates, guards, or corrections officials. Prison authorities took advantage of his background in the newspaper composing room, and assigned him to work in the institution's graphics shop. It helped keep him busy.

Then on April 27, 1988—two years after his arrest, and one year after his sentencing for engineering the murder of his wife—Spearman shouldered his way back onto newspaper headlines and television news reports. Florida Department of Law Enforcement officers and state correctional authorities revealed that he had been caught plotting a daring and melodramatic escape from the maximum-security Florida prison in a stolen helicopter.

He was also charged with conniving to have the assistant state attorney who had headed his successful prosecution murdered. He planned to pay hired guns to carry out the hit on Ms. Lasch. Spearman was no courtroom spitter, and he wouldn't be satisfied with insulting his nemesis by calling her "Miss Pointy Face." He wanted the prosecutor dead.

Spearman's two-pronged Machiavellian scheme to snatch back his freedom and violently avenge himself crumbled when the two fliers he was counting on to lead his escape bid revealed that they were undercover lawmen. He had agreed to pay $54,700 to the pilots for lifting him out of the prison yard in a stolen helicopter and flying him to an isolated nearby airstrip. There, he planned to complete his escape by personally piloting a stolen airplane to an undisclosed location far from the grim prison fortress at Zephyrhills. But his latest criminal mercenaries weren't criminals at all. They were working for the Florida Department of Law Enforcement. They were state cops.

Prison snitches reportedly passed the word to correctional authorities in March that Spearman was planning an elaborate escape attempt. Subsequently he produced a sophisticated color-coded map of the prison grounds with the landing site for the helicopter marked with an X, and passed the document on to the undercover officers. The map was produced in the prison graphics shop where he worked.

Spearman's outrageous escape plan had been carefully thought out and well crafted, and he was specific about the equipment he wanted to acquire to carry the caper off successfully. He told the men he believed to be his paid confederates that he wanted two machine guns and four hand grenades aboard the hijacked helicopter when it set down to make the dangerous pickup in the prison compound. The hand grenades weren't for the prison break. He planned to use them to even the score with the prosecutor who had put him behind bars for life.

He named a specific type of helicopter he wanted used because it was especially respected for its easy close-quarter maneuverability. He specified that the guns should be fully automatic M-16s, and he wanted the waiting airplane to be a Cessna or closely similar two-engine craft.

Spearman pinpointed three different dates for the breakout, but whichever day was chosen, the time would be the same—6:30 in the morning, when the institution was in the midst of breakfast preparations, and staff and inmates were just rousing themselves to begin the day's activities. He was waiting at the pickup site at 6:30 A.M. on the second of the three days he had stipulated, when corrections officers stepped in and informed him that they knew about his escape plot. When the inmate was searched, officers found $450, including four crisp, new hundred-dollar bills, in his pockets.

Prison informers revealed that Spearman had devised

an equally violent backup plan to put into action in case the men necessary to carry off the helicopter scheme couldn't be recruited. The plan called for outside accomplices to steal a heavy truck, and ram it at high speed through two barriers of eight-foot-high chain-link fencing to make the daredevil rescue from the prison compound.

It was obvious that although Spearman may not have been a couch potato, he could script an exciting television action plot. The trouble was, his scripts weren't thought out for the television screen. The violence, the blood, and the derring-do were all planned for real life. And it might have worked if Spearman had somehow figured out how he could hire criminal adventurers he could trust. Contracting with the wrong hired guns was an old bugaboo that had gotten him into serious trouble before.

State police spokesmen were bluntly honest about the workability of the diabolical scheme. As fantastically imaginative as it may have appeared to be, it could have worked, they admitted. It was just the type of exciting and hazardous caper that armchair adventurers dreamed about and real-life daredevils ventured to try. And helicopter prison breaks were successfully carried out before—and after—the Spearman debacle.

One of the most dramatic airborne breakouts occurred in South Carolina in 1985, when a woman hijacked a helicopter at gunpoint and forced the pilot to land in the Perry Correctional Institution recreation yard and lift out three convicts. Joyce Mattox and the escapees, who included a convicted murderer, were recaptured three days later in southern Georgia.

And less than three months after Spearman's thwarted Rambo-style escape, another woman hijacked a helicopter and forced the pilot to pluck three prisoners, including her convict sweetheart, out of the Penitentiary of New Mexico near Santa Fe. More than one hundred convicts in the exercise yard scrambled for cover as the helicopter lifted off in a hail of gunfire from the exercise yard. Beverly Shoemaker and the escaped prisoners were rounded up after a hair-raising aerial chase and ground search. The helicopter pilot was found unharmed, chained to the controls.

Corrections authorities throughout the country knew about those escapes, and others that had been successfully carried off both in the United States and Mexico. Some prisons, in fact, were already installing helicopter traps to guard against airborne breakouts. At Leavenworth, the maximum-security federal prison in Kansas, a ten-foot-high network of wires was stretched over the baseball and football fields and an oval running track in 1986. Similar security measures were soon installed at fourteen other federal prisons. Guards referred to the wiring system simply as their chopper stoppers.

Prosecutor Lasch wasn't an expert on helicopter breakouts, or chopper stoppers. And she didn't learn the full extent of her danger and other details of the shocking escape plot until she huddled with FDLE agents. The agents advised her that the imprisoned wife killer had worked out a complicated scheme to have hand grenades or other explosives planted in her car. He had also been trying from inside the prison to stockpile other weapons. And the concerned lawmen cautioned that he would continue to be a threat to her as long as he was alive and had the money to pay other people to do his dirty work. It was chilling information.

Spearman obviously wasn't as financially strapped as he had claimed to be. Or at least he was behaving as if there were money available that someone had squirreled away for him. Even after his imprisonment in a maximum-security institution, he was still promising big money for murder.

A few days before the escape plot was publicly revealed, Spearman was quietly transferred about twenty-five miles east from Zephyrhills to the nearby Polk County Correctional Institution in rural Polk City. He was locked up in solitary confinement in a maximum-security cellblock. His cramped single cell was furnished with only a bunk that was locked solidly to the floor, a sink, and a toilet without a lid or its own flushing mechanism. Spearman was put under extremely close scrutiny, and guards checked on him every fifteen minutes. The spartan cells provided maximum surveillance and control, and were used only for prisoners who were violent or considered to be serious escape risks.

He was in the Polk County lockup when officials filed formal charges against him of attempted escape, introduction of contraband into a correctional institution, attempting to place an explosive device with intent to cause bodily harm, and attempted possession of machine guns. All the charges were linked to his scheme to break out of Zephyrhills.

State police investigators also announced that they were looking for a Fort Lauderdale building contractor, Frederick Douglas Laurent, Jr., whom they identified as Spearman's outside contact for the escape plan. He was accused of passing the map showing the prison yard landing site, and a $4,700 cashier's check, to the undercover agents as a down payment for joining in the scheme. The thirty-seven-year-old Laurent was Spear-

man's stepson. Beverly ''Brandy'' Laurent Spearman
was his mother.

The undercover agents had demanded more money
up front during telephone negotiations with Spearman,
but he balked. He complained that he had been ripped
off by hired guns before. He wouldn't budge, even after
they left him waiting at the contact point in the compound, then told him that they hadn't flown in because
he still owed them fifty thousand dollars on the contract.

Yet, even with the collapse of his diabolical escape
and revenge scheme, Spearman still hadn't exhausted
his evil magician's bag of dirty tricks. He had proven
that he was a strong, ruthlessly determined man who
would do anything to get his way. On the last day of
April, he committed suicide. He was sixty years old,
and had spent the last twenty-four months of his life in
jails and prison.

A jail trusty who was preparing to give Spearman his
lunch discovered him hanging by a bed sheet at 11:20
on Saturday morning. One end of the sheet was tied to
the bars at the top of the cell. The other end was looped
in a tight noose around his neck. Spearman had spent
enough years of his life on tugboats, fishing skiffs, and
other small ocean craft to know how to tie a knot that
would do the job. Guards summoned by the other inmate immediately slashed through the sheet with knives
and cut Spearman down, but efforts to revive him were
unsuccessful. He had carried out the death penalty that
the Palm Beach County murder jury had been too com-
passionate to inflict.

Stunned prison officials reported that the convict had
not done anything previously to indicate that he was a
suicide risk. Nevertheless, spokesmen pointed out, a

guard had checked on him, and he was alive and well only fifteen minutes before the trusty discovered him hanging from the bars.

News of Spearman's final act was greeted with shock, sadness, and relief by the people who had known him, and who had intimate involvement with the investigation and prosecution of the sensational murder case. Some saw his suicide as a last act of defiance, an insolent thumbing of the nose at the law and society that he had sought to bend and manipulate. Others considered it to be a pathetic act of desperation by a broken man who no longer had hope.

Moira Lasch, who, along with her coprosecutor St. James, had fought hardest to send Spearman to death row for the murder of his wife, was relieved. She said Spearman had an obsession about killing her, and had been putting together personal information about her. She told one reporter that Spearman had ''that soldier-of-fortune mentality.''

Spearman's former in-laws in South Carolina were also clearly relieved. Anita's younger sister, Nancy Jones, said family members worried that he might harm them because of anger over the settlement of his murdered wife's estate.

Judge Harper said he was relieved for the prosecutor, because of the threats to her life. He added that although he realized Spearman was dangerous to others, he was surprised that he would deliberately harm himself.

Roth, who had visited with him at Zephyrhills only two months earlier, remarked that there had been nothing about his client to suggest that he was suicidal. The lawyer said that his entire experience with Spearman seemed more fictional than real.

Fenno, who had known Spearman since they worked together in the composing room at the *Post-Times* nearly thirty years earlier, was saddened. He observed that when he had visited at Zephyrhills the previous summer, his old friend was having trouble coping with prison life. And he was talking about getting out because he couldn't stand being locked up.

But Fenno also had a surprise to spring. On the Monday morning after his chum's death, the sixty-two-year-old West Palm Beach retired newspaper employee opened a safety-deposit box and removed a will and a sealed envelope. The envelope contained a copy of a letter written by Spearman to his loyal friend. It was postmarked January 10, 1987, and Spearman had scribbled instructions on the front that it was not to be opened until after his death. Fenno took the letter and the will to his lawyer to have them read.

Later, he told reporters that he cried while the letter was read. And he defended his old friend, who he continued to believe had been unjustly convicted after running afoul of would-be drug smugglers during the tugboat negotiations. Spearman alluded in his last testament to his reputed innocence.

Spearman asked in the letter that Fenno see to it that he was cremated as soon as possible, and his ashes dropped into the Gulf Stream. He suggested that he would appreciate it if his ashes could be taken out into the ocean aboard the *Equalizer*. Spearman stressed that he didn't want to be embalmed or to have an autopsy on his body.

Spearman also expressed deep concern for his mother and said that she and Fenno were the sole beneficiaries in his will. He asked his friend to reassure the old woman that her son loved her and would be waiting for her in the hereafter. Spearman said he read the Bible, believed in God and reincarnation, and if he was able to, he would pass along a sign to Fenno to prove that the soul continues to exist.

The quixotic man whose life of love and accomplishment had crumbled to ashes after he was accused of killing his wife also wrote that he was excited at the thought of dying because it meant that he would be with Anita again. He talked of how much he missed her.

Fenno may have sincerely wished to follow his late chum's wishes to the letter, but some of the requests were impossible to comply with because of factors out of his control. He couldn't immediately claim the body because pathologists with the Polk County Medical Examiner's Office had taken it to perform an autopsy on. And Fenno was quoted in the *Post* as saying he wouldn't be using the *Equalizer* to transport Spearman's ashes out to the Gulf Stream.

As generous as Spearman's intentions may or may not have been in his last bequest, it didn't appear there would be much, if any, money left for Fenno when all the financial affairs were settled. Blind and suffering from Alzheimer's disease, Spearman's eighty-five-year-old mother was in a Lake Park nursing home, and it seemed likely that any funds that might be remaining in his estate would be needed for her care.

Spearman's will provided a $125,000 trust fund to care for his mother, with any money that might remain after her death to go to Fenno. The document also stipulated that Fenno was to receive $50,000 in cash, and Spearman's personal belongings. Contrary to a statement in the letter written by Spearman and dated October 16 identifying his mother and Fenno as sole beneficiaries of his estate, the will also stipulated that

$50,000 was to be given to another longtime male friend who lived in Jupiter and had testified for him as a character witness.

But stipulating bequests on paper can be easier than producing the money. Inspection of Spearman's financial status at the time of his death indicated that he didn't have much money left. The whole question of how his fortune had so rapidly dwindled, even in the face of his backbreaking legal expenses, was an enigma that intrigued and challenged authorities. But even the most cursory glance at his manipulations of his money and property showed that he had worked hard to liquidate his assets, both before and after his trial.

In his will, Spearman left his prized Chevrolet Blazer to a man he referred to as "Doug." Police believed that Doug was Frederick Douglas Laurent, the former stepson accused as an outside accomplice in his prison break scheme.

Accompanied by a Fort Lauderdale attorney, Laurent surrendered to law enforcement officers in Dade City a few weeks after his former stepfather's suicide. He was charged with involvement in the conspiracy to help Spearman in the prison break scheme and held in the Pasco County Jail there under five hundred thousand dollars bail. A few days later, bail was reduced to one hundred thousand dollars, and Laurent was released.

Several months later, a Pasco circuit court judge accepted a plea of no contest, and ordered Laurent placed on one year of probation.

Chapter 12

Trial of a Murder Broker

It was two down and one to go for Moira Lasch and Kerry St. James. Only the accused murder broker himself, Richard "Doc" Savage, remained to go on trial—and he may have been as anxious as anyone to get the ordeal over with.

His life in county jails hadn't been easy. State and federal prisons are grim enough, but convicts at least have an idea what their future holds for them. They have their own permanent cells, develop friendships, and have the security of unbroken routine—some even have jobs—that can ease the burden of doing time.

But city and county jails, no matter how assiduously the corrections staff may struggle to maintain control and enforce regulations, can be sheer bedlam. Lunatic ax killers, homosexual rapists, drug dealers, and swaggering leaders of ruthless street gangs are jammed in uneasy proximity with car thieves, drunks, and runaway parents in numbers that almost always exceed the intended limits. The young and the old, the healthy and the infirm, the insane and the inhumane, exist side by side.

Prisoners cheat one another, threaten one another, rape one another, and beat one another. And the more crowded jails become, the more difficult it is for guards to prevent violence. On the day Richard Savage was beaten up, the Palm Beach County Correctional Center was averaging about 50 percent more in its daily population count than it was built to accommodate. And jailers were recording an average of more than two fights between inmates every day.

No one in jail fights by Marquess of Queensberry rules. Jail and prison inmates fight to cripple, maim, or kill. Fights among prisoners can lead to anything from a fist in the face to broken arms, legs, and ribs, or a piece of metal bedspring sharpened into a lethal jailhouse shiv shoved into an eyeball or a kidney. Prisoners fight over sex, gang membership, cigarettes, canteen rights, food trays, choices of bunks, bed sheets, telephones, old disagreements inside and outside the walls, perceived insults, or simply to establish dominance. Like a jungle animal, each prisoner quickly acquires his own place in the jailhouse pecking order.

Prison bullies typically pick on the weak, sexually vulnerable, the racially outnumbered, loners unaligned with gangs—and former law enforcement or correctional officers, or inmates locked up for especially celebrated crimes. Savage had been both a cop and a prison guard. He knew the dangers of his fellow inmates learning about his background. When he was jailed in Athens he pleaded to authorities to keep his secret. And when he was transferred to the Palm Beach Correctional Center to await trial in the Spearman killing, he also moved among his fellow prisoners as just another face.

Then ABC Television's popular news magazine show

"20/20" featured Savage and the activities of his klutzy killer gang on a segment of the weekly Thursday evening show titled: "Soldiers of Misfortune: Murder and Mayhem." Producers and camera teams had done a good job. They filmed portions of Spearman's trial; they interviewed police, lawyers, gang members, accused clients, the publisher of *SOF* magazine, and people who escaped assassination attempts.

Dana Free told an interviewer on the show that even though he escaped two murder attempts, the affair had literally destroyed his life. He learned a lot about fear. Norwood recounted the grenade bombing of his girlfriend's car, and his mad struggle for life when he was attacked by Buckley and DeLuca.

Buckley was especially apologetic and distraught. "I'm never really going to be able to live this down," he groaned. The gun-for-hire gang member said he was afraid that he would never be trusted again.

Lieutenant Swearingen, one of the University of Arkansas police officers who arrested Jackson, said it had been hard for him to believe that ads like Savage's could be run in magazines bought off any newsstand shelf. And interviewer Tom Jarriel claimed authorities had identified seven gangs like Savage's, and that they had been tied to seventy-five or so crimes around the country. It was a sobering thought. But that wasn't what got Savage in trouble with his fellow inmates. Initially it wasn't even his background as a police officer and prison guard. Only Jackson was identified on the "20/20" presentation as a former law enforcement officer.

There is a top gun attitude in jails and prisons, and convict toughs can earn respect from their peers by beating up on another inmate who is especially famous or notorious. Savage became instantly famous when crimes he was accused of engineering were featured on the national television show. His troubles were magnified when word was quickly passed through the jailhouse grapevine by inmates who suddenly recalled reading or hearing that he was also a former policeman and prison guard.

Early Friday morning, a few hours after broadcast of the Thursday night show, Savage was found in his bunk during a routine bed check, with his face bloody and swollen. He had been so brutally beaten that he couldn't get up. The beaten inmate was transported to Humana Hospital in West Palm Beach by ambulance and admitted for treatment of severe bruises and lacerations. Although painful, his injuries were not critical, and hospital spokesmen reported shortly after he was admitted that he was in stable condition.

Savage telephoned Ernest DePascale, his lawyer in Athens, from the hospital and told him about the beating. He pleaded for protection. But Sheriff Wille's corrections officers had already made new plans to protect their notorious prisoner. Guards kept the accused contract murder ringleader under close observation at the hospital until he was moved back to the jail, where he was locked in a special isolation cell.

Detectives with the Sheriff's Department Internal Affairs Division immediately opened an investigation into the beating. They learned that Savage had watched the "Soldiers of Misfortune" show in a day room, and as soon as the program was over, one or more of his fellow inmates had turned on him. A few days after the incident, a sullen nineteen-year-old inmate was charged with committing a felony, battery within a jail, for the assault on Savage. The husky youth said he punched the gang leader in the face.

Savage had more to worry about, however, than a mere beating, no matter how painful his injuries were. In a period of barely twenty-four hours before the beating, he and several of his accused fellow gang members were named on two separate federal grand jury indictments in Houston and in Fort Smith, Arkansas. The Houston indictments were tied to the bungled hand grenade attack on the home of Free's ex-wife and son; and the Arkansas indictment was linked to the murder attempts on Norwood.

When a newspaper reporter asked Norwood what he thought of Savage's beating, the gang leader's onetime murder target replied that he had only gotten a taste of what he deserved. The former policeman and prison guard turned law student said he wasn't surprised that Savage had become the target of street justice from other inmates.

The "20/20" program was later cited by Doutre's defense in the ultimately successful plea to move his trial out of West Palm Beach County because of pervasive publicity.

Widespread publicity was also cited by Savage's defense attorneys in their plea to move their client's trial on charges of first-degree murder, and conspiracy to commit first-degree murder, for the slaying of Mrs. Spearman outside the county. But the television show wasn't a significant factor. The lawyers focused on the local publicity generated by Robert Spearman's sensational trial the previous year, which they contended would make it impossible to select a fair and impartial jury from among local citizens.

But Palm Beach County Circuit Court Judge Thomas E. Sholts, who had been selected to preside at Savage's trial, instructed lawyers for both sides to try. There was one other new face among the leading court officers at the trial, in addition to Savage himself, Judge Sholts, and Birch. Attorney Brad Moores had been appointed to work as co-defense counsel.

One thing was exactly the same, however: The prosecutors announced that they were seeking the death penalty. Ironically, Savage had told a newspaper reporter in an Athens, Georgia, jailhouse interview that whoever murdered Anita Spearman should die in the electric chair.

The jury selection process for what was expected to be a three-week trial was predictably difficult and slow. Approximately two weeks after the first prospective jurors were questioned, a twelve-member panel and two alternates were seated.

During opening statements on a Tuesday morning in early August 1987, the prosecution repeated much of the same information called on in the previous two trials, although it was tailored to fit the charges against the new defendant.

Neatly dressed in a new pinstripe suit with a dark tie speckled with white, Savage listened and watched intently as Ms. Lasch described him and his hirelings as greedy, ruthless people who would do anything for a price. And she told the jury that he accepted a murder contract on Mrs. Spearman when her husband contacted him after reading a classified ad in *SOF* magazine. Subsequently, she said, Savage became a murder broker and dispatched Doutre to do the dirty work.

Birch agreed with many of the things the prosecutor accused his client of. He also conceded that evidence would show Savage wasn't a nice person. "He did run the ad, he did run the topless bar, he did steal twenty

thousand dollars, but he did not kill Anita Spearman,''
the bearded, bespectacled lawyer declared.

Instead, Birch said, Savage was no more than a con
man. Savage never intended for Mrs. Spearman to die,
but only planned to bilk her husband out of his money.
Then Doutre cut his own deal with Spearman and carried out the contract hit, the lawyer asserted.

Again the prosecution hauled out most of the same
familiar evidence and called many of the same witnesses featured at the earlier trials of Savage's accused
coconspirators in the Palm Beach Gardens slaying.
Telephone records, the Delta Airline ticket Spearman
had bought for the defendant, and the blown-up copy
of Savage's gun-for-hire ad in the *SOF* classified pages
were introduced as evidence. And the prosecutors called
on Emert, the confessed bagman in the contract murder, to testify once more as their star witness.

Although Emert's story was similar to the accounts
he had given before, Birch hit hard at his credibility
and repeatedly pointed out differences in his previous
testimony and other statements he had made earlier.
The big, bearded man on the witness stand appeared
unfazed. He had been through scornful cross-
examinations before.

Sergeant Johnson was also back in town, and for the
final time in court, recounted his arrest of Doutre on
the Sunday morning after Mrs. Spearman's bludgeon
murder. His testimony was used to introduce the shotgun and other evidence as prosecution exhibits. After
completing his testimony and walking off the stand,
Johnson and a law enforcement pal from the BATF office in Knoxville hurried from the courthouse to do
some deep-sea fishing. The Tennessee-based lawmen
had a boat waiting for them.

Prosecutors were three days into testimony before they produced the first new witness. The appearance on the stand of Brian Carney, a handwriting expert and former BATF agent, led to sharp exchanges between opposing attorneys. They argued over the state of Savage's mind when he provided samples of his penmanship to State Attorney's Office investigators, and its relevance to the case. Judge Sholts allowed the testimony, but cautioned jurors that distortions in handwriting samples taken after a defendant has been placed in custody should not be perceived as reflecting feelings of guilt.

Carney testified that he had examined and compared handwriting provided with a personal history when Savage had applied for a liquor license, and samples taken after the defendant's arrest. He said distortions in the writing pattern Savage provided to the state attorney indicated he was deliberately trying to disguise his penmanship.

In a curious twist to the labyrinthian homicide case, Debra Mattingly, who was a key witness for the state in the successful prosecution of Spearman and Doutre, turned up at the Savage trial on the side of the defense. And she provided virtually the same testimony that she had given at the earlier two proceedings.

Savage's chunky longtime live-in girlfriend said that Spearman and Doutre made their own deal that led to the horrendous bludgeon murder. Later in her testimony, she said that Savage advertised in *SOF* because he wanted jobs as a courier or bodyguard to make extra money. When readers began telephoning with offers to pay him to kill, he decided to bilk them out of their money by agreeing to their murder-for-hire schemes, then welching on the contracts, she said.

Before the witness was called to the stand, Ms. Lasch attempted to block some areas of the testimony that would be harmful to her case. The story told by Ms. Mattingly was damnably incriminating to the defendants during both the earlier trials. But the same story, repeated in its entirety with no alterations, portrayed the current defendant as a confidence man, not a killer.

"The rules of the game change when there's a severance of the defense," the lead prosecutor argued. But the judge permitted the witness to testify, without the restrictions.

Ms. Lasch struck next at the credibility of the woman who had once been such an effective prosecution witness, pointing out that Ms. Mattingly lived with the defendant for eight years.

"I care about what happens to him, but I'm not in love with him," the witness said.

The prosecutor snapped back that Ms. Mattingly had testified the previous summer that she was, indeed, still in love with Savage.

"That was a year and a half ago," Ms. Mattingly replied.

The witness's temper briefly flared as the assistant state attorney stubbornly continued her attack on her credibility, while pointing to the defendant's guilt. During one rancorous exchange, Ms. Mattingly declared: "You can convict him of racketeering all day long, but you can't convict him of a conspiracy or a murder he had nothing to do with."

Testimony was moving uncommonly fast—much more rapidly than questioning of prospective jurors—and forty-four witnesses appeared during the first three days. Another twenty-four were called to the stand during the next four days, before testimony was concluded. Only six of the witnesses were called by the defense.

Once more during summations, Ms. Lasch dragged out the grisly color blowups of the victim's bloodied and broken skull to show to a jury. With the horrendous photograph propped accusingly on an easel in front of them, she told the jury that greed was the motive for Mrs. Spearman's murder. "Everyone involved had a price for this crime," she said. Calling Savage and Spearman "cowards," she told the jury that they plotted an innocent woman's death for the same reason: money.

She pointed out that Savage had a long relationship with Doutre, and not only paid the rent on his apartment, but provided him with a MAC-11 machine pistol as well as other guns. Investigators suspected the machine pistol may have been the weapon used to club the sick woman to death.

"Why all the firepower if it's just a con?" she asked.

Birch insisted, as he had from the beginning of the trial, that his client had never intended for the woman to be killed and that Doutre had acted on his own. He claimed Mrs. Spearman wasn't murdered when Doutre made his first trip to West Palm Beach with Emert because Savage had instructed them not to hurt her.

"We may not like Richard Savage and we may not like the scam he set up, but it was really a perfect con," the lawyer declared.

The defense lawyer also made a meal of the prosecution's troubles with their former key witness, Debra Mattingly, pointing to their attempt to limit her testimony. "How is it she can be telling the truth one time and not another?" he asked of the witness.

After receiving instructions from Judge Sholts, the

jury left the courtroom to begin its life-or-death deliberations. The ordeal for Ms. Lasch and St. James was
almost over, and the last of three trials was only hours
away from ending. The lead prosecutor's dentist husband, Alan Lasch, was in the spectator seats watching
the windup. The defendant's mother, Muriel Savage,
had also come to Palm Beach County for the last few
days of her son's trial and spent much of her time seated
quietly in the hallway outside the courtroom.

The jury deliberated two hours before the panelists
were sent to a West Palm Beach hotel to spend the
night. The next day they deliberated seven hours before
reaching a verdict. They found Savage guilty of second-
degree murder, and conspiracy to commit first-degree
murder.

The verdict was less than a total victory for the prosecution, but it was close enough. Ms. Lasch told reporters that she was satisfied with the jury's decision.
Birch was quoted as saying he felt there had been sufficient evidence to win an acquittal.

Savage was poker-faced. In May, a few months earlier, he had pleaded guilty in Arkansas to federal
charges of conspiracy and interstate travel to commit
murder for the attempts on Norwood's life and was sentenced to a twenty-five-year term in a federal prison.
And he was still facing serious charges in other states
that were likely to draw long prison sentences. There
were only so many years in prison that a thirty-eight-
year-old man could serve.

According to sentencing guidelines in the Florida
State Criminal Code, Savage could expect to receive
terms of from twelve to seventeen years for the crimes
he was convicted of. But the guidelines were only rec-

ommendations, and were not binding. Judge Sholts could exceed them if he wished.

The judge scheduled sentencing for September 2. After a few brief words with his lawyers, Savage was returned to the jail in handcuffs to await sentencing.

On September 2, less than two weeks after the jury verdict, Savage was sentenced to forty years in prison. The jarring sentence included a thirty-year term on the second-degree murder conviction, and another ten years for conspiracy. The judge specified that the sentences should be served consecutively. Savage would have to complete the longer sentence before beginning the ten-year term. However, the judge did say that Savage could serve his sentences in Florida and in the federal prison concurrently.

Explaining his stern justice, Judge Sholts pointed to the motive of greed, and said there was no reasonable excuse for the appalling crime. He talked of the cold-blooded and brutal nature of the murder, and of the victim's frail vulnerability.

"The severity of this sentence is necessary to protect the public. Richard Savage has shown no remorse, and rehabilitation is not possible," the jurist declared.

Nevertheless, Savage had drawn a slightly lighter sentence than his two major coconspirators in the murder of Mrs. Spearman. Judge Sholts took notice of that in his remarks, pointing out that Savage's second-degree murder conviction was a lesser offense than the first-degree murder convictions of his cohorts. The judge added that Savage was also "the least culpable of the three defendants."

Authorities were still waiting in line in several other states to prosecute Savage for crimes reputedly tied to his advertisements in the classified pages of *SOF*.

The attempts he had masterminded on Norwood's life in Arkansas had already saddled him with three stiff federal prison sentences. Following guilty pleas, U.S. district court Judge H. Franklin Waters ordered terms of five years for conspiring to commit murder; twenty-years for traveling across state lines with intent to commit murder; and ten years for attempting to intimidate a witness. Judge Waters ordered the last term to be served concurrently with the first two so that the total prison time under the three sentences would be twenty-five years. The judge ordered the harsh sentences even though Savage tried at the last minute to withdraw his guilty plea and change attorneys.

About a year after his conviction in West Palm Beach, he was transported to Houston, Texas, to face trial in U.S. district court there for his alleged role in the hand grenade bombing of the house in Pasadena.

Unfortunately, the timing for putting Savage on trial in Houston was awkward. One of the civil lawsuits filed against *SOF,* after contract killings or murder attempts were linked to the controversial ads in the magazine's back pages, was in the process of being settled amid widespread local publicity. And of the first sixty-six men and women called from the jury pool as potential jurors to hear Savage's trial, sixty-one said they had read or heard news accounts of the *SOF* civil trial.

Reluctantly, U.S. district court Judge James DeAnda agreed to a motion by Savage's court-appointed defense attorneys for a change of venue because of the publicity. He announced that he would move the trial to one of three cities, San Antonio, McAllen, or Brownsville, and ordered a three-week delay while he checked out the available facilities at each of the prospective sites.

Judge DeAnda said that he would preside. A few weeks later the trial was moved to Brownsville.

Brownsville is Texas's southernmost city and is the lower Rio Grande Valley's gateway to Mexico. Snuggled against the dirty gray waters of the Rio Grande, it is a twin city with Matamoros, a rowdy Mexican border town just across the river where gangs of machine-gun-toting desperados and fearless *pistoleros* shoot one another down in street-corner gunfights with about the same regularity that the sun sets at night. The crime gangs smuggle drugs, antiquities, exotic animals, guns, and people over the porous border into the United States, and the violence follows hand in hand.

The activities of an amateurish gang of murder-for-hire bumblers, who botched more killings than they carried out successfully, could go virtually without public notice among the heady violence of the rambunctious border towns. Few people there had heard of the *SOF* civil suit so recently settled in Houston. And fewer yet had any idea who Richard Savage was, or cared, when his trial opened on nine separate counts of violating federal laws by masterminding the gang's final murder attempt on Dana Free's life.

Authorities didn't take any chances with their prisoner, however, and he was handcuffed and secured with leg and body chains whenever he was moved between the Cameron County Jail in Brownsville and the courtroom. At least two guards were also with him during the moves. At one time during the court proceedings, eight deputy marshals were standing by inside the courtroom.

Assistant U.S. Attorney Scott Woodward advised the judge, before the first witness was called to the stand, that he had information the prisoner had planned to escape during his transfer from Houston to the Texas border town. Savage had reportedly planned to murder a deputy marshal if it was necessary to make good on his getaway scheme, he added.

Although the carefully guarded prisoner might have been a stranger to most residents of Texas's lower Rio Grande Valley, government prosecutors had rounded up an impressive rogues' gallery of witnesses who knew all about him. Jackson, Buckley, and Ms. Breeden had all agreed to testify against their former boss. In a plea agreement, Ms. Breeden had admitted her part in the hand grenade assault on the house in Pasadena, and Buckley had pleaded guilty to that attack as well as to attempting to kill Free by blowing up his car in Marietta. The young woman was serving three concurrent four-year sentences at the minimum-security federal prison at Lexington. Buckley would disclose under cross-examination that he was awaiting sentencing after pleading guilty in the Texas case and had agreed to testify in return for a recommendation for leniency from the prosecutor. The testimony of the three defectors made the outcome of the trial almost a foregone conclusion.

Jackson testified that after he placed his ad in *SOF* looking for assignments as a bodyguard, Savage contacted him and asked him to go to Georgia and wire hand grenades under Free's car. The witness claimed that he refused to help with the wiring in what was the bungling gang's second attempt to kill Free, and agreed only to act as a lookout. Nevertheless, Savage gave him two thousand dollars for his help, he said.

Ms. Breeden's testimony was equally incriminating as she described how she and Buckley accepted a murder assignment from Savage and subsequently tossed hand grenades into the Pasadena home of Free's former wife. The tomboyish witness added that she was never paid for the aborted murder attempt, and wasn't sure why she even agreed to take part in the scheme.

"I guess I was just stupid—I just went," she said. "It bothered me, and it still bothers me to this day."

Defense Attorney Michael Brown asked if she had thrown the grenade just "for the heck of it."

"I guess that's the way it looks now." She shrugged.

In Buckley's testimony, he retraced his part in the aborted murder attempts on Free's life, both in Georgia and in Pasadena. And he softly conceded that he had spent a few weeks in a mental institution when he was a teenager.

Lambeth testified briefly about his role in the murder schemes against Free. He had been sentenced about a year earlier by Judge DeAnda to a five-year prison term after pleading guilty to conspiring to illegally transport explosives used in the grenade attack in Pasadena.

At the time of Savage's Texas trial, Lambeth's longtime friend Mrs. Brado was already dead. She died of emphysema in the federal prison in Lexington, Kentucky, in October, shortly after sentencing to a five-year term after pleading guilty to buying the murder contract on her former boyfriend. At her sentencing, she told the judge that Free had broken his promise to invest her life savings, and she wanted to collect on the life insurance policy he had taken out to guarantee her money.

Free also testified, explaining that on October 24, 1984, at Mrs. Brado's insistence, he took out a half-million-dollar life insurance policy on himself and named her as his beneficiary. She was identified on the policy as his fiancé. The witness, who had moved back to Colorado, said they were business partners and had a brief romantic relationship. A few weeks after taking out the policy, he left Colorado for Georgia, where he began receiving telephone threats warning him that he was "a dead man," the building contractor added.

Concerned about opening the door to more testimony harmful to his client, Brown did not call any witnesses in Savage's defense. He later confided to reporters that he didn't want to give the prosecution an opportunity to bring up Savage's previous convictions or charges he was still facing in other states.

The Houston lawyer, however, conducted spirited cross-examinations of the prosecution witnesses, and he gave a rousing closing statement in a last-ditch effort on behalf of his client. He claimed that the trial was the biggest comedy of errors he had witnessed during his eleven years of law practice, and he hit hard at the credibility of the witnesses.

"There's no evidence other than testimony from murderers, bomb throwers, and nuts," he declared. "We don't send people to prison on the basis of those witnesses."

Assistant U.S. Attorneys Gary Cobe and Scott Woodward, who were the prosecutors, painted Savage as the depraved mastermind of the murder schemes and the man who sent the others out to kill. He was the pivotal man in a nationwide network of contract killers, they said.

"By the grace of God, Dana Free was not killed in any of these attempts," Woodward declared. "His life is a shambles, as you can imagine. He's scared to death, he has no home, he has no job."

The trial ended three days after it began. The jury deliberated only ninety minutes before returning a verdict finding Savage guilty of masterminding the aborted murder plot against Free. Judge DeAnda greeted the verdict by remarking that the evidence against the defendant was "overwhelming." Savage was returned to the Cameron County Jail in Brownsville in handcuffs and leg chains.

While awaiting sentencing, Savage filed a handwritten motion asking for a new trial, claiming that Brown had provided him with an ineffective defense. He criticized his court-appointed lawyer for refusing to call witnesses whom Savage wanted to testify in his defense.

Approximately six weeks later, Judge DeAnda ordered the maximum penalty, sentencing Savage to a total of forty years in federal prison. The stern jurist ordered that the sentence was to be served after Savage had completed the twenty-five-year prison term he was currently serving in Arkansas, and the forty-year term still facing him in Florida. Savage was represented by a Brownsville attorney at the sentencing hearing, and the judge appointed yet another lawyer to help him with the appeal.

The former Oklahoma policeman and Kentucky prison guard was nevertheless already looking at a staggering 105 years behind bars. The charges of conspiracy to murder filed against him in the plot against Lamey in Clarke County, Georgia, had been dropped. Clarke County Superior Court Judge James Barrow ordered the dismissal, while ruling on a defense motion demanding that Savage be given a speedy trial or released.

But charges were still pending against him elsewhere. The courts weren't yet through with the star-crossed strip club operator and hired-gun gang leader.

Barely nine months after Savage was sentenced in

Brownsville, a U.S. district court jury in Atlanta returned guilty verdicts against him and his former client, Bruce M. Gastwirth, in Braun's ambush murder. Describing Gastwirth's offense as a "dastardly crime," Judge Marvin S. Shoob ordered the Georgia businessman to serve a forty-year prison term on the charge of interstate commerce in commission of murder for hire. "This was not done on the spur of the moment. This was a cold, calculated attempt over a long period of time to kill someone," the jurist declared. "I cannot give you a modest sentence."

About a month earlier, Savage had been sentenced to another life prison term for his part in the murder plot. And Doutre was given a twenty-five-year term on charges of murder and of conspiracy to murder, for serving as the triggerman.

Earlier, in separate proceedings, Gastwirth was given a ten-year prison term after his conviction on charges of mail fraud and fraud by wire for his manipulations while he was an officer of Reliance Capital Services Corp.

Moore also pleaded guilty to his part in the conspiracy and was sentenced to a ten-year prison term.

Chapter 13

More Criminal Trials

Mary Alice Wolf had all the fighting spirit of a cornered vixen protecting her kits. And she needed every bit of her spunk and determination when her trial opened in U.S. district court in Lexington on charges that she paid a gang of professional killers to murder the wife of the man she loved.

The Louisville woman won an initial victory when U.S. district Judge Scott Reed granted her motion to be tried separately from the six codefendants indicted with her for reputedly taking part in the abortive schemes against the life of Victoria Morgan Brashear. It was mostly downhill for her after that.

Prosecutors had assembled an intimidating array of evidence and witnesses for their effort to win a conviction. And a recorded statement she had given to a federal agent in Louisville, confessing that after finding Savage's gun-for-hire ad in *SOF,* she paid him to have her love rival killed, was among the most damaging weapons in their legal arsenal.

During opening statements in the trial that, curiously, attracted few spectators who were not directly involved in the proceedings, Assistant U.S. Attorney Robert Trevey traced a tragic picture of a young woman whose vulgar obsession with her former sweetheart lured her into a twisted devil's pact with killers for pay.

As the plump, frizzy-haired defendant watched from the defense table, the woman she had reputedly targeted for murder, and the reluctant object of her twisted affection, each testified about the months of near nonstop harassment they endured, which even the courts seemed to have been unable to interrupt.

Mrs. Brashear told about how the troubles with her husband's jilted former sweetheart began before her marriage, then continued on after the wedding. She told of the false birth announcement placed in her hometown paper by Ms. Wolf. And she told about the strange man who came to her home in August 1985 after she and her husband moved to Lexington and tried to talk her into opening her glass door.

"I thought, maybe I'm being silly, but I won't open the door for nobody," she said. The witness, who was slim and pretty with lustrous shoulder-length blond hair, identified a photograph of Doutre as that man. He was one of Ms. Wolf's codefendants expected to be put on trial later by government prosecutors.

The witness said she didn't learn that someone was trying to have her killed until she was telephoned at work by an FBI agent who advised her that three attempts had been made on her life. The federal lawman warned that she might still be in danger.

Alan Brashear told the jury about the romance with Ms. Wolf that began when they met at summer camp and which he tried to end about two years later, after he met Ms. Brashear.

"I tried everything in the world to get out of the relationship, but she didn't want it to end," the witness declared. Despite his assertions that he wanted out, he said, she continued to telephone him about once a week, and also frequently showed up at his apartment.

An employee of the nearby Lexington–Blue Grass Army Depot, the balding young husband said that Mary Alice once told him that if he died, she would dig up his body to make sure he was dead.

Brashear also testified about Ms. Wolf hounding him with stories that she had given birth to his child, and that it had died during infancy. He never saw any evidence to prove that the story about the baby's birth and tragic death was legitimate. But he said that after he talked with a California lawyer, he considered the possibility that the tale could be true.

During cross-examination, defense attorney Steve Milner asked him why he thought there could have been some truth to the paternity claims.

"I'm human," the witness responded. "I'm not an animal." The court-appointed attorney wanted to know more.

"You were with her from time to time after 1981?" he asked. Brashear said that it was true—until the time of his marriage.

Brashear revealed that Ms. Wolf also talked to him about Savage, another of her codefendants in the murder conspiracy case. He quoted her as saying that she was seeing him, and that he was a hit man. Ms. Wolf cautioned him that federal agents would probably be talking to him soon about her new friend and his criminal profession, he said.

Joan Steele, advertising director for *SOF*, testified briefly, confirming that Savage had placed a gun-for-hire classified in the August 1985 issue of the magazine.

Buckley had already pleaded guilty to his part in the grotesque murder plot, and agreed to testify for the prosecution. At that time, he still hadn't been sentenced. But he was a key witness. And the defendant made it obvious that she didn't appreciate or agree with his testimony. As Buckley calmly related his version of the reputed murder conspiracy, she whispered with her attorney, squirmed and rocked in her chair, shook her head from side to side, and rolled her eyes with all the expressive disapproval of a roly-poly mime.

Buckley's testimony was devastating. He told of the effort by Savage and himself to divert Ms. Wolf from killing the schoolteacher, by suggesting they murder her crippled employer instead. But he said she was determined that Victoria Morgan Brashear should be the one to die.

And Buckley told of how he made two trips to the Kentucky horse country to murder the pretty blond schoolteacher, once with Doutre and once with DeLuca. Trevey asked why the defendant wanted Mrs. Brashear killed.

"If we killed Vicki, then Vicki's widower would turn to Mary Alice for consolation," he explained.

Debra Mattingly and Jackson also testified as prosecution witnesses. DeLuca, who had been apprehended in Hamilton, Ontario, and returned to the United States, was summoned as well. The federal charges against him had been dropped because he was still a juvenile at the time he was reputedly sent to Kentucky on the murder mission. He nevertheless invoked his constitutional rights against self incrimination and refused to testify. When Judge Reed asked him if his refusal had anything to do with fears for his own safety, he replied that it did.

But the most ruinously effective testimony against the defendant was her own—the perniciously damaging statement she made to BATF agent Ed Verkin while she was in jail in Louisville. The prosecution played it for the jury.

The panel of eight men and four women listened intently as Ms. Wolf's voice was heard on the tape telling the federal lawman she had paid five thousand dollars to have Mrs. Brashear murdered, then called off the killing because she was tormented by feelings of guilt.

She also charged in the appalling thirty-four-minute statement that her former sweetheart suggested the contract killing because he wanted to be together with her again, but wouldn't even consider divorce. Alan Brashear told her to look in *SOF* for a hit man, and she found Savage's ad in the classifieds, she claimed.

When Verkin asked why Brashear would want his wife killed, she replied that she believed that an insurance policy was a factor. "I honestly believe that the man still loved me," she added, however. Most of the jurors listened to the tape-recorded confession stonefaced. But one woman pressed a wrinkled hankie to her mouth as if she were attempting to suppress a gasp of shock and revulsion.

The statement was a powerful indictment against the defendant, and cast her as a devastating, though reluctant, witness against herself. But when she was called to testify, she also provided the most dramatically emotional appeal in her defense. Her attorney quickly turned to the key question of the ominously damaging statement she had given to Verkin. She claimed the government lawman scared her into making the incriminating statement.

"I would have lied to Mr. Verkin about my mother that day," she declared. "I was terrified of Ed Verkin. I would have told him anything he wanted to hear to get away from him. I was told I wasn't going to get out of that room until I told him what he wanted to hear," she said. She claimed that Verkin had intimidated others who testified against her, as well.

The witness wriggled in her chair as she talked. Her voice rose shrilly, then dropped suddenly as if she had just won a personal struggle to remain reasonably composed. Tears streamed down her smooth moon face through much of her testimony. Twice during the agonizing ordeal, she was permitted to step off the stand for a few moments to regain control of her emotions.

Testifying was obviously an arduous emotional experience for her. It was a fierce test of endurance that she seemed perilously close to failing several times during the approximately two hours that she testified. But she was firm about the statement she had given to Verkin: She insisted she had lied in a desperate move to satisfy the BATF agent because he frightened her.

Ms. Wolf admitted that she gave money to Savage, but insisted that the transaction had nothing to do with jealousy or a wish to have her old boyfriend's new love murdered. She said the money was a loan she made to him after he revealed that he was thinking about leasing a Knoxville nightclub. She explained that she borrowed six thousand dollars from Hickerson, her quadriplegic home-care client in Indiana, and handed over four thousand dollars to her new friend.

She also had some good things to say about the na-

tionally notorious former strip joint operator who had
been identified in newspapers, magazines, and on television as the ringleader of a gang of cutthroat killers
for hire. The shrillness in her voice that had seemed
about to erupt into hysteria at any moment when she
was testifying a few minutes earlier vanished as she
turned to her relationship with Savage. Her voice became softer, and coquettish.

"When I first met Richard, he was so attractive. He's
got big gorgeous blue eyes, and he's got a very soft-
spoken Tennessee accent," she coyly explained. "And
the more time I spent with Richard, the more time I
wanted to spend with him."

She firmly denied that she and the handsome, blue-
eyed Tennesseean were brought together by an ad in
Soldier of Fortune magazine. She insisted that they met
in a nightclub at the Hyatt Regency Hotel in Louisville
in May 1985. They were instantly attracted to each other
and began getting together often after their fateful en-
counter at the night spot, she claimed.

The prosecution called Verkin as its lone rebuttal
witness, and he denied coercing Ms. Wolf into making
the jailhouse statement she had accused him of wring-
ing out of her with intimidation and threats.

When the trial opened, Savage was expected to testify for the defense. Although the murder broker had
been brought to Lexington for the trial in response to a
defense subpoena, after a few minutes of conversation
in Judge Scott Reed's chambers, he walked out of the
federal building without testifying. He invoked his constitutional rights to refuse to testify, on grounds of protecting himself from self-incrimination. Although
Savage had wanted to testify, his attorney advised him
against the move. U.S. marshals returned the cuffed

and chained prisoner to the Fayette County Jail in Lexington.

In a bare-fisted and brutal summation, Trevey portrayed the fickle defendant as a self-confessed perjurer, liar, and lover of a hit man who was an admitted killer. "This is the man Mary Alice Wolf wants to spend the rest of her life with," the prosecutor declared. "I submit to you that Mary Alice Wolf is an obsessed, demented, misguided, and dangerous person."

The jury deliberated about an hour before notifying the judge that they wanted to listen once more to the taped statement that Ms. Wolf had given to the BATF agent. A few minutes after listening to the tape for the second time, the panel reported reaching verdicts.

They found her guilty of all four charges against her: conspiracy to commit murder for hire, and three counts of traveling in interstate commerce to commit murder for hire. The three matching charges were linked to the three times that hit men were sent by Savage to murder the schoolteacher. The defendant's round face paled as the verdicts were read, but she maintained a gritty hold on her emotions until federal marshals handcuffed her and prepared to take her to jail. Then the tears flowed.

Her lawyer's plea to permit her to remain free on bail until her sentencing was rejected by the judge. Trevey had argued that she should be locked up because she might flee, and could be a danger to the community. Before walking unsteadily out of the courtroom with a federal marshal on each side, she peeled off her watch and a diamond ring and handed them to her lawyer. She had said earlier that the ring was a gift from Savage.

The prisoner was facing the possibility of up to twenty years behind bars if Judge Reed chose to stack the sentences and rule that they had to be served consecutively. Each of the offenses carried sentences of up to five years imprisonment.

Two weeks after the jury verdicts were returned, Ms. Wolf was sentenced to a total term of fifteen years in prison. The sentence included three consecutive terms of five years each, and five years probation on the other. Judge Reed also ordered the prisoner to participate in a mental health program during her incarceration.

Two years after Ms. Wolf was imprisoned, the U.S. Court of Appeals for the Sixth District overturned her conviction, claiming that her confession had been unlawfully obtained and consequently was inadmissible as evidence. Several months earlier, the Cincinnati-based federal appeals court had upheld her conviction, but ultimately ordered a new trial after being told by the U.S. Supreme Court to reconsider the case. After two and a half years behind bars, Ms. Wolf was freed on bail to await a second chance at convincing a federal court jury that there wasn't sufficient evidence to prove she had tried to have her love rival killed by professional hit men.

When her new trial convened in Lexington near the end of April 1990, she had the same defense attorney and the same prosecutor. But there were some important changes, including a different judge and loss to the prosecution of the formidably incriminating statement she had given to the BATF agent while she was in the women's jail in Louisville. The appellate court decision had ruled it inadmissible as evidence. There were also some changes in the lineup of witnesses. This time she didn't testify. But Savage did.

In his testimony, Savage told primarily the same story the defendant had told at the earlier trial about their meeting at the Louisville nightclub, their romantic relationship, and the four thousand dollars that each claimed she had loaned him to open a bar in Knoxville. Savage said there was never any talk between them about doing anything to hurt Victoria Morgan Brashear. And he said that Doutre and two other prosecution witnesses who had already testified that he had sent them to Kentucky to kill the woman were lying.

Savage admitted placing gun-for-hire advertisements in *SOF,* but insisted that it was merely part of a scam to cheat clients out of their money. There were never any plans to kill anyone, he insisted. It was a story he had repeatedly told before to law enforcement and to court authorities.

Most of the testimony was a repeat of the earlier trial, and the outcome of the three-day proceeding was the same. Once more, the jury found her guilty of conspiracy and other charges for setting the murder plot against her rival in motion. And once more, she was sentenced to fifteen years in prison, despite her attorney's plea for mercy. Milner pointed out that she had already spent thirty-six months in prison and asked that she be sentenced only to time served. But U.S. district Judge Henry Wilhoit denied the request.

Despite his defection and damaging testimony against former cohorts in the contract murder schemes, including the client from Louisville, Buckley still had to pay the piper in the blue-grass-country conspiracy case. He was sentenced to a four-year prison term after his guilty plea.

But his testimony against Savage during the gang leader's trial in Brownsville for the Pasadena house bombing didn't help him much, despite the prosecutor's recommendation of leniency. Judge DeAnda jolted him with a ten-year term for possession of hand grenades, and five years each on charges of conspiracy and of interstate travel with intent to murder. And he not only stacked the terms on top of one another, but ordered as well that they should be served consecutive to prison sentences he had drawn in other jurisdictions.

The jurist said that he wanted to be as sure as he could be that Buckley didn't commit other serious crimes in the future. He pointed out that he believed the prisoner participated in the deadly scheme against Free's life for thrills, rather than for money. Judge DeAnda also ordered that Buckley undergo a psychiatric examination.

When Buckley was led out of the U.S. district courtroom in Houston in chains, he was facing a mind-boggling fifteen years from his convictions in Arkansas; ten years from his sentence for the grenade bombing of Free's car in Georgia; and four years for his part in the murder conspiracy in Kentucky.

Authorities had long ago settled affairs with one of Buckley's old acquaintances in Texas. In June 1986, a few months after his arrest, Thielman pleaded guilty in U.S. district court in Austin to charges of placing a destructive device aboard an aircraft, and of damaging an aircraft. Federal prosecutors disclosed at the time that in return for the guilty pleas on the more serious counts tied to the aircraft bombing, they had agreed not to pursue any charges against him involving fire damage to the house under construction in Georgetown.

The grim-faced defendant was returned to the Federal Correctional Institute in nearby Bastrop after his brief appearance before U.S. district Judge James Nowlin to await sentencing. He faced possible imprisonment for up to forty years, a half million dollars in fines, and could also be ordered to pay more than twelve hundred dollars for damage to the aircraft.

At his sentencing a few weeks later, his court-appointed attorney, Rip Collins, pleaded for leniency, blaming Thielman's fierce addiction to cocaine for the crime. Collins asserted that during eight months behind bars, his client had ended his drug dependency, and was no longer the same man he was when he attempted to blow up the airliner, the passengers, and crew.

But the assistant U.S. attorney argued for a harsh sentence, pointing out that Thielman had put in motion a coldly calculated plan to murder his wife, children, and 147 other innocent people. "Gambling, drugs, nude models was the life he chose," the prosecutor asserted.

Judge Nowlin imposed the maximum prison sentences: twenty years for each offense. The contrite prisoner, who shifted uneasily from foot to foot as the penalty was imposed, would become eligible for parole in ten years. The judge did not order a fine or restitution, pointing out that Thielman had no money to pay. Although the confessed bomber's wife and children had visited him regularly at the prison, they were not present at the sentencing. Collins said Thielman asked his wife not to attend.

In Arkansas the criminal justice system was also busy settling accounts for the conspiracy and attempts on Norwood's life.

Investigators had learned a lot about Gray and the sinister scheme he was accused of setting in motion to murder the mild-mannered young law student he blamed for replacing him in his estranged wife's affections. Buckley had claimed that he met with the Tulsa businessman and was given specific instructions that after killing Norwood, he was to plant evidence to make it look as if the victim had gotten into trouble with drug dealers.

Detectives also learned how Gray had managed to so handily breeze through the polygraph test he passed shortly after Norwood advised police that he thought his lady friend's estranged husband was behind the attacks on him. Gray had reportedly questioned experts about how to pass the polygraph, and taken several practice tests. Savage and Jackson weren't the only people whom the Tulsa businessman had approached about murdering Norwood, police also revealed.

Gray and his reputed coconspirators entered guilty pleas to several of the charges against them. Then, shortly before they were scheduled for sentencing, the Tulsa businessman and Savage attempted to change their pleas to not guilty. Their last-minute moves were rejected, and Judge Waters proceeded with the sentencing. He ordered a fifteen-year prison term for Gray for causing persons to cross state lines with the intent to kill; and a ten-year term for causing persons to use a telephone in a murder scheme. Savage's sentence totaled forty years, although the judge juggled the terms so that the maximum to be served would be fifteen years less. The charges filed against the thirty-nine-year-old businessman in the Arkansas state courts were dropped.

Jackson was ultimately sentenced to a long term behind bars, and was sent to a federal prison in Texarkana to serve time for his crimes in Arkansas and in Georgia. But authorities still weren't through with him.

He drew additional prison time for his free-lance activities in three different attempts to murder a fellow Texan, Anthony Bennie Hunicke. Police investigators said that Jackson tried unsuccessfully to kill Hunicke on November 22, 1985, by placing a pipe bomb under his pickup truck; on December 13 by firing a shot at him from a silencer-equipped .45-caliber pistol; and on December 19 by spraying twelve to fifteen rounds at him from a silencer-equipped 9-mm semiautomatic rifle. The bumbling would-be killer pleaded guilty to illegally manufacturing a bomb.

Federal prosecutors charged John George Noppinger, Jr., with paying Jackson $10,000 for the proposed contract killing after spotting his advertisement in a copy of *SOF*. And they argued at the trial that a love triangle was behind the murder conspiracy. Noppinger, however, claimed in his defense that he and Jackson first met in mid-December at a bar near the Houston area's Hobby Airport and struck up a friendship because of mutual interests.

The forty-two-year-old defendant was ultimately convicted of six weapons offenses tied to the ill-fated murder plot and sentenced to a fifteen-year term in federal prison.

The bizarre interlocking relationships in the multistate investigation of the activities of Savage's grotesque brotherhood of bombers and killers were a nightmare for police and prosecutors to deal with. Yet somehow they were managing to cut through the labyrinthian tangle and one by one put the sad sack criminal mercenaries and their avaricious and vengeful clients behind bars. But the investigation and subsequent trials spotlighted some curious alliances and kinships.

Mary Alice Wolf traveled from Kentucky to Minnesota to testify as a defense witness in Richard Lee Foster's federal court trial for hiring the Knoxville-based gang to move interstate to bomb or burn out his business rival. She told the U.S. district court jury in Saint

Paul that she was with Savage near Louisville in early June 1985 when federal prosecutors claimed he was in Rochester scheming with Foster.

She also claimed that she was in a Kentucky motel with Savage on August 11 when the Knoxville strip club owner was reputedly in Rochester with Foster, Buckley, and Jackson trying to bomb Harry's 63 Club out of business.

During cross-examination, Assistant U.S. Attorney Joan Ericksen asked if it was true that Ms. Wolf had previously told authorities she didn't meet Savage for the first time until August 1985 after reading his advertisement in *SOF*. But the witness's attorney refused to permit his client to reply to any questions about the magazine, citing her constitutional protection against self-incrimination.

Jackson told the jury that Savage recruited him for two bombing capers in August 1985 after finding his advertisement in the *SOF* classified pages. He claimed that Savage told him Foster supplied the hand grenades wired under Free's car in the bungled assassination effort near Atlanta on August 2.

The witness said that a week or two after he returned to his home in Texas from Georgia, Savage telephoned and asked him to travel to Rochester and blow up a tavern. He said that after the first bombing try that he and Buckley collaborated on misfired, Foster helped him obtain parts for a new bomb and watched him put the explosive device together. But that effort failed, as did the third and final bombing attempt, Jackson said. After three tries to bomb Harry's 63 Club without success, the witness testified, he left town.

Both Buckley and Ms. Mattingly also recounted their activities and observations during their trips to Minnesota while Savage was dealing with Foster. At one point during her testimony, Savage's former girlfriend identified Foster as the man the adventurers had traveled from Tennessee to meet with. "Rick Foster, in the gray suit and black tie," she said as she pointed her finger at the defendant.

During opening and closing statements, prosecutor Ericksen contended that the defendant was a vicious and vengeful man who tried to destroy Harry's 63 Club after buying The Pub from Hayes because he resented the competition.

Showing a copy of the June 1985 edition of *SOF* to the jury, she claimed that Foster had shopped through the magazine's classifieds to find someone who could do his dirty work for him. She said he found Savage's ad, and they made some deals.

Foster was portrayed by the prosecutor and state's witnesses as a weapons enthusiast who supplied submachine guns and hand grenades to criminals, and was deeply involved in an illegal drug-trafficking operation centered at the poultry farm in northwestern Minnesota.

Witnesses called by Foster's defense attorney during the three-week trial depicted his thirty-two-year-old client to the jury as an honest, nonviolent man who worked hard. The defendant's mother, his girlfriend, and a former girlfriend testified for him as character witnesses. "He don't explode. He don't hurt people. He's not a vengeful person," said his mother, Pat Foster. "He wasn't raised like that."

Foster became his own most dramatic witness when he testified that he had never conspired with anyone to burn the chicken barn near Fertile, or to bomb his competitor's bar in Rochester. The witness conceded that he was disturbed when his longtime friend opened another bar. "It was like somebody dropped a ton of bricks on me," he said. "I didn't think he would do it. But it was more a hurt upset than a get-out-and-get-him upset."

The defendant testified that his own dealings with Savage were over a bar they had considered buying together. Foster claimed that he first met Savage at a *Soldier of Fortune* trade show in Las Vegas in 1982, and got together with him in Knoxville in 1985 to discuss the possible bar partnership.

The jury deliberated two days before returning a verdict of guilty of all charges on the seven-count indictment accusing him with conspiring to obstruct interstate commerce in the arson bombing scheme. Approximately ten weeks later, U.S. district court Judge Paul Magnuson sentenced him to a twelve-year term in federal prison.

In Georgia, it was more than four years after Sean Doutre was picked up by sheriff's police in Morgan County with a mini arsenal of high-powered weapons in his car before the courts at last closed the books in the murder conspiracy against trucker Bruce Lamey. Early in September 1990, Major pleaded guilty to conspiracy to commit murder, and to two counts of possession of a firearm during the commission of a crime, in the sordid plot against his onetime friend and business partner. He was given a twelve-year sentence, with five years of the term to be served in prison.

Prosecutor Gerald Brown later explained to reporters that the relatively light sentence was a compromise negotiated with Major's defense attorney. Brown pointed out that the state's chances for a successful prosecution at a jury trial would have been closely tied to Doutre's cooperation. But Doutre wasn't cooperating, and there was little or no room for the prosecutors to negotiate with a prisoner who was already serving life in prison with no chance of parole.

Chapter 14

Free-Lancers

Unfortunately, members of the loose-knit gang operating out of the Continental Club, and their sporadic associate Jackson, weren't the only criminal rowdies who had contracted murders or offered sinister assignments through the classified pages of *Soldier of Fortune* magazine.

Other killers, madcap adventurers, and shady clients had been using the magazine's classifieds for devilish purposes as well. And not all the aspiring killers were as amateurishly mediocre as Savage's gang of slipshod muddlers.

One of the most industrious and murderously effective of the free-lance hit men was a boyishly handsome Texas-born drifter, part-time truck driver, and random photographer with the macho name John Wayne Hearn. The husky ex–marine sergeant surrendered to law enforcement officers on March 20, 1985, exactly one year to the day before Detective Springer sat down in the BATF office in Knoxville to talk with Emert about the brutal bludgeon murder of Anita Spearman.

By that time Hearn had already carried out three contract killings, including the shootings of two men in Florida and the slaying of a south Texas housewife, after running a series of ads in *SOF* late in 1984. One of the classifieds read:

World Security Group. Ex-Marines, Nam vets, weapons specialists, jungle warfare, political . . . high-risk assignments in U.S. or overseas.

A telephone number was also listed.

Hearn's first ads were run in conjunction with his roommate, another marine veteran of Vietnam who was a former drill instructor. But when calls began coming into their apartment from people who wanted them to help out with bombings, drug running, dealing and transport of high-powered weaponry, kidnap, and murder, Hearn's alarmed pal dropped out. He was looking for adventure, not a criminal career.

But the sinister calls didn't bother Hearn. He continued advertising on his own after dropping the phrase "ex–drill instructor" from his classified description. He was scrupulously high-principled about the way he worded his ad. He didn't want to overstate his qualifications. He was less high-principled about the kinds of assignments he took. He slipped into the murder business.

At thirty-eight years old, the three-year veteran of Vietnam was a baby-faced bundle of insecurities, a four-time loser in the marriage stakes who cried when things went bad for him, and a Walter Mitty dreamer with a shaky hold on reality. Hearn, who lived in an austere, sparsely furnished apartment in suburban Atlanta, was the proverbial accident waiting to happen.

The accident was Debra Banister, and the star-crossed meeting that started them on a deadly downward spiral to disaster occurred on a sunny day in November 1984 when they got together at a Shoney's restaurant in south Georgia after she read one of his ads in the *SOF* classifieds.

At twenty-nine years old, Debra was the mother of a son and a daughter, and was a few years into a luke-warm marriage to her second husband, Joe Banister. He was a placid forty-one-year-old telephone installer who had worked for the same company for more than fifteen years. The Banisters lived in the north-central Florida town of Starke, which is best known for the dismal gray prison fortress that houses the Sunshine State's notorious death row.

The firebrand housewife and bank employee in nearby Gainesville had many of the hard qualities that Hearn didn't. She was the eldest daughter and a leader in the close-knit family of her parents, Franklin and Iris Sims. She was also audacious, aggressive, and ruthless about getting what she wanted. And she wanted her younger sister's ex-husband murdered.

Debra's sister Marlene was on her third marriage, and she was locked in a nasty child-custody fuss with her first husband, Cecil Batie, over their two boys. It sounded like a good idea to her when her big sister told her that after looking through a copy of *Soldier of Fortune* magazine, she had talked with a man who could take care of Marlene's problem with Batie.

Hearn had seemed to be a bit surprised when Debra talked to him about a contract killing, but she sealed the bargain when she leaned over the restaurant table and gave him a warm, wet kiss on his nose. He was also up to his neck in a custody battle with an ex-spouse. He needed money, and it was a time to be practical. He said he would do the job for thirty-thousand dollars.

Debra shared the information with her sister and their parents. She said she knew a nice man who had agreed to kill Cecil Batie if the price was right. When Mrs. Sims heard about the big money the would-be hit man was asking for, she teased her eldest daughter about losing her sex appeal. Soon Debra reported back that the handsome Vietnam veteran had dropped his fee to ten-thousand dollars. The sisters invited their unsuspecting grandmother to Gainesville for a pre-Thanksgiving visit, then burned down her house in Santa Rosa Beach for the insurance money.

Even then, Batie wasn't the first one of the men in Marlene's life to experience serious violence at her hands. Her current husband, Larry Watson, was hospitalized with a head injury after she ran him down with a van. She claimed to authorities that the construction worker had hit her and she struck him with the vehicle as she was trying to get away. The rambunctious couple had been married less than a year when the fight occurred. Police investigated, but no charges were filed.

The family collected the insurance money on the burned house on January 2, and two days later Debra met with Hearn at a Gainesville motel and gave him ten thousand dollars in hundred-dollar bills. He quickly spent some of the money to buy a twelve-gauge shotgun advertised for sale in the *Gainesville Sun,* and picked up a box of shells.

It was Friday, and Marlene picked her boys up at their father's house across the street from her parents' trailer home for their weekend visit. Then she brought her husband, Larry Watson, home from the hospital, and they all got together for a barbecue.

It wasn't yet daylight on Sunday morning when Hearn stepped out of the shadows in front of the picture window at Batie's house, and peered at the man sleeping inside on a couch with the television on. Then he lifted the gun and fired two blasts through the window into the sleeping man.

Members of Batie's family immediately suspected that Marlene was behind her ex-husband's cold-blooded murder, and passed their hunch on to investigators with the Alachua County Sheriff's Department. Marlene didn't bother to attend the funeral. And she was upset when she inquired about his thirty-thousand-dollar life insurance policy and learned that she had recently been dropped as a beneficiary.

Meanwhile Debra's relationship with the handsome hit man had developed into a full-blown romance. They even opened a joint checking account together, and Debra signed her last name on the banking documents as "Hearn." Traveling between the Atlanta area and north Florida quickly became too much of a bother for the illicit lovers, and Hearn moved to Gainesville and settled down in a motel.

A few days after Batie was shot to death in his front room, Hearn received a telephone call from an out-of-work electrician who lived in the sleepy rural settlement of Sleephollow, in Brazos County, Texas, and had seen one of his ads in *SOF*. Robert Vanoy Black, Jr., was also a marine veteran of Vietnam, who had risen through the ranks from private to captain before leaving the Corps. At first he asked about the possibilities of working with the World Security Group. Then, as the initial call was followed up with a series of telephone chats between the two men, the talk ventured into discussions of a gun collection Black had to sell, their experiences in Vietnam, the marines—and murder. Black told his telephone pal that he wanted his wife murdered. But Hearn said he wasn't interested.

The telephone calls to the one-man World Security Group didn't mark the first, or the last, time that Black approached someone to talk about murder. He had been trying for months to have his wife killed.

Throughout his childhood in the west Texas towns of Haskell and Snyder, and into the early years of his marriage, Black would have seemed to be an unlikely candidate to one day be shopping around for a dial-a-killer to do away with his wife. He grew up in a loving family, was a fine son, good student, and spent years as a Boy Scout who reached Eagle rank. From every indication, he appeared to be a straight arrow with a bright future when he met Sandra Kay Eimann, while they were students at Texas A&M University. He had just completed his junior year when he enlisted in the marines. He and Sandra Kay married while he was home on Christmas leave.

His life with Sandra began to sour after he left the Corps and returned to Texas. He had difficulty holding jobs, and that led to money problems, which led to domestic quarreling. Some of the fussing was extraordinarily violent. One time during a nasty quarrel at the home of his mother-in-law, Margie Eimann, the burly husband picked his wife up and tossed her across the living room, through the front screen door, over a porch, and onto the sidewalk. They fought, then they patched things up, then they fought again.

By the early 1980s, Sandra was running the day-care center in nearby College Station that her mother started

years earlier. The uneasy marriage was still limping
along in April 1984 when Bob Black, Jr., ran across
Teresa Hetherington, his twenty-nine-year-old first
cousin from Apple Valley, California, at a family reunion in Houston. In the thirteen years since they had
last seen each other, the young teacher's aide had become an attractive woman, and he was a handsome
man. Despite the irksome fact that both were married
to other people, they began a love affair.

A month after Black's ill-fated reunion with his
cousin, he left his wife and child and rode off across
the country on a motorcycle headed for California. He
stayed in Apple Valley for four months, rendezvousing
regularly with his cousin. By the time he decided it was
time to ride back to Texas, the sweethearts had agreed
they would get divorces so that they could marry each
other. But he didn't want to go through the nasty and
expensive ordeal of a divorce. And he wanted his wife's
life insurance money, as well as his freedom.

Back in Brazos County, the wandering husband convinced his wife that he was ready to resume their marriage. But while he was going through the motions of
settling back into married life, he started shopping for
a hit man.

He had found a job with an electrical contracting
firm, and one of the men he worked with was an ex-
convict. Black asked him to murder Sandra Kay. Black
gave him five hundred dollars for the job, but the ex-
convict welched on the deal. Eventually he returned
seventy-five dollars. The cash-strapped schemer's initial foray into the murky world of contract murder had
been an expensive dud, but he didn't learn his lesson.

He approached the brother of the ex-convict who had
already turned him down, and asked if he was inter-

ested in taking on a contract murder. Black had been doing some thinking about the best way to have his wife killed without being caught. He had come up with plans to murder her and cover his tracks by staging phony accidents with their car, with his motorcycle, or a hit-and-run. He also considered the possibilities of killing her and rigging a bogus burglary, then covering up her murder by setting a fire. But the former convict's brother didn't want any part in a murder scheme either, no matter how it might be staged. He flatly refused to get involved.

Black next asked his former boss to help him murder Sandra Kay and cover up the slaying by making it look as if she died in a car accident. He offered to pay fifty thousand dollars, half of the money he expected to collect from her life insurance policy. His former boss didn't want to get involved in a murder scheme any more than the brothers had. His answer was an unequivocable "no."

So Black turned to World Security Group, where he was also turned down. But he didn't give up, and continued telephoning Hearn to talk about matters of mutual interest, and the murder contract he wanted to take out on his unsuspecting wife. Eventually they decided to make another deal. Hearn agreed to fly to Texas to make a deal on the gun collection Black was offering to sell. But when Hearn showed up, Black backed out of the deal.

Hearn was upset, and before he caught a flight home, he told Black that he didn't plan to come back unless he was reimbursed for his trip. He estimated that the round-trip flight and the short stay in Texas was worth at least one thousand dollars. Black didn't pay the thousand dollars, but he continued to telephone Hearn in

Florida to talk about life in the marines, guns, and murder. The scheming husband was unaware of it at the time, but he had an ally in Florida.

Hearn would later testify in court that Debra talked him into reconsidering the Texas murder plot. And she asked her boyfriend to do another killing, as well. She offered to pay him to kill her forty-one-year-old husband, and even had a plan worked out. She explained that she and her spouse were planning to attend a dinner party in the town of Palatka about forty miles southeast of Starke, and would be returning home in separate vehicles. She suggested that Hearn could run Banister off the road and make him crash into a steep ditch.

The conniving wife also had a backup plan in case her lover couldn't stage the killing as an accident, or Banister wasn't killed in the crash. She arranged for Hearn to take her husband's .22-caliber survival rifle from the trunk of her car a few days before the planned hit. Then, if it was necessary, Banister could be shot with his own gun.

When Debra shared her dark secret with her younger sister, Marlene was worried. It was too soon after Batie had been shot in his sleep, and she was afraid that if Debra went ahead with the plans to get rid of Banister, police would link the killings to each other. If that happened, homicide investigators could be led straight to the two Sims sisters. But Debra was determined to have her husband killed, and Hearn had agreed to go ahead with the hit to keep her happy. Debra did her part to keep her sweetheart's interest high, by getting together with him every day in his motel room for torrid lovemaking sessions while waiting for the fateful Saturday night of the dinner party.

She was driving back home from the party at about

10:00 P.M. when Hearn saw her car and motioned to her to stop. He wanted to know if she was sure that she wanted her husband killed. She responded by telling him that they didn't have time to waste, because Banister was not far behind her in his pickup truck, Hearn would later tell investigators. She still wanted him killed.

Despite the late hour, when Banister drove by, there was too much traffic for Hearn to take a chance running him off the road. So he followed the unsuspecting husband, hurriedly assembling the rifle as he drove with one hand. A few minutes after Banister turned off the highway onto a lonely back road, Hearn squeezed off the first shot from the rifle. The bullet crashed through a window of the pickup and creased Banister's neck. The truck was veering crazily along the road when Hearn fired the second and final shot into Banister's head.

About midnight a state trooper discovered the truck nosed into a ditch with the dead man inside. But it was Monday morning, when an autopsy was performed, before a Bradford County pathologist found the bullet hole, and police were able to confirm that Banister had been murdered. At the funeral the next day, the new widow attended the rite with a handsome stranger who introduced himself as her cousin. He had helped with the funeral arrangements. The curly-haired man was friendly and comforting, and he snapped several photographs of Banister's grieving survivors. One of the pictures he took was of the widow, standing in front of the fresh grave with a single red rose in her hand.

The dead man's family members weren't as naive as Debra apparently thought they were. They were upset at the new widow's brassy flaunting of her new man at her husband's funeral. And Banister was hardly in his grave before they were talking with Bradford County sheriff's homicide investigators about the mysterious stranger who claimed to be Debra's cousin. A homicide investigator with the Alachua County Sheriff's Department also shared information with his brother officers in Bradford County about the recent murder of Batie. Curiously, the Alachua County detective observed, a man named John Wayne Hearn had started being seen in the company of the Sims family just about the time that Batie was murdered.

In less than a month, two men who had been married to the former Sims sisters had been mysteriously shot to death. And relatives of both victims had noticed the same stranger hanging around at about the time of both shootings.

When detectives talked with the sisters and with their parents, however, they were told that Hearn was an old friend they had all known for years. Hearn told a similar story when investigators talked with him. He added that he hadn't even been in Florida that weekend, because he had gone to South Carolina to visit with his mother, Mary Watson, and his teenage son.

A few minutes after talking with the detectives, Hearn used a nearby pay telephone to place a call to Texas. He agreed during the call to murder Robert Black's wife for ten thousand dollars. Black quickly mailed a thousand-dollar cashier's check to Hearn to pay back expenses for the earlier trip to Texas. And he promised another thousand dollars in expense money, over and above the ten-thousand-dollar murder contract fee, when Hearn returned to the Lone Star State.

The homicidal husband planned to pay for his wife's murder with a chunk of her life insurance. Sandy Kay had carried two life policies worth a total of seventy-five thousand dollars on herself, but late in January Black talked her into increasing the amount to one hundred thousand dollars. There would be more than enough money to pay her killer, and he would still have a small fortune left over.

Black was still hopeful that his wife's slaying could be staged as a car accident. But he was worried that it would be difficult to catch her alone and unaccompanied by their son later in the week. He didn't want their only child hurt. And he explained in a polite handwritten note he included with the check that he planned to spend that weekend with the boy in Houston, so it would be a convenient time for the murder.

"If there is any way you could schedule your plans to coincide with my being alibied out-of-town this weekend, it would help considerably," he wrote.

Black never referred directly to murder in the one-page note, and he addressed his coconspirator as "Skipper." It was a code name they had agreed on. The ruthless cutthroats, sinister footpads, and darkling executioners who moved in the shadowy world of mercenary murder preferred code names, or no names at all.

There were also other reasons for Black's impatience. There were a few days late in February when the effective dates on the old insurance policies on his wife's life, which were being canceled, would overlap with the new policies. For a few days her total life insurance worth would be $150,000, before dropping to $100,000. And Black was also in a hurry to get on with the killing because his girlfriend's divorce was scheduled to become final on February 23.

Hearn returned to Brazos County on February 20,

too late to follow through with Black's wishes to schedule the killing for the weekend. But they were determined that it was time for Mrs. Black to die, and the two men huddled together to work out the details of the murder plot. The two-time killer quickly ruled out a harebrained scheme by his client for Black to knock his wife unconscious, load her body into her van, then set up a fatal car crash. Black explained that he could drive the van to a lonely stretch of road, set the cruise control, and jump into a car that Hearn was driving alongside. The van with the unconscious woman inside would continue on at high speed until it crashed.

Hearn also turned thumbs down on a proposal to shoot both Sandra Kay and her mother while they were taking an afternoon stroll together on the campus of Texas A&M University in College Station. Hearn rejected the ruthless scheme because the campus would be crowded with students. The two men finally agreed that the safest way to kill the woman and cover up their tracks would be to shoot her in her home and make it look as if she had surprised a burglar.

With the method of execution settled, Black cashed a thousand-dollar money order, and handed over ten hundred-dollar bills to the hit man for expenses. He promised that the contract fee itself would be paid as soon as settlement was made with the insurance companies.

Late that afternoon, on February 21, Hearn and his dial-a-death client were in the Black home, busy ripping open drawers and tearing up beds to make it appear as if a burglar had been at work. At Black's suggestion, Hearn stuffed some of his targeted victim's jewelry into his pockets, to help make the alibi-crime look more believable. Black also gave the trucker-turned-contract-killer his wife's .22-caliber revolver to shoot her with.

Finally Black telephoned his wife at the day-care center to make arrangements to pick up his son and ask when she was coming home. Less than an hour later at about 5:30 P.M., the hired gunman was lurking in the late afternoon shadows inside the house when Sandra Kay Black opened the door and walked in carrying an armload of groceries. She had just set the sacks down in the kitchen and turned to return through the door she had left open, to bring in more groceries from the van, when he shot her in the head. Then as she lay sprawled on the floor, he fired another shot into her eye, executioner-style, to make sure she was dead. She never saw her killer.

The hired gunman fled from the murder scene in his victim's van, and drove it to the grocery store parking lot, where he switched to the rental car. Then he tossed the .22-caliber pistol he had used for the killing into Lake Conroe and drove to the Houston Intercontinental Airport to catch a flight home.

The thirty-six-year-old homemaker's body was discovered by her fourteen-year-old-son, Gary Wayne Black, when he arrived home with his father later that afternoon. Robert Black sent the unsuspecting teenager into the house ahead of him to make the gruesome discovery. It was part of the alibi the victim's diabolical husband had worked out.

Hearn was pitifully weak-willed, and easily led or pushed, but he was no bumbler at contract killing. He had accepted three assignments, and left three dead victims in his wake. But the cruel slaying of Mrs. Black was his last deed as a professional hit man. Back home in Florida, homicide investigators had been busy since their interview with him, and they were rapidly closing in.

Although Hearn's mother had backed up her son's alibi when detectives traveled to South Carolina to talk with her, and even claimed to recall what he had eaten for supper at her home the night Batie was shot to death hundreds of miles away, the investigators were suspicious of her story. When they returned to Florida, they continued their probe into the perplexing murder, and called on some of the same investigative techniques that Springer and other members of Sheriff Wille's Rent-A-Wreck squad used to help tie down the case against Spearman.

Under the direction of Don Denton, chief investigator for the Bradford County Sheriff's Department, they subpoenaed records of telephone bills, and quickly found a link between Debra Banister, Hearn, and his advertisements in the *SOF* classified pages. Checking records of Hearn's calls from his motel room in Gainesville, they also found that he had telephoned Debra at her house three times in the early morning hours immediately after her husband's ambush murder. The detectives went back to South Carolina to talk with Mrs. Hearn once more, and this time they put the pressure on.

Faced with the unsettling prospect of being charged as an accessory to murder, Hearn's mother changed her story. She admitted that her son wasn't at her home on the night that Batie was shot to death along the quiet Florida country road. She also produced an unexpected bonus. She gave the investigators the note that Black had included with the thousand-dollar cashier's check he had sent to her son.

Homicide investigators with the Brazos County Sheriff's Department had also been busy with their investigation of Mrs. Black's shocking murder. Although at first glance it had appeared that she was killed by a burglar, detectives began to take a closer look at her husband as a possible suspect after they found a copy of *SOF* in the house. A circle had been drawn around Hearn's classified ad. So it fit right in with their suspicions when sheriff's investigators in Florida telephoned to tell them about the letter and check they had uncovered from Robert Black.

Brazos County sheriff's detectives arrested Black on March 10 on charges of capital murder. Five days later Hearn surrendered at a truck stop just outside Huntsville, after telling Brazos County sheriff's deputies during a telephone conversation the day before that he wanted to give himself up. His sister, who had set up the telephone call, was with him in the truck stop parking lot along Interstate 45 when deputies handcuffed him and took him into custody. Investigators who searched his pickup truck found some of Mrs. Black's jewelry inside.

Settled on the northwest edge of the Sam Houston National Forest, Huntsville is only about forty miles east of Black's Brazos County home. Ironically, the somber old prison at Huntsville houses the Texas state correctional system's death row.

But for the time being, Hearn was held without bail in the Brazos County Jail in Bryan on a charge of capital murder. Sheriff Ron Miller told reporters that the prisoner was linked to a group of people who reportedly handled high-risk assignments, and was being sought by law enforcement agencies in at least one other state.

At a hearing a few months later on a motion to establish bail for Black, his former coworker at the electrical contracting company revealed that the defendant had also tried to set up his girlfriend's husband for murder. The ex-convict said Black first mentioned that he wanted the husband killed, then switched targets and suggested several plans for murdering Sandra Kay. Hearn also appeared at the hearing, and testified that he murdered the woman at the direction of her husband. The bond request was denied.

Within a few hours after Hearn's surrender the previous March, he had confessed to shooting three people to death in two states during one terrible seven-week period. And the lovesick mercenary was soon tattling on his girlfriend, her sister, and their parents, telling police everything he knew about the role they had played in the crazed contract murder spree. He agreed to testify for the prosecution against his accused coconspirators in all three cases.

Hearn and his hot-blooded lover were indicted in April by a Bradford County grand jury on charges of first-degree murder for Banister's slaying. Seven weeks later an Alachua County grand jury indicted Hearn, Debra, Marlene, and their parents on charges of first-degree murder and conspiracy to commit murder in the Batie slaying. Hearn testified before the panel, prior to the indictments.

The remorseful hit man agreed to enter guilty pleas to the charges in all three slayings, and was the prosecution's star witness in the trials against his accused coconspirators. It was a desperate tactic that would eventually net him three life prison sentences, but enable him to sidestep the death penalty in the Florida and Texas contract murders. Texas and Florida rank number one and two in that order among states with the death penalty, in carrying out executions since they had been resumed about ten years earlier.

Hearn dabbed at his eyes with a handkerchief, and big tears rolled down his chubby, baby-plump cheeks when he testified at his former sweetheart's trial in August 1986 about the first kiss she had given to him during their fateful meeting at the Shoney's restaurant. Prosecutor Thomas Elwell also played a tape recording for the jury, of the defendant and her onetime lover plotting to stage her husband's ambush murder as a traffic accident. Hearn was at his mother's home in South Carolina when the incriminating conversation was taped, and had installed an automatic recording device on the telephone as part of the battle with a former wife over custody of their son.

Debra's defense attorneys attempted to show that she had ended her affair with Hearn on the day that her husband was killed, and knew nothing about her lover's crazed scheme against Batie's life. The jury decided otherwise, and returned a verdict of guilty to second-degree murder. The widow Banister was sentenced to a seventeen-year prison term.

Early in 1986 Hearn once more returned to Texas. But this time he was handcuffed and chained, and accompanied by two Florida sheriff's detectives. He was there to testify against his former client in Black's capital murder trial in the state district court in Bryan, for engineering the contract slaying of his wife. Hearn was an unsteady witness. He was able to recall for the jury that his advertisements in *SOF* led to his meeting with Black, but he couldn't remember his first wife's name or how many times he had been married. He admitted shooting Mrs. Black, however. "I wanted to kill her instantly," he said. "I didn't want her to suffer."

Hearn also recalled the defendant's cold-blooded proposal for a double murder, to include Mrs. Eimann. "He said if I could kill both of them, he'd have no problem with it," the hit man blandly testified. "He offered me fifteen thousand dollars to kill her mother too."

Several members of the jury looked away from the witness and swiveled their heads to look at the defendant as Hearn replied to District Attorney Bill Turner's question asking why Black wanted his wife dead.

"So Bob Black could have the house, the insurance money, and so he could have his girlfriend," Hearn matter-of-factly replied.

Black sat quietly at the defense table during the chilling testimony, showing little emotion and moving only occasionally to swipe at an imaginary speck of dust on his suit coat, or to whisper to one of his attorneys.

Hearn claimed that the first time the Texan telephoned, he said he had a gun collection for sale. Black called after finding the World Security Group ad in the *SOF* classifieds. The talk of contract murder didn't come up until later telephone conversations, Hearn told the jury. Black had told a similar story to Brazos County sheriff's detectives about contacting Hearn because he wanted to sell his gun collection.

Teresa Hetherington testified about her affair with the defendant and the plans they made to marry before Black was accused in the contract murder of his wife. She said she later backed out of the affair, and Black threatened to commit suicide.

Black instructed his attorneys, Bob Scott and Keith Swim, not to present any evidence in his defense. But the defense lawyers worked hard to undermine the credibility of the star witness, and to draw an alternate scenario of how Mrs. Black was killed.

During cross-examination Scott confronted Hearn with glaring contradictions in his courtroom testimony and statements and depositions he had given to police and prosecutors' investigators in Texas and Florida. Hearn had initially denied that he played any part in Mrs. Black's ambush slaying. Then he claimed that he was merely the wheelman for a mysterious triggerman he knew as "Doug," who actually shot the woman. Eventually he admitted that he was the killer.

Hearn blandly explained that he had simply been trying to protect himself and throw investigators off track with his earlier claims.

But the defense also had developed a possible explanation for the murder that left the victim's husband out of the picture as an active member of the plot. Swim suggested to the jury that after the deal to buy the gun collection fell through, Hearn might have decided to steal them, and Mrs. Black was killed when she stumbled onto the burglary.

In the prosecution's closing statements, however, District Attorney Bill Turner labeled Swim's suggested explanation for the shooting as ridiculous. He pointed out that the gun collection wasn't stolen. And if the confessed killer was working alone, he would have faced a long six-mile afternoon walk in the sun between his parked rental car and the house.

The Brazos County jury deliberated for only three hours before returning a unanimous verdict of guilty to capital murder. As Judge McDonald read the verdict, Black slammed his fists sharply against the defense table.

Black's defense attorneys paraded fifteen character witnesses to the stand during the sentencing hearing, in their last-ditch effort to save the convicted wife killer's life. The witnesses talked about the good he did as an assistant Boy Scout leader; about his friendliness, and about the exemplary life he led as a young man. But the most poignant testimony came from his heartbroken father.

Spectators and some jury members openly sobbed as Robert V. Black, Sr., desperately pleaded for his son's life. "I love my son," he said. "I'll show you how much I do if you let me. I'll go over and kiss him on the cheek if you let me. That's my boy."

When the elder Black stepped from the witness stand a few moments later, his weeping son stood up as he approached, and they hugged each other.

During closing statements, Scott also pointed toward the inequity that would seem to accompany an order for his client's execution, when the triggerman—who had admittedly murdered three people for pay—was expected to escape the death penalty altogether.

Assistant District Attorney Margaret Lalk had a different picture from the emotional scene played out by the father and son to draw for the jury. And she was determined to show that regardless of Hearn's punishment, Black deserved the death penalty. She cited testimony from the ex-convict about the old murder contract offer, to point out that the defendant had plotted his wife's murder for at least four years. "While Bob Black was trying to teach young boys the ideals of scouting, he was also paying five hundred dollars to have his wife killed," she declared. "Robert Black used her gun to kill her, Bob Black used her jewelry to pay for the killing. Bob Black used their child for the alibi."

The jury deliberated for nine hours over a two-day period after the sentencing hearing, before recommending the death penalty. The convicted killer's son broke into tears after the verdict was announced and hugged relatives on both sides of his family.

But relatives of the slain woman were grim-faced and dry-eyed a short time later as Texas State district Judge W. T. "Tom" McDonald, Jr., complied with the jury's wishes, and sentenced the husky, curly-haired widower to death.

Brazos County sheriff's deputies drove the cuffed and chained condemned killer the forty miles to the ominous old state prison at Huntsville. In Texas, the death penalty is carried out by lethal injection. But condemned men and women in Texas, like those in other states with the death penalty, spend years awaiting the outcome of appeals before the dread sentences are carried out—or repealed. There are no John Wayne Hearns in the criminal justice system to make the killing quick.

On May 22, 1992, Black's time ran out. His appeals exhausted, he was strapped to a gurney and injected with a lethal dose of cyanide.

The same day Black was condemned to death, Hearn was given a life sentence in the same court as part of his prearranged bargain to testify against the man who masterminded the woman's murder.

In Florida, a few weeks after the second anniversary of her ex-husband's death, Marlene Watson agreed to a bargain by her attorneys and prosecutors and pleaded no contest to arson in the burning of her grandmother's house, and to a scaled-down charge of conspiracy to commit first-degree murder in Batie's shooting. She was given a five-and-a-half-year prison sentence.

Soon after their youngest daughter's plea was accepted by the courts, Franklin and Iris Sims entered pleas of no contest to charges of being accessories after the fact. They were each put on five years probation.

Finally Debra entered a plea of no contest to conspiracy to commit first-degree murder in Batie's slaying. She was given a thirty-year prison term, to be served consecutively with the sentence she had already received for concocting her husband's murder. With credit for good behavior, she could look forward to possible parole in less than nine years.

By early 1986, *SOF* was out of the business of accepting the type of personal classifieds used by Savage and Hearn. Spokesmen for *SOF* and its parent company, Omega Group Ltd., explained to inquiring news reporters from around the country that the ads had stopped beginning with the April issue. One spokesman said that the magazine's board of directors ordered the ban as part of a routine review of the content of the magazine. Another stressed that the magazine had never knowingly accepted classifieds that made it obvious the advertiser was soliciting someone to break the laws. "We're pretty strong on law enforcement," he observed.

The spokesmen insisted, however, that the change in policy regarding the personal services ads was not tied to any reputed link between the controversial classifieds and murders, murder plots, or other alleged crimes.

Whatever the reasons were for stopping the ads, it was too late for Anita Spearman, Richard Braun, Sandra Kay Black, and others. And the ads had even put the future of the paramilitary magazine itself in peril. At *SOF*'s headquarters at Boulder, Colorado, the buzzards were already coming home to roost.

Chapter 15

An Accounting

During the middle and late 1980s lawsuits were exploding around the Boulder offices of Omega Group Ltd. with the regularity of North Vietnam Army rockets around a company of U.S. Army grunts dug in at Khe Sanh.

The mother and son of the late Sandra Kay Black filed a whopping civil damage suit in the U.S. district court in Houston charging that *Soldier of Fortune* was negligent in running the ad that led to the murder contract between her husband and John Wayne Hearn.

Brothers Michael and Ian Braun filed a similar action in U.S. district court in Montgomery, Alabama, where they moved after the machine-gun murder for hire of their father in front of his suburban Atlanta home.

Norman Douglas Norwood filed a $2 million damage suit in U.S. district court in Fayetteville against the magazine and five men he claimed were responsible for the attempts on his life. And other civil suits were filed against *Soldier of Fortune,* and/or its parent company, Omega, in other cities around the country.

People had been killed, and others were injured or had their lives threatened, in a dizzy reign of terror that the survivors were blaming at least in part on Colonel Brown's popular combat and paramilitary magazine, and they wanted an accounting. Some of the angry litigators made no bones about their desire to run the former Green Beret–turned–publisher out of business, along with his magazine.

The amount of money sought in the lawsuits was staggering. And the federal court suits filed by Mrs. Eimann and her grandson Gary Black, by Norwood, and the others posed important legal questions that carried implications of a major First Amendment battle over the rights of a free press, as well.

Other publishers, including many who were not especially friendly to *SOF,* considered the lawsuits to be tests of their rights and responsibilities in regard to the advertisements they ran. High American courts had already ruled that publishers were not liable for criminal or false ads, if they had no reason to suspect wrongdoing. And media spokesmen pointed out that if publications or the electronic media were held legally responsible for damages linked to ads, it could become extremely difficult to attract advertisements because of difficulties verifying each and every ad. They were watching the federal court trial in Houston closely, as they would watch appeals that were expected to be filed if the magazine lost.

It was the kind of First Amendment case known for setting legal precedent. And a precedent-setting case such as the lawsuit in Houston, or any of the others filed against the magazine, could wind up in the appeals process for years. Costs of legal counsel to defend the magazine could zoom to backbreaking proportions in no time.

Brown wasn't facing the kind of brushfire litigation that publishers of newspapers and magazines have become so used to in America's modern society of lawyers and lawsuits. He was neck-deep in a make-or-break firefight for survival.

Sandra Black's survivors asked $22.5 million in the federal court lawsuit that went to trial before U.S. district Judge David Hittner in Houston early in 1988. And during the three-week media spectacular, the family's lawyers declared that they wanted to get *Soldier of Fortune* off the magazine racks.

Witnesses for the family claimed that Hearn's use of the phrase ''high-risk assignments'' and similar key words used by other advertisers made it obvious that they were making themselves available for criminal undertakings.

And forensic psychiatrist Dr. Park Elliott Dietz testified that the use of the term ''high-risk'' in the classified meant that the advertiser was willing to commit a crime. He said he conducted a study of the magazine's ads that ran before the personal services classifieds were dropped and concluded that many of them were offers to commit crimes. He claimed that many of the ads appealed to paranoids.

Dr. Dietz, who headed the federal forensic team that studied John Hinckley after the youth shot President Reagan, said it would have been easily apparent to readers of *SOF* that the controversial ads were linked to crimes. ''It was obvious there were people who were lunatics, criminals, involved in all kinds of illegal acts, and that they were using the magazine for their forum,'' the Charlottesville, Virginia, criminologist told the jury.

But the testimony of the victim's mother and son was the most poignant of the complex and emotional civil trial. Mrs. Eimann told the jury of six people and two alternates that her grandson was so shaken by the ruthless murder of his mother that for eighteen months he wouldn't sleep alone or enter his house by himself. She said he suffered from agonizing headaches, and constantly twitched.

During Gary Black's testimony, the clean-cut high school senior told the jurors that his mother was a kind and understanding parent.

But a deposition that Hearn gave to attorneys from his jail cell the previous October provided the most spectacularly shocking moments of the trial, and opened the window on the possibility of his involvement in lunatic schemes to assassinate Canada's top government leader and participate in the invasion of a non-hostile South American country.

The signed statement, which was read in court, was important to the family's case because he said that although he was looking for bodyguard and security work, about ninety-percent of the calls he received in response to the ad involved illegal activities. Callers wanted him to kill or beat other people, set off bombs, and help prisoners break out of jail. But some of the contacts were from people who wanted him to play a violent hand in the political affairs of foreign nations and at least one unconventional domestic religious leader, he said.

He claimed that he had a proposal to assassinate the ''king'' of Haiti, and to bomb the headquarters of the controversial Bhagwan Rajneesh in Antelope, Oregon.

Ominously, one of the calls he received was from a man who wanted him to "kill the president of Canada."

In Houston, however, the interest of the federal court jury was not on talks of coups or assassinations of foreign leaders, but of a murdered housewife and the question of responsibility. And the proceedings weren't going well for *Soldier of Fortune* magazine and the Omega Group, Inc.

The magazine's lawyers didn't deny that Hearn's ad in *SOF* made it possible for him and the victim's husband to meet. But they argued through witnesses and their own opening and closing statements that executives of the magazine and the parent company had no way of knowing that the ad would be used to drum up illegal work assignments.

They pointed out that Black had planned on killing his wife for months before responding to the World Services Group ad, and he talked to Hearn several times before contracting with him for the slaying. The responsibility for the woman's death rested on the shoulders of her husband and the hitman, they contended, not with the magazine.

Lieutenant Colonel Brown declared that the personal services ads had legitimate use for helping Vietnam veterans who had served in an unpopular war and were having trouble getting work find honest employment as couriers, bodyguards, or mercenary soldiers in foreign hot spots. The publisher testified, nevertheless, that he would have stopped the ads earlier if he had known that they were linked to criminal activities. He said he hadn't read news stories in national magazines linking *SOF* to several crimes.

And a glittering array of retired military officers and

American patriots, including retired Colonel Charles Beckwith, testified that the magazine was a legitimate military journal. Colonel Beckwith led the ill-fated attempt to rescue American hostages in Iran in 1980.

But the final witness called by the family's lawyers told the jury that an *SOF* editor had known at least since 1982 about a criminal act linked to one of the magazine's ads. James Levine, a former Harris County assistant district attorney, testified that James Graves, who was *SOF*'s managing editor, signed an affidavit in a 1982 case in Houston dealing with a man who used the magazine's classifieds to advertise for an expert in poisons to kill his wife.

The ads were placed by William Chanslor, a Houston lawyer who was using the alias of John G. Thompson, and ran in the October, November, and December 1981 issues. Chanslor was convicted in the scheme at the conclusion of a trial in August 1982.

Even one of the magazine's own expert witnesses provided damaging testimony under cross-examination when he said that he was aware of a half dozen major cases of crimes that had links to *SOF*'s classified ad section. But Neil Livingstone, who had served as a consultant on terrorism to the U.S. Senate and written several books on that subject and on warfare, said he couldn't be specific about individual crime cases.

Livingston, however, also provided testimony that rebutted Dietz's translation of the term "high-risk" that was so popularly used in the controversial classifieds. Livingston said the term referred to a willingness to work in a war zone. And he refuted claims by attorneys for the plaintiff that the word "mechanic" was a euphemism for "hit man" when used in the ads. He described the word's meaning as much less exotic or sinister. It referred, he said, to someone who repairs equipment. Several other words and phrases popularly used in the cryptic ads were dismissed by the witness as "Hollywood terms."

Calling on the jury to award $20 million in punitive damages to Mrs. Black's survivors, attorney Ron Franklin asserted during summations that the mark of a civilized society was the amount of the value placed on human life. And he accused Brown and *SOF* of teaching the magazine's readers "how to contact and hire a professional hit man."

"What would it mean for a fifteen-year-old boy to walk into the kitchen and see, lying on the floor, in her own blood, his mother with two bullets in her head?" the family lawyer asked the jurors.

The jury deliberated three days before returning a verdict finding that the magazine was grossly negligent in printing the ads, and recommending an award totalling $9.4 million to the mother and son of the victim. The panel called for $7.5 million in punitive damages, and compensatory payments of $1.5 million to Gary Black and $400,000 to his sixty-four-year-old grandmother. The magazine knew or should have known that the advertisement was offering the services of a contract killer, the jury had decided. Mrs. Eimann hugged each of the jurors after the verdict. "I just want to thank every one of you for doing what you did for Sandra," the white-haired grandmother said. "We loved her so much."

Jury Foreman Herman Castex later told the press that the panel wanted to set a monetary award that would set an example for other publications considering similar ads. A few weeks later, Judge Hittner issued his formal judgment ordering the magazine and its parent company to pay the award. He ordered payment of an additional fifty-seven hundred dollars for Mrs. Black's funeral and burial expenses.

SOF attorney Larry Thompson, however, responded to the verdict by vowing that the legal duel was far from over. "This fight goes three rounds like a lot of First Amendment cases," he declared, in referring to plans to file appeals. "We lost the first round, but put your money on us in the next two rounds."

But it's impossible to place a bet on someone if there's no money to play with, and appeals can be incredibly costly. So the old soldier did what he had to do: He organized a rescue mission. Colonel Brown appealed for help from his readers and supporters. It was time to marshal his forces and dig in for an all-out battle against the assault on *Soldier of Fortune* magazine and the Omega Group.

The feisty folk hero and publisher, whom staff members fondly refer to as "Uncle Bob," formed the "Omega First Amendment Legal Fund." And editors wrote editorials in *SOF* calling for contributions from readers, and reiterating its defense in what publications around the country were recognizing as an important First Amendment case.

The editors cited editorials in daily newspapers and other publications expressing fears that the decision could ultimately lead to a crackdown or negligence suits over ads for everything from kitchen knives to rubber lifeboats and lonely hearts.

Contrary to the belief of some people, they wrote, *SOF* was not a deep-pockets publication. Much of the money earned by Omega and the magazine was passed on to support their special causes such as the POW/MIA project, projects in Afghanistan and El Salvador,

and refugee relief. And they warned that without the
financial help of readers and other supporters, the magazine might indeed disappear from newsstands. And
that was exactly what leftist liberals and other enemies
of *SOF* wanted.

Early in June 1989 a three-judge panel of the Fifth
U.S. Circuit Court of Appeals in New Orleans heard
arguments on *Soldier of Fortune* and the Omega Group
Ltd.'s appeal. Each side had twenty minutes to argue
its case. The appeal focused heavily on a pretrial ruling
in Houston that the magazine did not qualify for full
First Amendment protection in the matter because of
the commercial nature of the ad. Judge Hittner's decision indicated that advertising wasn't entitled to First
Amendment protection equal to what he termed "core
speech" or ideological expression. And attorneys contended that even if the jury did rule negligence had
occurred, the finding should be against the advertiser,
not the magazine.

Approximately six weeks after the hearing, the appeals panel overturned the Houston jury's award, striking down the $9.4 million judgment. The jury had
imposed too high a standard on the magazine, the high
court declared. Holding the magazine responsible would
place too much of a burden on publishers to screen ads
that were worded ambiguously. The magazine "owed
no duty to refrain from publishing a facially innocuous
classified advertisement when the ad's content—at
most—made its message ambiguous," the judges stated
in their unanimous decision.

Although the constitutional right to a free press was
a cornerstone of the appeal, the court based its ruling
on Texas liability law. Nevertheless, the magazine's ju-

bilant attorneys described the appeals court ruling as a victory for the First Amendment.

In January 1990 the U.S. Supreme Court refused to reinstate the $9.4 million award to Mrs. Black's survivors. They permitted the federal appeal panel's decision in New Orleans to stand, without comment. Colonel Brown had just returned to Colorado from Panama when he learned of the high court's decision. The news was a nice present for his return home, he told the press.

In Montgomery eleven months later, a U.S. district court jury found *SOF* liable for damages in the ambush slaying of Richard Braun and ordered a payment of $12.4 million for his sons, Michael and Ian. The five-day trial had been a close rerun of the proceeding in Houston. And like the Houston trial, the decision of the federal jury in the $120 million lawsuit didn't mark the end of the case.

Attorneys for the magazine appealed, and Michael Braun, who was to receive the lion's share of the award, agreed to a reduction of $7.6 million in punitive damages. U.S. district Judge Truman Hobbs had ruled that the $10 million in punitive damages was excessive. The brothers would have been faced with another trial if Michael hadn't agreed to accept shaving down of punitive damages to $2.375 million.

Norwood had agreed to an out-of-court settlement with the Omega Group and *SOF* a few days before the case was scheduled to go to trial in Fayetteville in June 1987. The suit against Gray, Savage, and the former strip club owner's hirelings was dropped "without prejudice," because they were imprisoned and without funds. The "without prejudice" stipulation permits a possible refiling of the suit in the future.

The amount of Norwood's settlement with the magazine was not publicly disclosed. Although he was quoted by a reporter as saying he wound up with enough to retire on, he continued to keep his job for a time as a deputy prosecutor in Bentonville, Arkansas. By early 1991, however, he had gone into private practice in Springdale. And he was still keeping his Magnum handy.

Compelling True Crime Thrillers
From Avon Books

BADGE OF BETRAYAL
by Joe Cantlupe and Lisa Petrillo

76009-6/ $4.99 US/ $5.99 Can

A KILLING IN THE FAMILY:
A TRUE STORY OF
LOVE, LIES AND MURDER
by Stephen Singular with Tim and Danielle Hill

76413-X/ $4.95 US/ $5.95 Can

LOSS OF INNOCENCE:
A TRUE STORY OF JUVENILE MURDER
by Eric J. Adams   75987-X/ $4.95 US/ $5.95 Can

RUBOUTS: MOB MURDERS IN AMERICA
by Richard Monaco and Lionel Bascom

75938-1/ $4.50 US/ $5.50 Can

GOOMBATA:
THE IMPROBABLE RISE AND FALL OF
JOHN GOTTI AND HIS GANG
by John Cummings and Ernest Volkman

71487-6/ $4.99 US/ $5.99 Can